MOST
USEFUL.

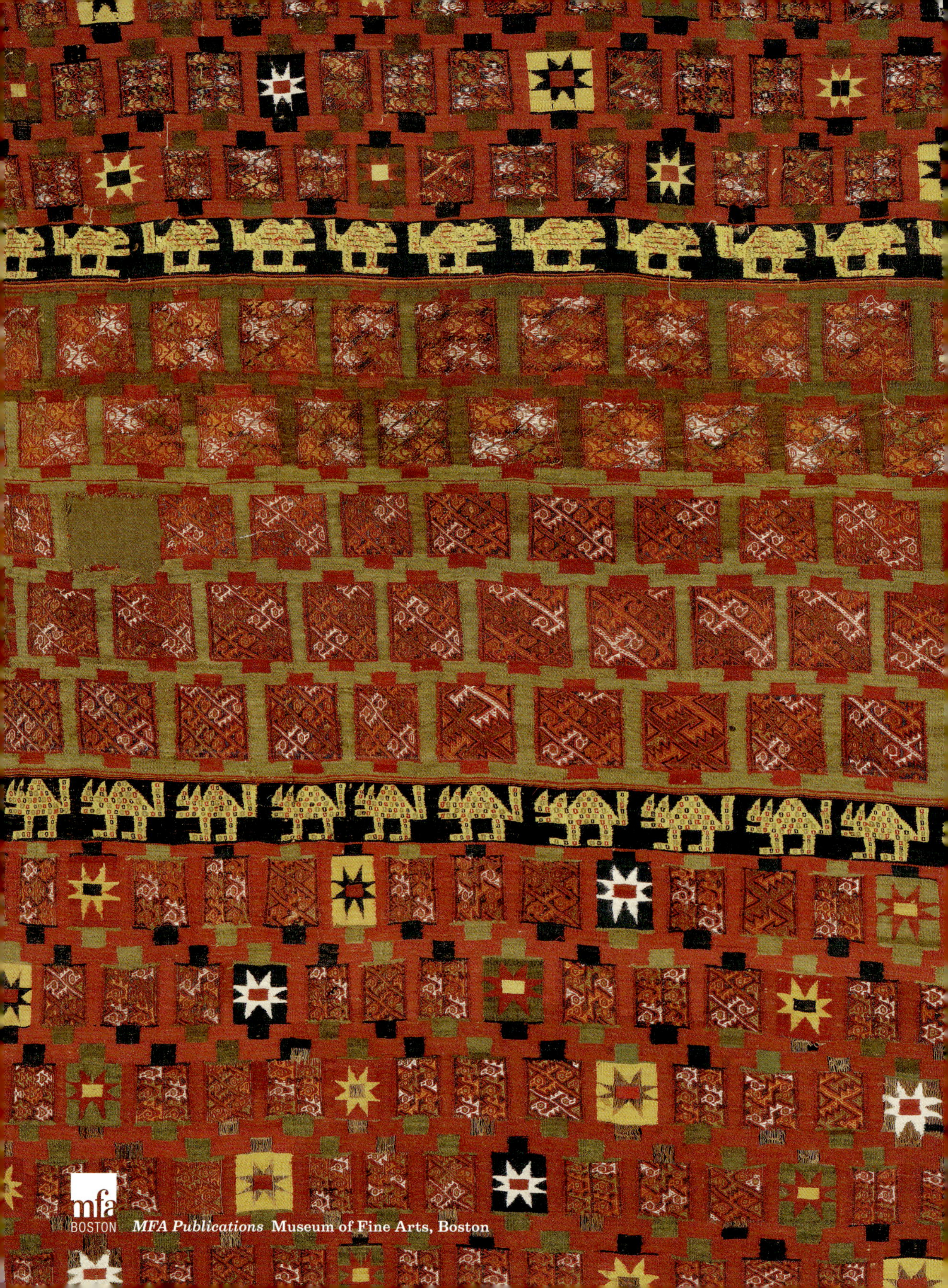
mfa
BOSTON
MFA Publications Museum of Fine Arts, Boston

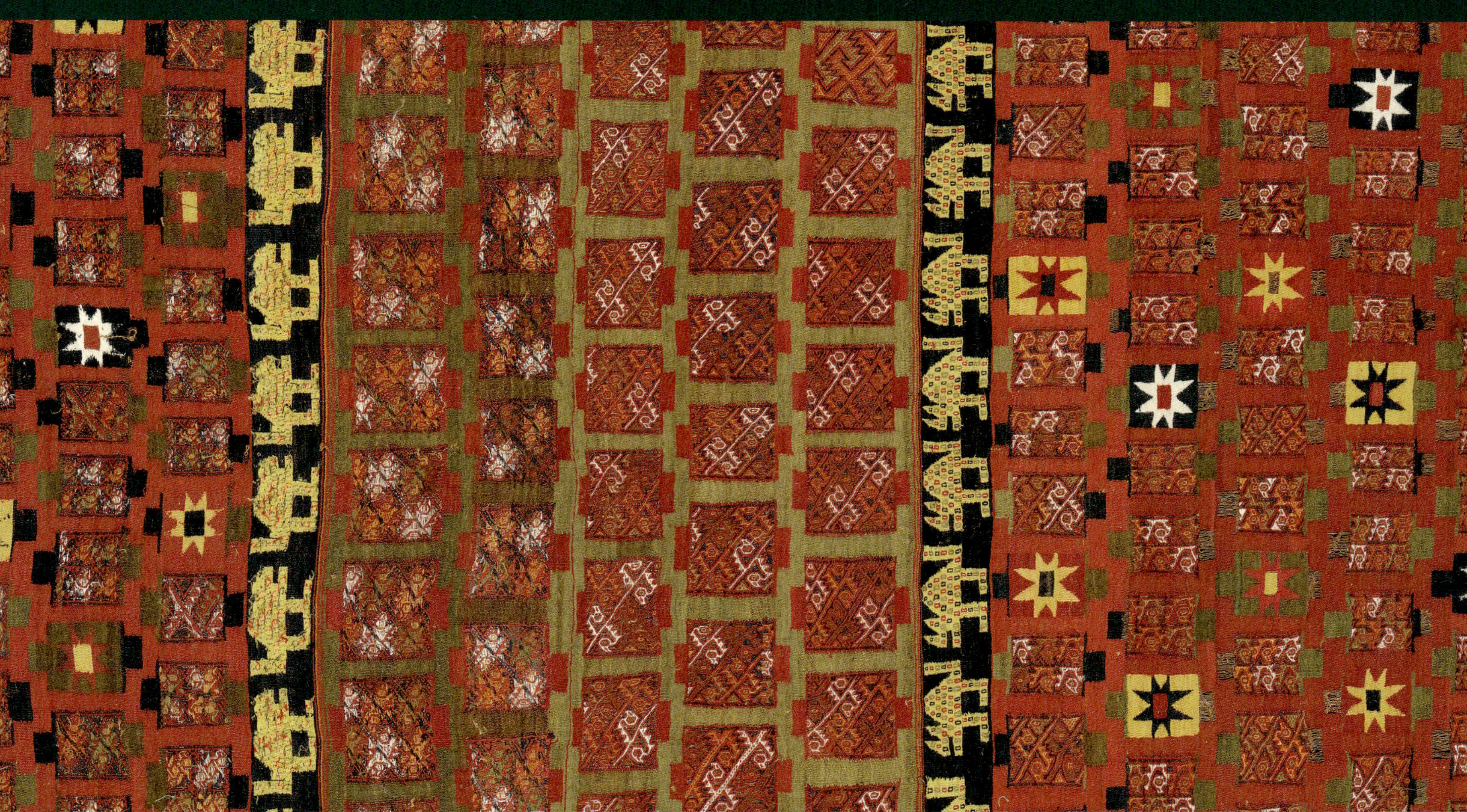

MFA HIGHLIGHTS arts of the ancient americas
Dorie Reents-Budet
Dennis Carr

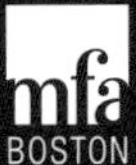

MFA PUBLICATIONS
Museum of Fine Arts, Boston
465 Huntington Avenue
Boston, Massachusetts 02115
www.mfa.org/publications

Generous support for this publication was provided by the Landon T. Clay Fund.

© 2019 by Museum of Fine Arts, Boston
ISBN 978-0-87846-741-9
Library of Congress Control Number: 2019930803

The Museum of Fine Arts, Boston, is a nonprofit institution devoted to the promotion and appreciation of the creative arts. The Museum endeavors to respect the copyrights of all authors and creators in a manner consistent with its nonprofit educational mission. If you feel any material has been included in this publication improperly, please contact the Department of Rights and Licensing at 617 267 9300, or by mail at the above address.

While the objects in this publication necessarily represent only a small portion of the MFA's holdings, the Museum is proud to be a leader within the American museum community in sharing the objects in its collection via its website. Currently, information about approximately 400,000 objects is available to the public worldwide. To learn more about the MFA's collections, including provenance, publication, and exhibition history, kindly visit www.mfa.org/collections.

For a complete listing of MFA publications, please contact the publisher at the above address, or call 617 369 4233.

All illustrations in this book were photographed by the Imaging Studios, Museum of Fine Arts, Boston, except where otherwise noted.

Edited by Gerald W. R. Ward and Jennifer Snodgrass
Proofread by Kathryn Blatt
Typeset by Fran Presti-Fazio
Design and production by Christopher DiPietro and Terry McAweeney
Series design by Lucinda Hitchcock
Production assistance by Jessica Eber
Printed and bound at Verona Libri, Verona, Italy

Distributed in the United States of America and Canada by
ARTBOOK | D.A.P.
75 Broad Street, Suite 630
New York, New York 10004
www.artbook.com

Distributed outside the United States of America and Canada by
Thames & Hudson, Ltd.
181A High Holborn
London WC1V 7QX
www.thamesandhudson.com

FIRST EDITION
Printed and bound in Italy
This book was printed on acid-free paper.

Contents

Director's Foreword

The collections of the MFA explore the world's limitless diversity of creativity and communication that delight, unsettle, expand, probe, refocus, and enrich mind and spirit. Among these is the ancient Americas collection, which represents more than forty cultures and two thousand years of expression in the region extending from present-day Mexico to Bolivia before the arrival of Europeans. These objects and images in clay, stone, fiber, and precious metals challenge our assumptions about beauty, visual narrative, and aesthetics. They also illuminate the cultures, histories, and philosophies of the native peoples of the Americas, whose unique perspectives and ingenuity are a vital part of the story of both civilization and consciousness.

In 1912, the MFA was among the first institutions in the United States to exhibit ancient American objects within the context of an art museum, presenting the works as art rather than anthropological touchstones. The collection had its foundation some thirty years earlier, in 1878, in an exchange with Harvard University of artifacts from the two institutions' respective excavations in Egypt and the Americas. Acceptance of these objects sparked the first donations of other works from the ancient Americas by members of the public, many of them women who were philanthropists and intellectual leaders in the community. Over the next 140 years, the Museum has continued to build its collection, often through generous gifts from subsequent donors. By sharing the artistry of the ancient Americas in this volume, we encourage visitors and readers to discover the creative, social, political, and religious narratives expressed in these remarkable works of art.

Matthew Teitelbaum
Ann and Graham Gund Director
Museum of Fine Arts, Boston

Acknowledgments

Hard work is enjoyable when outstanding individuals come together and contribute their expertise to the project. This book is the result of such an endeavor, and I am grateful for the efforts of the large number of colleagues at the MFA who contributed. Foremost among them is Dennis Carr, Carolyn and Peter Lynch Curator of American Decorative Arts and Sculpture, who has been a steadfast force on this project over many years. He is the personification of colleague, curator, scholar, and friend, as well as contributor of curatorial insights to the chapter on regalia. Pam Parmal, Chair and David and Roberta Logie Curator of Textile and Fashion Arts, Jennifer Swope, and Meredith Montague shared their viewpoints on the fiber arts, a prime artistic medium in the ancient Americas. Darcy Kuronen, Department Head and Pappalardo Curator of Musical Instruments, and Michael Suing took the lead in the chapter on performance. Their deep knowledge of world musical forms shed light on fugitive musical traditions through a discussion of the sound qualities of the surviving instruments. Jayme Kurland assisted with complementary details of the musical instrument collection. Emily Stoehrer, Rita J. Kaplan and Susan B. Kaplan Curator of Jewelry, is thanked for her informative comments on body adornments. The editorial virtuosity of Gerald W.R. Ward, Katharine Lane Weems Senior Curator of American Decorative Arts and Sculpture Emeritus, molded the dense text into an accessible jaunt through the complexities of ancient American art and culture.

I am grateful to colleagues past and present in the Art of the Americas department who have assisted this project throughout its long development in ways too numerous to list. Elliot Bostwick Davis, the former John Moors Cabot Chair, piloted the department over many years and supported the multiculturalism of art in the Americas. Special thanks to former graduate research intern Laura Cunningham, who uncovered the long-buried early history of the MFA's ancient Americas collection. I also extend deep gratitude to Victoria Reed, Monica S. Sadler Curator for Provenance, for her research and guidance in art provenance investigations.

The excellent work by the staff of the Conservation and Collections Management department has significantly broadened our understanding and appreciation of the ancient American collection. It has been my pleasure to work closely with Pamela Hatchfield, Robert P. and Carol T. Henderson Head of Objects Conservation, as well as Jessica Arista, Gerri Strickler, Mei-An Tsu, and Richard Newman.

This publication would not have been possible without the dedicated efforts of the MFA Publications team, including the former director Emiko K. Usui, Anna K. Barnet, Jessica Eber, Anne Levine, Terry McAweeney, Chris DiPietro, Jennifer Snodgrass, and Hope Stockton. They have paid careful attention to thousands of details yet kept a schooled eye on the final outcome. Thank you from a most grateful author.

Invaluable direction and support for this project have come from Ben Weiss, Director of Collections and Leonard A. Lauder Curator of Visual Culture; Christraud Geary, Teel Senior Curator Emerita of African and Oceanic Art; Alex Irving, and Kay Satomi. Grateful thanks for the impressive work of the MFA's photography studio, whose staff includes John Wolff, Michael Gould, Greg Heins, and Jared Medeiros. Marietta Cambareri, Senior Curator of European Sculpture and Jetskalina H. Phillips Curator of Judaica, is a valued curatorial colleague and friend whose camaraderie makes my working trips to the MFA a professional and social delight. Finally, my gratitude is extended to Malcolm Rogers, Ann and Graham Gund Director Emeritus, and Matthew Teitelbaum, Ann and Graham Gund Director, as well as to Katie Getchell, Kelly Hays, and Julia A. McCarthy, for their efforts to progress the museum in countless ways.

Scholars and friends outside the MFA have shared knowledge and insights that deepen our understanding of the ancient Americas collection. Special thanks to Rebecca Bailey, Ronald L. Bishop, John Burkhalter, Arnd Adje Both, Mary Clarke, Alphonse Jax, Barbara and Justin Kerr, Matthew Looper, Barbara MacLeod, David Mora Marín, Sofía Paredes Maury, Robert B. Pickering, John Pohl, Yuriy Polyukhovych, and Franco Rossi.

Special mention and deep gratitude are given to Suzy Forster and Claude Cernuschi, who have hosted me during working trips to the MFA for twenty years. Martha Richardson, too, has extended friendship and hospitality over the years. And the generosity and friendship of Leigh Braude-Borowski have proffered memorable times in her Boston home and at the MFA. The camaraderie and counsel of Timothy Phillips—not to mention his dedication to the MFA's collections—have been invaluable.

The Museum's donors are sincerely thanked for their generosity and vision. Beginning in 1878, they recognized that great art was created in the ancient

Americas and should be part of the MFA. Special recognition is given to Landon and Lavinia Clay, Leigh Braude-Borowski, Hanne and Jeremy Grantham, and Timothy Phillips. And last but far from least, *millones de gracias* to my husband, Ricardo Budet, for his endless support and encouragement over the years (yes, he does know what's wrong with my computer).

This publication is dedicated to Landon T. Clay, friend and mentor. As a true Renaissance man, he exemplified the perceptive collector. Landon not only focused on aesthetic quality but also sponsored scientific investigations of artworks to illuminate the creativity and history they embody. From 1968 to 2007, he helped build the MFA's ancient Americas collection and sponsored its scientific research. Today the ongoing support of the Clay family continues his vision and legacy. Generous support for this publication was provided by the Landon T. Clay Fund. Landon is missed, but he lives on in these artworks.

Dorie Reents-Budet
Consulting Curator, Art of the Ancient Americas
Museum of Fine Arts, Boston

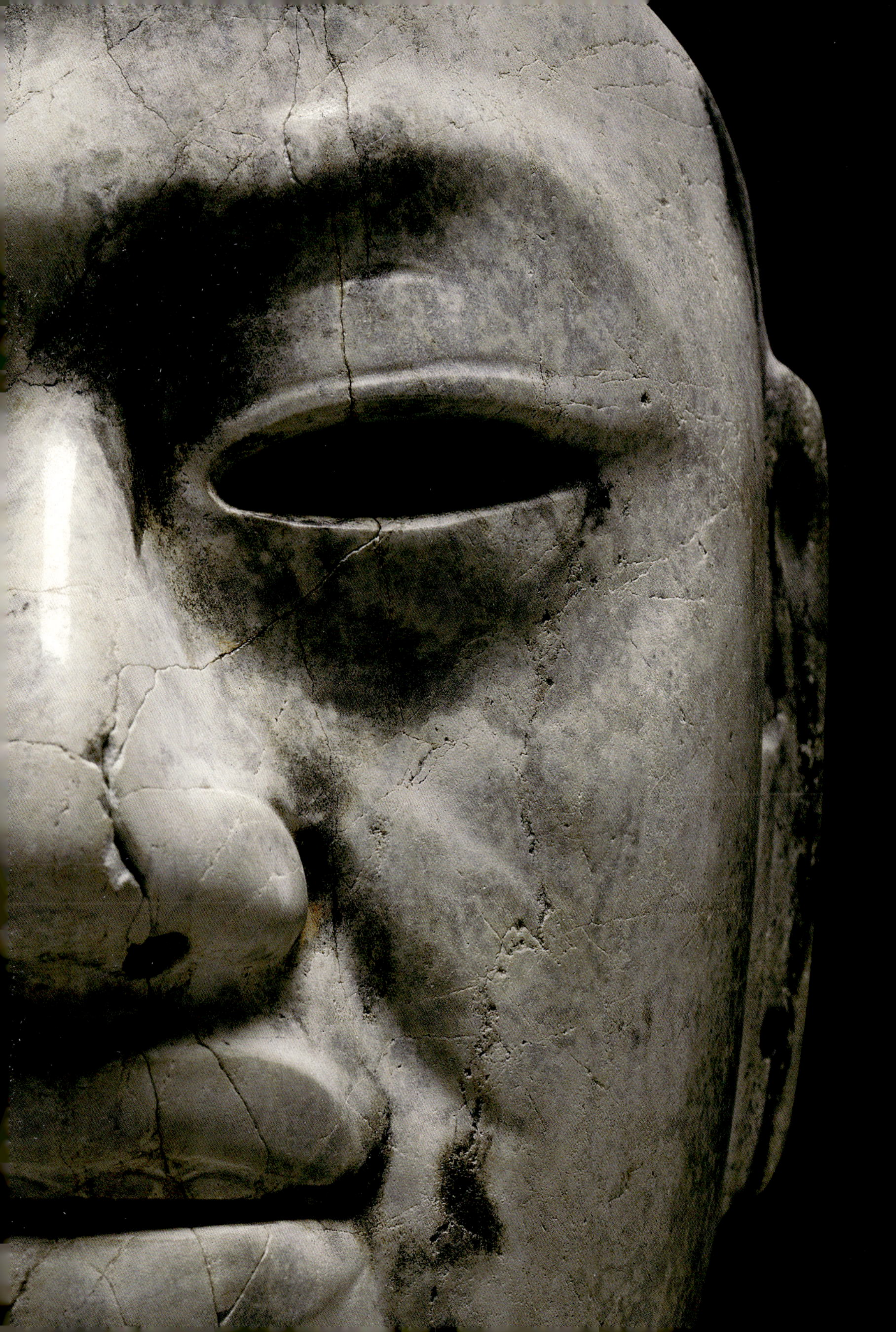

The Earliest American Arts

Dorie Reents-Budet

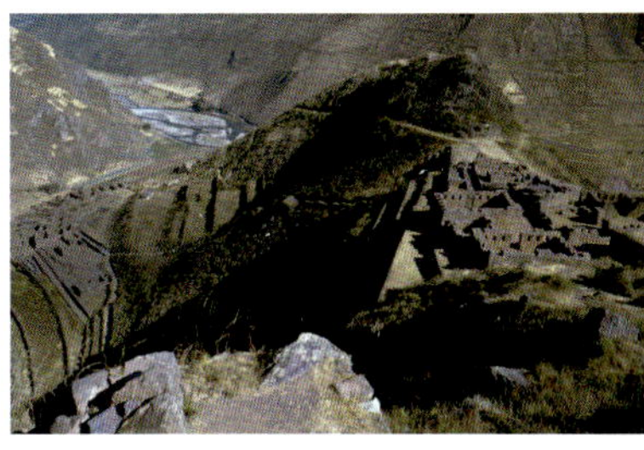

fig. 1. View of the Inti Watana residential group at Pisaq, the estate of the Inka ruler Pachacuti (1438–71)

All human cultures make art because it is the primary visual means by which we convey our fundamental beliefs and values, transforming soul into substance. The ancient Americas is no exception; its magnificent art and architecture preserve the intellectual and spiritual grandeur of the hemisphere's first civilizations (fig. 1). From northern Mexico to Chile, rich natural resources and varied environments nurtured more than 350 distinct cultures. Today, in excess of 130 native languages and dialects are spoken in Peru, Bolivia, and Chile, while 290 enliven the cultural landscape in Mexico, Belize, Guatemala, and Honduras. Myriad ancient art styles reflect the cultural diversity of the ancient Americas, and many have provided national emblems and inspiration for later artists. For example, the shape of a nineteenth-century glazed earthenware bottle made in England mimics the characteristic spout-and-bridge-handled vessels of the Nasca people and other ancient Peruvian cultures (fig. 2). The works presented here display the technical mastery and creativity of the hemisphere's first artists in what today is Latin America. But more importantly, these artworks reveal the people who made and used them.

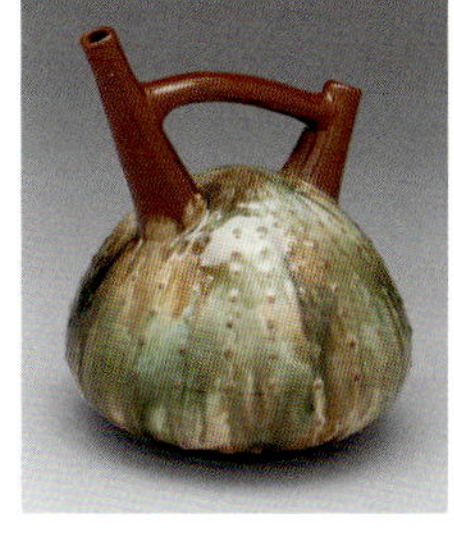

fig. 2. Double-spouted vessel, designed by Christopher Dresser, about 1879–82

The ancient Americas is one of six "cradles" of civilization along with Egypt, the Near East and Mesopotamia, the Indus Valley, North China, and Southeast Asia. All developed at roughly the same rate, although the Americas matured later than those of the other five regions. From Mexico to Bolivia, towns with formal civic architecture and established craft traditions appeared during the fourth millennium BCE. Social and political complexity quickly followed, culminating in large urban centers with distinctive art traditions by the end of the first millennium BCE. Anthropologists have traditionally identified six traits as markers of civilization: agriculture, animal husbandry, a class-based society, public buildings, writing, and metallurgy. Ancient American peoples developed the first four but are unique for constructing splendid civilizations largely without writing and the use of hard (e.g., bronze) metals. In the Andean world, gold, copper, and silver were used to fashion body adornments and tools, including sewing needles, fishing hooks, and small knives. Absent, however, were bronze and iron. Metallurgy was not known in Mesoamerica until well into the first millennium CE, when only a limited repertoire of techniques and materials (copper and gold) was used to fashion primarily personal adornments. Picto-logographic writing systems were found only in Mesoamerica, and the Maya devised a true writing system, defined as the graphic representation of spoken language, shown here on an earthenware vessel (fig. 3). Andean cultures never developed writing, although they created a complex recording system using knotted strings. Thus the cultures of the ancient Americas were simultaneously in step with, and unique among, the world's great civilizations.

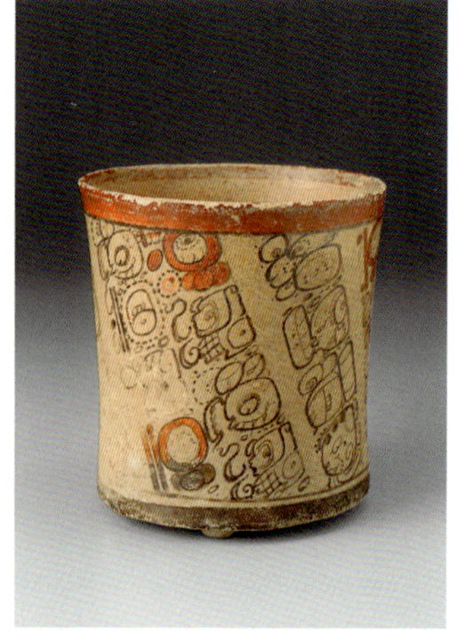

fig. 3. **Drinking vessel,**

Maya, 675–750 CE

Five major culture regions make up the Americas—North America, Mesoamerica, Central America, Andean South America, and Amazonia. These modern-day divisions give order to the complex cultural landscape of the hemisphere. Each region is distinguished by unique languages, social and political systems, and religions, all of which are expressed through unique art and architectural styles. Mesoamerica, Central America, and Andean South America were home to what anthropologists call "complex societies" because of their multifaceted levels of social and political organization.

Mesoamerica ("Middle America") stretches from Mexico to northern Central America. When the Spanish arrived in the sixteenth century, Mesoamerica was populated by more than a million people; its vast geographic diversity was matched by that of scores of distinct cultures. The Spanish, who encountered only the contemporary societies in the late fifteenth and sixteenth centuries, had little notion of the region's previous three thousand years of cultural history.

Mesoamerica's first complex society was that of the Olmecs, who developed Mexico's first state-level political system (a confederacy of independent political groups) sometime around 1200 BCE. They established long-distance trade networks and devised the intensive agricultural system known as *chinampas* (raised fields), which survives today as Mexico City's famous "floating gardens." The Olmecs initiated key Mesoamerican traits such as hieroglyphic writing and the pyramid-and-shrine as the conventional model for sacred architecture. They formulated Mesoamerican cosmology (the nature of the universe) and religious philosophy, including the divine basis of social hierarchy and rulership. Artists developed ingenious techniques to fashion spectacular objects without the use of metal tools, especially jadeite carvings which are among the most accomplished artworks in the ancient Americas.

Olmec culture paved the way for the dynamic Classic period (250–900 CE), during which Teotihuacan became Mesoamerica's preeminent force and first quasi-empire, its influence stretching from New Mexico to Costa Rica. Teotihuacan religion, politics, art, and architecture accompanied its extensive trade and governmental enterprises, occasionally supported by warfare. At its sixth-century peak, Teotihuacan was the second-largest city in the world, covering more than eight square miles (21 square kilometers) and inhabited by as many as 120,000 people. Its massive Pyramid of the Sun was the Western Hemisphere's tallest building until the completion of New York City's Empire State Building in 1931. Other powerful Classic period cultures include the Maya of southern Mesoamerica, renowned for impressive temple pyramids towering above the jungle and finely crafted artworks. The Maya also are famous for their writing system. Its decipherment in the late twentieth century has provided a wealth of historical and ideological information about the ancient Maya, whose territory extended over what is today southern Mexico, Guatemala, Belize, Honduras, and El Salvador.

The Mesoamerican cultures of the Classic period collapsed in the tenth century due to soil depletion, overpopulation, long-term drought, and the failure of leaders to address the resulting agricultural and social problems. New political organizations, backed by innovative religious beliefs, arose during the Post-Classic period (900–1521), culminating in the Aztec empire of the fifteenth century. The people of this empire called themselves the Mexica and exercised astute politics and warfare to quickly absorb societies from coast to coast and establish a new world order. To confirm its rightful place in history, the Aztec state mined earlier artistic traditions to invent an antiquity that conveyed its prophesied supremacy. Focusing on nearby Teotihuacan, which lay in ruins and clouded in myth but whose memory of divine glory survived, the Aztecs named the ruins Teotihuacan, the "city of the gods," believing that it was here the gods created the new sun of the Aztec age. The still-impressive metropolis was a source not only of artworks to adorn the Aztec capital but also of inspiration for Mexica artists.

The so-called Intermediate Zone of Central America, extending from Nicaragua to Panama, physically bridges Mesoamerica and Andean South America. The peoples of this cultural crossroads absorbed influences from north, south, and east. They were related to cultures of northern South America and the Caribbean, sharing a common linguistic base and relying on manioc (*Manihot esculenta*) as the staple food. Yet Central American societies comprised independent cultures, each with its own distinctive social, religious, and political systems. Their individuality was expressed in diverse art styles, although formal similarities indicate commonly held beliefs. Pottery, jadeite, basalt, and gold were primary materials from which extraordinary objects were produced (fig. 4).

Understanding of the ancient history of Central America lags behind that of Mesoamerica and the Andes for many reasons. First, the native population declined by more than 90 percent soon after European contact due to disease, forced labor, and destruction of the social order. As a result, the few sixteenth-century accounts by Spanish writers are mostly brief and imprecise. Many ancient traditions were lost, and the surviving peoples' beliefs and lifeways are but a faint shadow of the past. And last, only sporadic scientific attention has been paid to Central America's archaeological remains.

Yet the region was a key player on the ancient American stage. Beginning before 200 BCE, its peoples forged relationships in Mesoamerica indicated by the use of jadeite to express status and power. Trade brought Mesoamerican artworks to Costa Rica, and vice-versa. And the Central American knowledge of gold-working, which had been adopted from peoples in Colombia, was introduced to Mexico sometime after 750. Objects from both regions reveal a shamanic undercurrent, reflecting the belief in spiritual transformation and its use to validate political authority. Central American artists met the challenge of portraying the shaman's un-representable visionary experience, bringing to the everyday world the innermost revelations of spiritual practice.

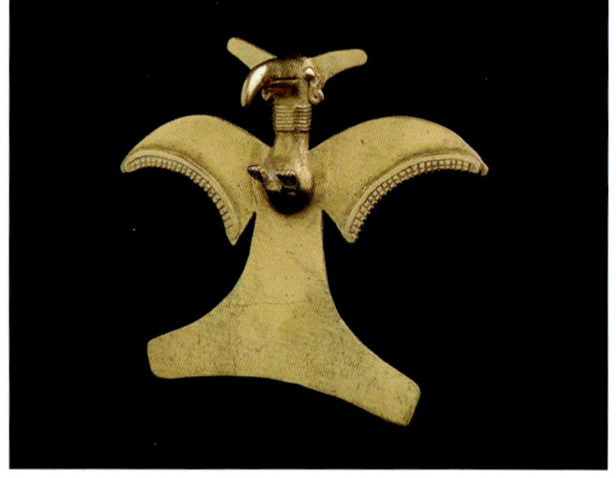

fig. 4. Bird effigy pendant, Veraguas–Gran Chiriquí, 1st–4th century CE

The Andean region of western South America nurtured many cultures with distinct languages, political systems, religious practices, agricultural and culinary customs, and art traditions. Yet all shared the belief in an animated cosmos composed of binary opposites (male-female, sun-moon, earth-spirit world) and the importance of maintaining balance to ensure universal life. Reverential offerings were made to Pacha Mama (Earth Mother) to ensure her ability to reproduce. Gold was a prime artistic medium because it signified the divine solar force necessary for Pacha Mama's fertility, and it was paired with silver to express the cosmic principle of binary oppositions. This philosophy shaped Andean aesthetics, embodied by the foremost Andean medium—the fiber arts with its warp and weft opposites.

By 4500 BCE, societies from Peru to Chile had created America's other great cradle of civilization by harnessing the region's dramatically different environments—from cold alpine highlands to the world's driest coastal deserts. The potato was the dietary staple, although maize was used to make beer. Camelids (including alpacas, llamas, and vicuñas), the only native American beasts of burden, also provided wool fiber, blood for religious offerings, and sometimes meat. By 3200 BCE, massive public architecture and the aesthetic principles of bilateral symmetry, image metaphors, and shifting forms to portray the supernatural were well-developed. Chavín culture (1800–900 BCE) fully articulated these forms and served as the foundation for regional expressions such as the spectacular Paracas funerary textiles of Peru's South Coast. The later Nasca culture (1–700 CE) expanded Paracas subject matter to slip-painted pottery, and the North Coast Moche (100–700 CE) expressed political power with gigantic adobe mounds and expertly crafted artworks recounting human events and deeds of gods, often blurring the distinction between them.

The Middle Horizon (500–900 CE) marks the appearance of the first Andean empire, composed of the interconnected Tiwanaku (Bolivia) and Wari (Peru) states, linked by a vast system of paved roads from Ecuador to northern Chile. Wari art is standardized yet visually complex. The artworks seek to convey the official Wari message across the empire's language and culture boundaries by using a common symbol system. Yet the imagery is rendered in a highly intricate—if not obscured—format to distinguish the imperial artworks from those of its subject societies.

The ensuing period from the year 900 until 1470 witnessed the rise of regional powers whose mass-produced works of art reflect a more secular and diffused political authority. Textile arts became particularly important, with artistic specialization meeting the increased demands for status-bearing goods. The opulent tombs of leaders, particularly those of the Sicán and Chimú states of the North Coast, contained massive quantities of artworks, including golden beer-drinking cups, ritual sacrificial knives, and towering headdresses.

Onto this stage stepped the obscure Inkas (1400–1534) rising, like the Aztecs in Mexico, from humble origins. By 1500, they controlled the largest territory in the world, surpassing the contemporaneous Ming and Ottoman empires. Inka territory extended 3,400 miles from Quito, Ecuador, to Chile, the Inkas having enlarged the old Wari transport network to more than 20,000 miles of mostly paved roadway. Inka architecture features massive shaped boulders (some exceeding sixty tons) fitted perfectly together without mortar. Inka walls stand today while colonial and modern buildings crumble in the region's frequent earthquakes. Although the Spanish were impressed by Inka architecture, the buildings' resplendent sheaths of gold and silver drew the greatest attention. None survives, although the metals live on as gold-encrusted altars and silver chalices for High Catholic mass, coinage, and European-style adornments.

The power of the Inka state stemmed from their weaving together the many cultures of the western Andes into an orderly, well-managed organism of interlaced parts across social, cultural, and linguistic divides. They did so by leaving intact local traditions and political organizations as long as each group met its labor and military obligations to the Inka state. This imperial strategy is reflected in Inka art, which melds local and earlier traditions with Inka forms to create a standardized style grounding Inka supremacy in the exalted past. Although most Inka gold and silver artworks were lost to the Spanish forges, thousands of painted and modeled ceramics, portable stone and wood sculptures, and opulent textiles—not to mention massive stone architecture—survive to bear witness to the magnitude of the Inka empire.

For centuries, the art of the ancient Americas (known as pre-Columbian art) garnered little interest other than as curiosities of the "primitive." It was not until the nineteenth century that broader interest developed due to two primary factors. First, Latin America embarked on independence efforts, and many new countries looked to their ancient cultures for symbols to express national identity. Second, the emerging field of anthropology viewed the Americas as fertile ground for testing theories of social development. Yet it was not until the advent of modern art that ancient American artifacts began to be considered art, culminating with midcentury collectors and artists, especially in Mexico and California, who deemed these works equal to any great art tradition.

Boston institutions, the Museum of Fine Arts among them, conducted archaeological field projects during the late nineteenth century. Harvard University began one of the first academic departments of anthropology with archaeology at its core in the United States. Artifacts from field projects helped to build early collections in Boston, and the MFA and Harvard also exchanged artifacts from their field projects (Egypt and the ancient Americas, respectively). Donations also brought works to the MFA, the first being made in 1878 by Edward William Hooper, Treasurer of Harvard College, who gave forty-five Peruvian textiles and one pottery vessel.

The first purchase of ancient American artwork occurred the following year, comprising five Peruvian pottery vessels acquired from C. A. Wellington (fig. 5). The associated Wellington Art Rooms enterprise was aligned with the city's Women's Club, and most ancient American donations during the next thirty years came from women collectors and philanthropists, including Miss H. Louisa Brown, Mrs. John Thorndike, Mrs. Charles Greely Loring, Mrs. Charles Amos Cummings, and the Misses Norton. These early acquisitions were groundbreaking in the museum world because the MFA accepted and displayed the artifacts as art.

A momentous gift from Harvard professor Denman Waldo Ross in 1910 founded the Museum's spectacular collection of Peruvian textiles, which Dr. Ross continued to build during the next fifteen years. Joining the more than eleven thousand artworks he donated to the MFA's growing encyclopedic collection, these fiber masterpieces constitute a stellar collection and remain among the finest outside Peru.

In 1912 the MFA presented what may be the first exhibition in the United States of ancient American objects in an art museum. It featured Maya pieces from the Peabody Museum's excavations and was curated by Harvard professor Alfred M. Tozzer and Denman Ross. Tozzer's goal was to show visitors that "there was something in this country in pre-Columbian times worthy of the name of art" (*Museum of Fine Arts Bulletin*, 1912). The next exhibition, in 1932, featured Peruvian textiles from the Ross donations, curated by the Bostonian Philip Ainsworth Means, who earlier had donated an exceptional Nasca pottery vessel. Means was a distinguished archaeologist and ethnohistorian at Harvard University who had served as director of the national archaeology museum in Lima, and one of the first scholars to insist that the artifacts of the ancient Americans belonged in the category of world art. More than three decades later, the MFA mounted its next ancient Americas exhibitions—*The Gold of Ancient America* (1968) and *Ancient Art of the Americas from New England Collections* (1971), culminating in *To Weave for the Sun: Andean Textiles in the Museum of Fine Arts, Boston* (1992) and *Painting the Maya Universe: Royal Ceramics of the Classic Period* (1994). In 2010, two galleries were dedicated to the ancient Americas.

The MFA's collection of precious metal artworks from Central America and Colombia commenced in 1922–24 with purchases from the Walter Channing Wyman collection. Fifty years later, Catherine Coolidge Lastavica and former Trustee Landon T. Clay broadened the holdings with superb gold artworks. Clay's donations in 1971 and 1975 are noteworthy for having come through the Conte family of Panama, whose land encompassed the archaeological site of Sitio Conte. It was excavated by Harvard University and the University of Pennsylvania during the 1930s, with the three principals dividing the artifacts among themselves.

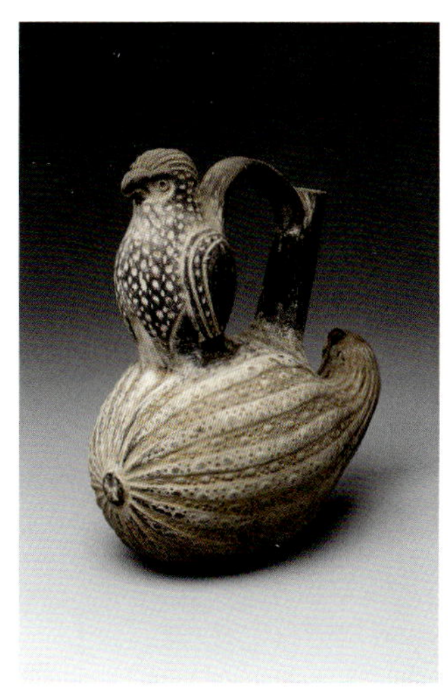

fig. 5. **Effigy bottle,**
Lambayeque (Sicán)
or early Chimú, 900–1470

Pivotal change for the collection occurred in the 1970s when Clay began donating significant ancient American pottery. He was especially impressed by the painted Maya ceramics, and sought through his donations (including the renowned November collection) to elevate the world's perception of Maya pictorial pottery to that of great paintings. Together with his wife, Lavinia De Nood Clay, he gave hundreds of artworks exhibiting the finest aesthetics and techniques in pottery, precious metals, textiles, and jadeite. The Clays embraced the same aesthetic doctrine as Denman Ross's belief that similar principles are found in textiles as in paintings, and that the only important question is to what extent a sense of beauty has been expressed.

The MFA continues to build its collections while strictly adhering to current professional standards. The Museum particularly seeks to include underrepresented cultures and their art traditions, exemplified by the recent donations of ceramic artworks from Central America and West Mexico by Trustee Timothy Phillips. The MFA's diverse collection has led to the organization of this publication around themes, rather than by culture and chronology. By so doing, the objects are freed from archaeological service and take center stage as works of art. Drawing from Ross's writings on art, this volume aims to "discover the manifold expressions of life" of the diverse ancient American societies embodied by these objects.

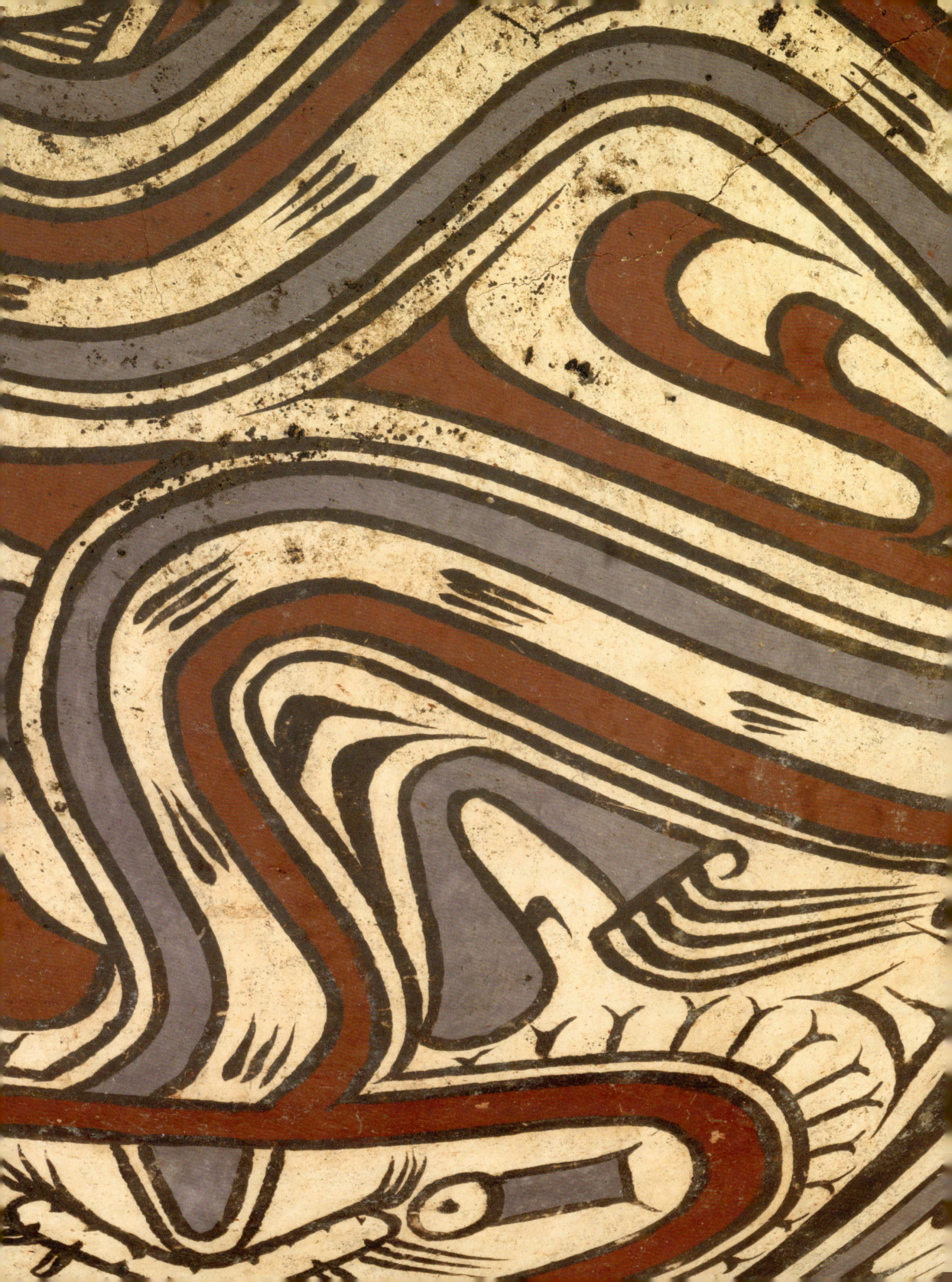

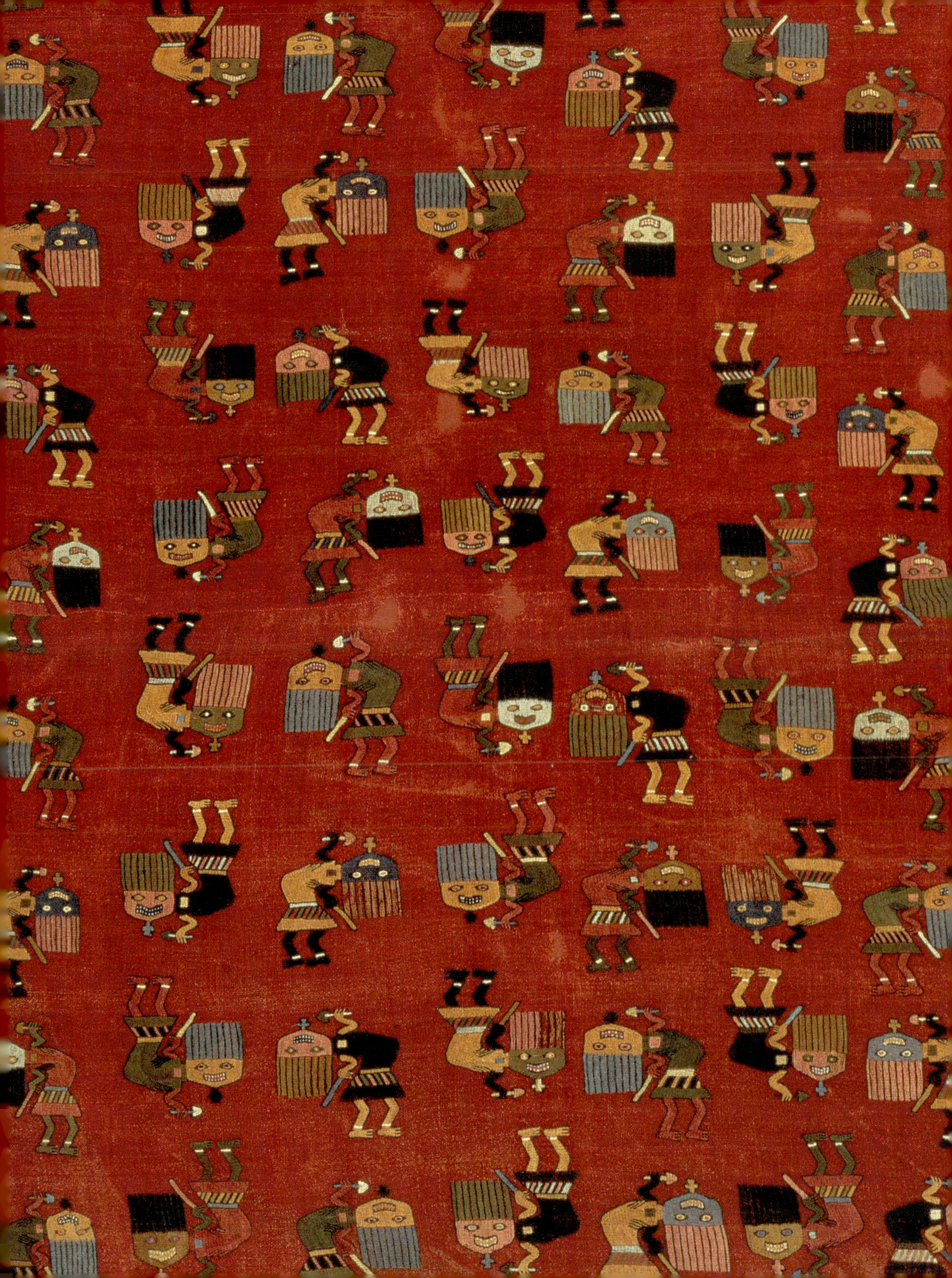

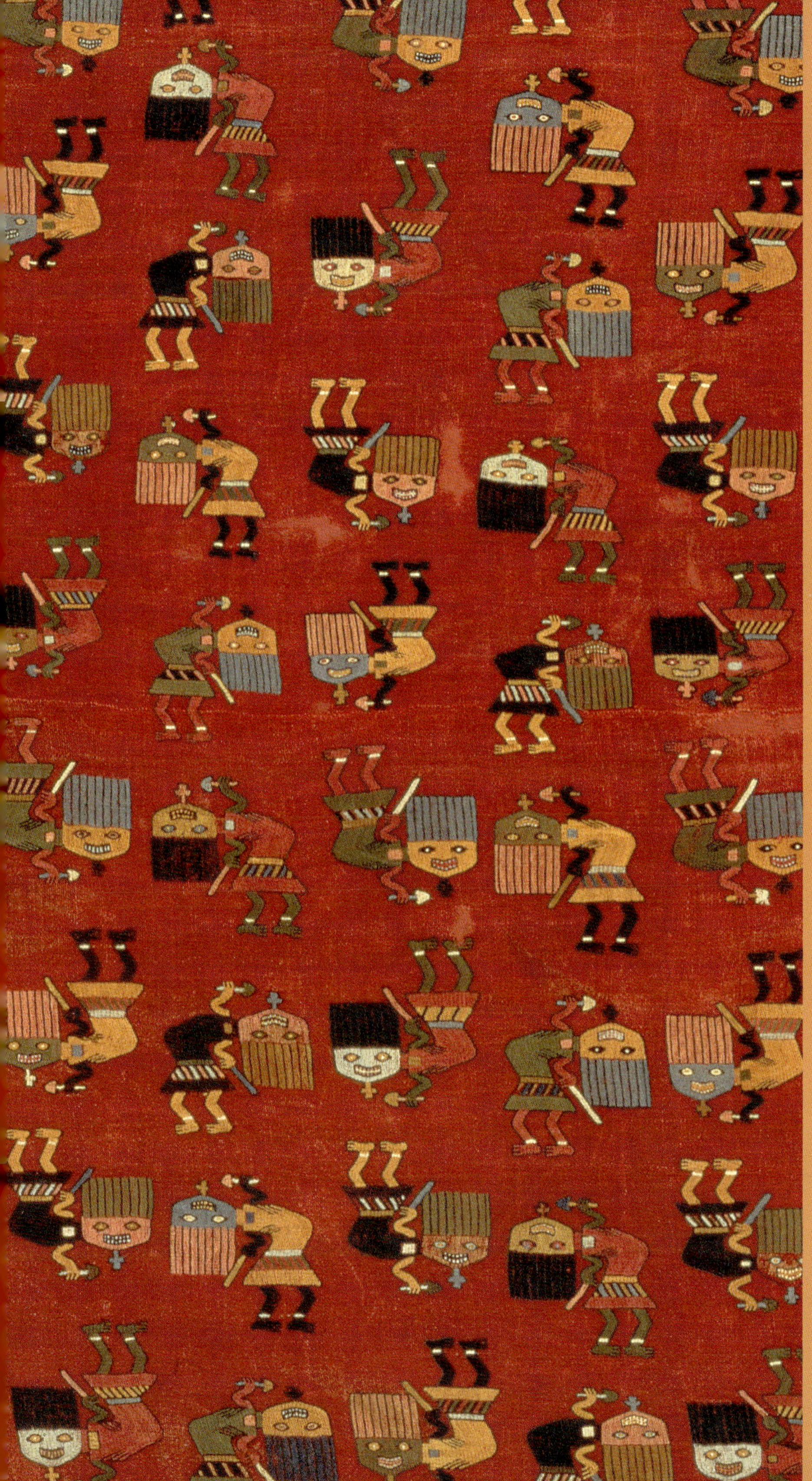

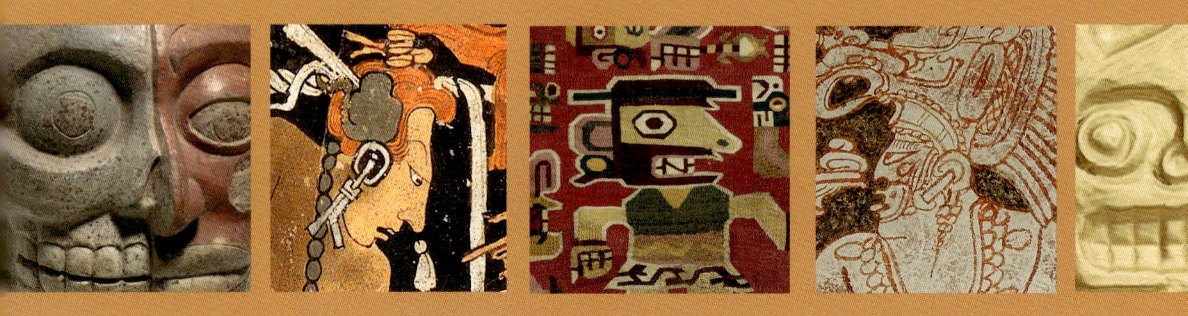

All societies develop religion and philosophy to address the mysteries of existence. In the ancient Americas, unique doctrines gave form to the cosmos and humanity's place therein. No overarching religious philosophy prevailed across the ancient Americas, but much like the Jewish, Christian, and Islamic faiths, fundamental principles were shared among related societies.

Foremost among these is the belief in a world animated by spirit forces. Natural phenomena—such as rain, earthquakes, and the movement of celestial bodies—were believed to be manifestations of the divine principle driving the universe. A second widespread belief is the human ability to interact with, and even affect, these universal forces via ritual practice. For example, in the Andes, ancestors were considered living beings existing in the spirit realm. When a person died, he/she became a sacred ancestor whose descendants could petition for divine power to address earthly needs. For this reason, among Peruvian cultures, the body was preserved in a bundle of tightly wrapped cloth that also encased personal items of adornment and occupation. The ancestral bundle was housed in special enclosures, and was brought out for consultation and participation in important gatherings. The quantity and quality of the cloth wrappings reflected the supernatural potency of the ancestor and the social status of the family.

A third common principle is that of shamanism, a religious doctrine based on the belief in spirit companions and the shaman's ability to take on their form and characteristics. The shaman travels to the preternatural realm as her/his animal companion and acquires supernatural powers to wield on earth for such purposes as healing the sick, vanquishing enemies, and ensuring life-giving rains. A shaman achieves a spirit form through a variety of techniques commonly used throughout the world. In the ancient Americas, these included repetitive motion, hypnotic sounds, and the ingestion of mind-altering substances such as psychotropic plants, alcohol, and neurological toxins (usually animal poisons). Some artworks from Mexico and Central America suggest that shamans, too, relied on yoga-like positions and meditative exercises. The shaman's spirit journey is likened to the transition from life to death, although the shaman has the ability to return to the world of the living. Today in Mexico and Central America, shamans call the spiritual journey the "sleep of death."

Ancient American artists grappled with the challenge of portraying that which cannot be seen. A common convention for depicting nature's divine forces is the composite animal-human form. These representations, which we often refer to as gods or deities, are a graphic way to illustrate something lacking physical form. To picture the shaman's transformation, artists would combine human and animal features based on the belief that shamans have animal companion spirits and, while in the spirit realm, they acquire the animals' characteristic powers. The shamanic forms feature such animals as crocodiles, jaguars, raptors, and bats (see, for example, pp. 86–87). With these points in mind, the art of the ancient Americas becomes more understandable as a symbolic visual language describing divine principles of the universe. Without some degree of graphic literacy, these portrayals appear simultaneously simplistic and incomprehensibly complex.

Among many ancient American cultures, sacrifice was essential for life and balance in the universe. Andean ideology expressed this balance as paired opposites—light and dark, male and female, hot and cold, day and night, sun and moon, gold and silver, etc. The tension between opposing forces caused the universe to be created and continues to animate it. Humanity plays a key role in preserving the balance through proper rituals and social conduct, especially acts of blood sacrifice, which regenerate the earth. Similarly among Mesoamerican cultures, universal balance was maintained by the exchange of life-giving liquids—blood from humans and animals to nourish the gods who bestow rainwater and fertility.

Throughout the Americas, rulers, as formidable shamans, were believed to have special relationships with the spirit world because they possessed the ability to tap into its sacred forces for the benefit of society. This divine sanction was the foundation of social and political hierarchy and created the moral platform from which a sovereign enjoyed expansive secular powers. A noble's blood sacrifice was not the odious practice of primitive people, but rather was the paramount metaphor for rulership as resolute service to society and a way to ensure continuity of universal life.

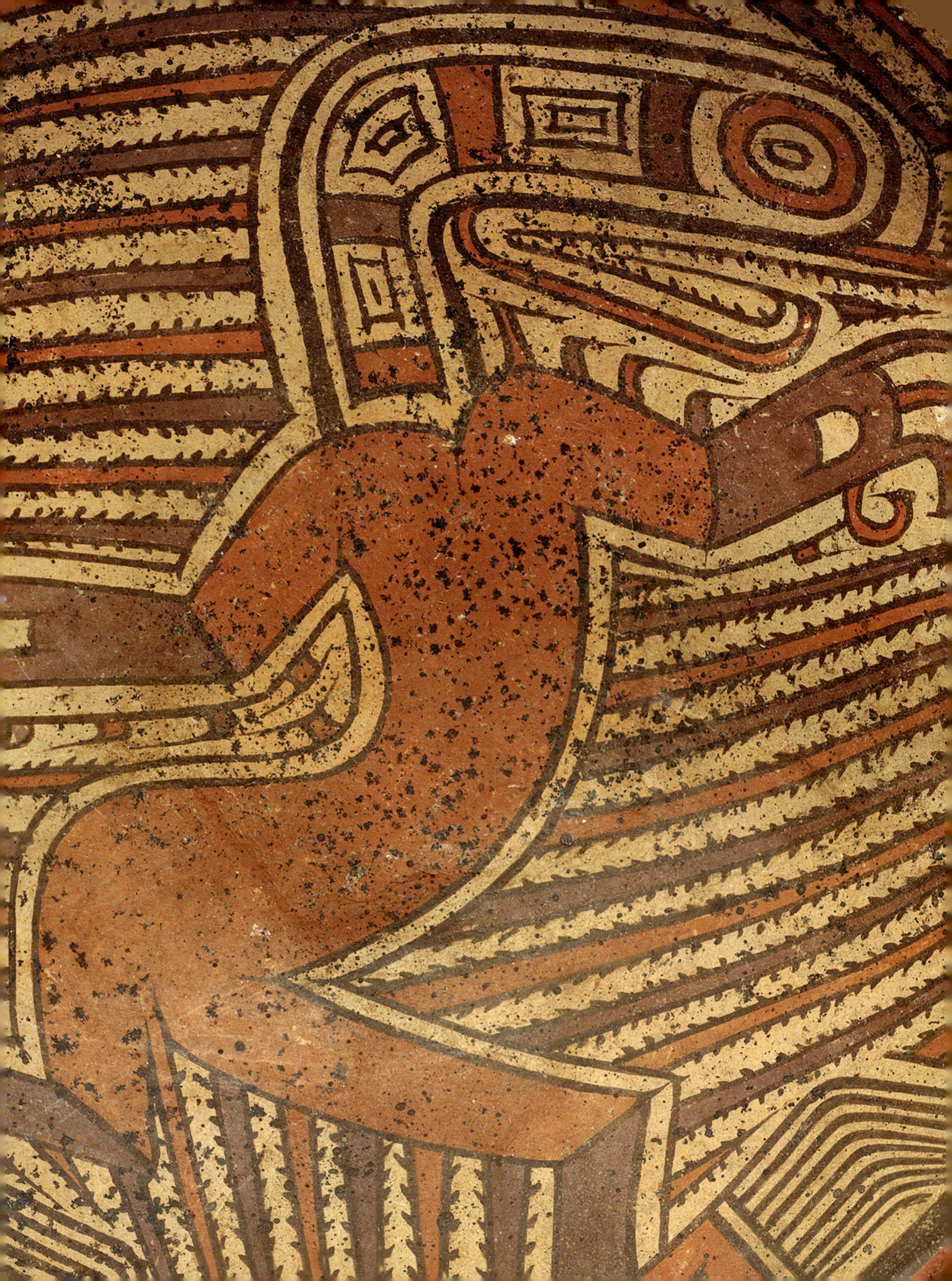

Plate

Maya, Late Classic Period, 680–740 CE
Nakbé area, Mirador Basin, Guatemala

This plate is a superb example of the distinctive
"codex-style" pottery, so named because its palette
and fine-line painting recall those of the four surviving ancient Maya books or "codices." Codex-style
pottery was made exclusively in the Mirador Basin
of northwestern Guatemala and royal workshops
at nearby Calakmul, in southern Mexico. The hieroglyphic text at the top of the plate's scene names its
owner Toham K'awiil, who ruled in the Mirador Basin
during the early eighth century.

The scene illustrates a prime epic in Maya religion that also was key to royal power. It portrays the
Maize god's resurrection from death, rising from the
underworld due to the clever and magical efforts
of his heroic twin sons Juun Ajaw and Yax B'ahlam.
They pour water on the earth, symbolized by a turtle
shell, which cracked and released the Maize god.
This myth is an allegory of the natural cycle of maize
as it sprouts each year in the once-dry fields now
nourished by the spring rains. Just as a young maize
plant emerges from death (the hard, dry seed planted
underground), so too is the Maize god resurrected
from the underworld when his sons water the earthly
shell.

Earthenware with red and black on cream slip paint
H. 5.8 cm (2¼ in.), w. 32 cm (12⅝ in.)
Gift of Landon T. Clay   1993.565

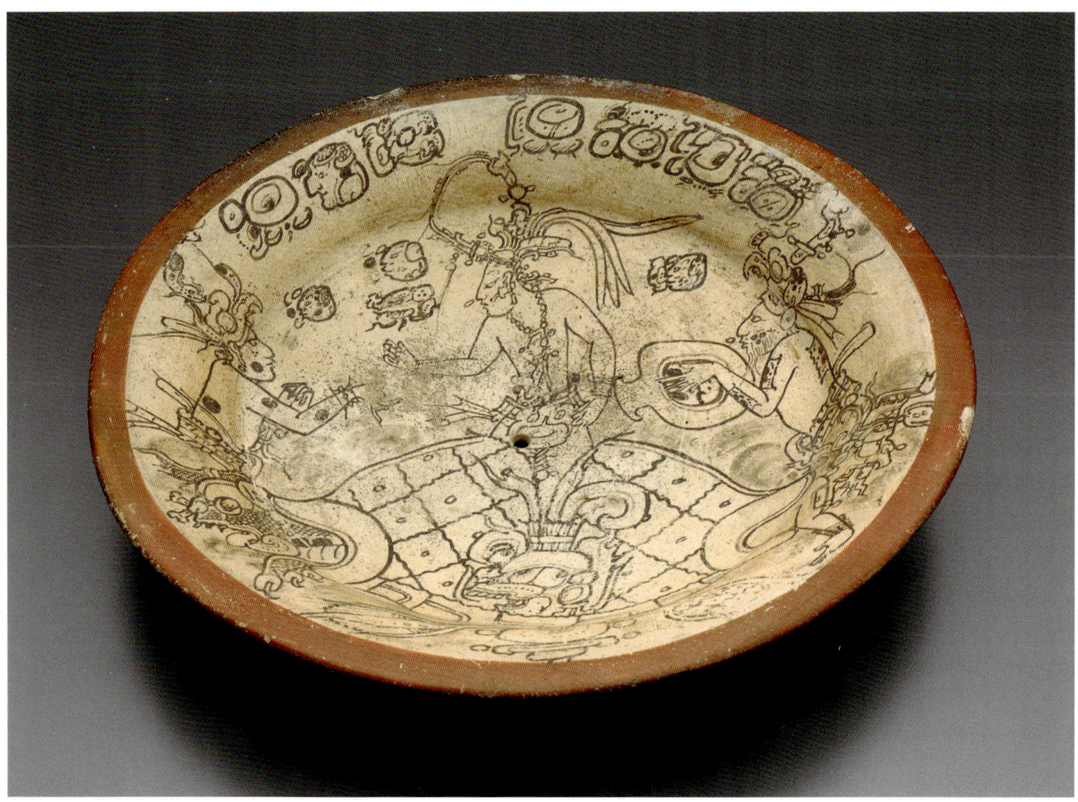

Drinking vessel

Maya, Late Classic Period, 755–780 CE
Motul de San José area, Lake Petén Itzá region,
Department of El Petén, Guatemala

Considered one of the preeminent artistic achievements of Maya vase painting, the dramatic imagery on this vase combines two seminal myths expressing the universal cycle of reciprocity of life—the sacrifice of the Baby Jaguar being, and the birth/resurrection of the Maize god. The scene wrapping around the vessel is unified by the jaguar deity's white umbilical cord, and the artist used a black background to indicate the event took place during pre-creation times. Here the Maize god rises from the mythical maize mountain, rendered as a bearded saurian with a maize leaf adorning its earflare. A pair of supernatural beings greets the newborn god (although he is rendered in adult form), their wrists and ankles wrapped with sacrificial blood-splattered paper or cloth.

The short hieroglyphic text records the details of the event beginning with its date indicated by the day and month positions in the 260-day Mesoamerican ritual calendar. Unfortunately, most of the date was lost when a small piece was broken from the vase's rim; only the month name *Mak* survives. The text goes on to name the Jaguar Baby–Maize god and identifies the location of the birth—a mythological place named Naah Jo' Chan Tz'am Xaman (first-five-sky altar [of the] north). The complex form of the "altar" hieroglyph looks very much like the saurian-mountain on which the deity rises, thereby indicating that the locale is both a geographic location and the mythical "first-five-sky-altar-north" place.

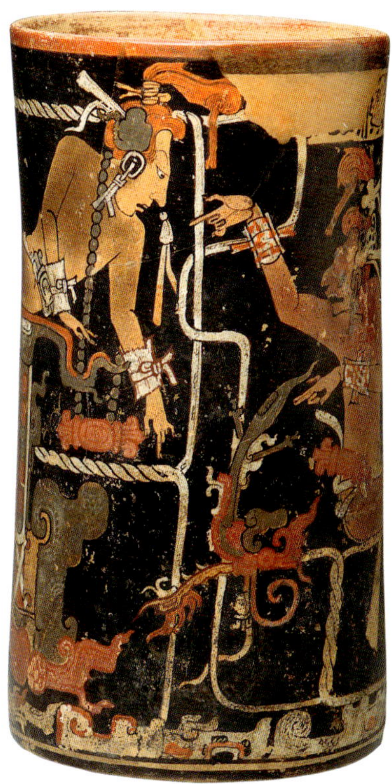

Earthenware with red, orange, ocher, brown, gray (originally green), and black on cream slip paint
H. 22.5 cm (8⅞ in.), diam. 12 cm (4¾ in.)
Gift of Landon T. Clay   1988.1168

Panel

Wari, Middle Horizon Period, 500–700 CE
Peru

This tapestry panel teems with colorful forms that repeat a seemingly simple illustration of a standing male figure and a feline or camelid (likely a llama). Closer inspection reveals this to be an account of the Andean principle of a universe animated by creative life forces. This principle lies at the heart of ancient Andean cosmology and served as the spiritual foundation of social and political hierarchy, including that of the Wari state. The Wari created the first empire-like political organization in the Andes and sponsored the production of opulent textiles, as both personal and architectural adornments, to express their civic and religious configurations.

The standing male figure is the so-called Sacrificer, one of three main Wari supernatural beings embodying the creative forces in nature and conduit to the supernatural realm. The Sacrificer's long staff is topped by a U-shaped finial, and he wears a headdress of pierced white rectangular sequins. Versions of these items made from silver have been found in elite burials at the Wari site of Espíritu Pampa in southern Peru, which suggest that those in official positions in the Wari state wielded the Sacrificer's divine powers.

Another prominent entity pictured on this tapestry is the so-called Winged Staff Bearer, who always appears in profile and flanks a frontally portrayed personage (here the Sacrificer). This rendering is unusual in Wari art for its being fully zoomorphic rather than the typical human-animal composite being. Also notable is the absence of the Winged Staff Bearer's requisite staff. Instead, the zoomorph grasps the neck of a trophy head hanging at the rear of the Sacrificer, which links visually and conceptually this crucial pair of supernaturals in Wari state ideology.

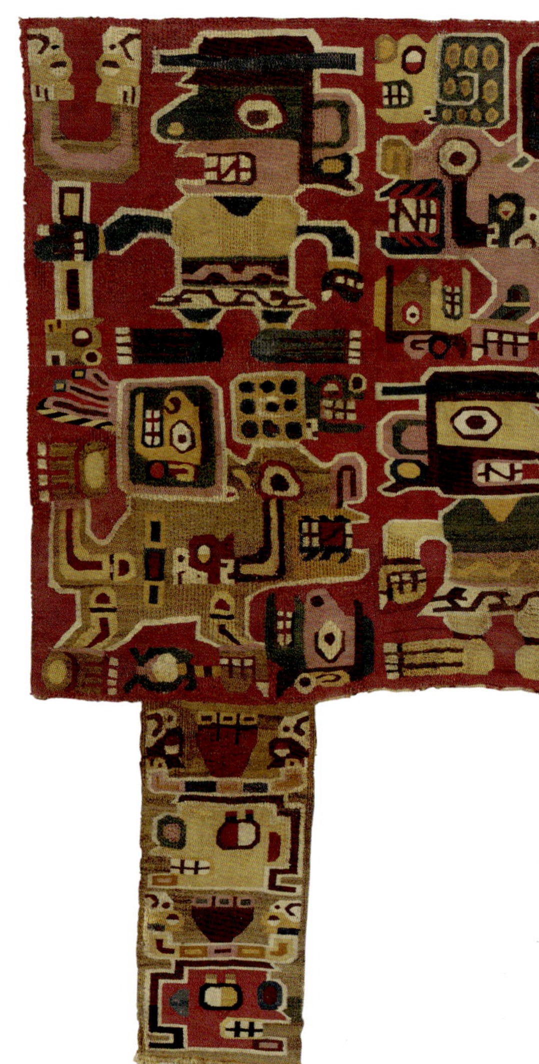

Wool (camelid) and cotton tapestry weave (predominantly interlocking)
H. 70.5 cm (27¾ in.), w. 117 cm (46⅛ in.)
Charles Potter Kling Fund   1996.50

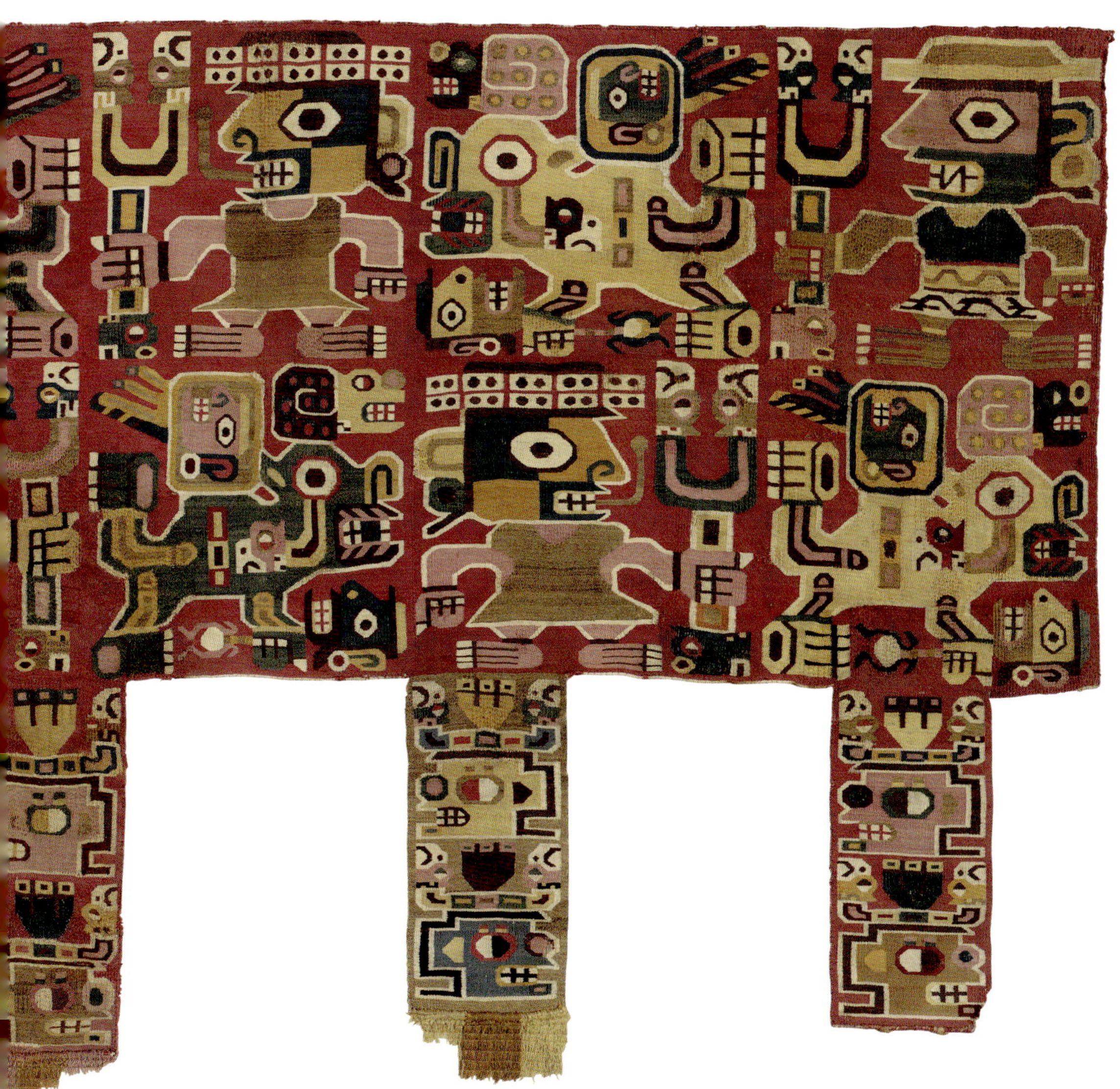

Seated figure

**Mezcala, Late Formative to Early Classic Periods,
400 BCE–300 CE
Guerrero, Mexico**

Hundreds of abstract figural sculptures purport-
edly came from the Balsas River Valley of central
Guerrero in western Mexico. The unique art style
and the unknown culture that produced them
were named for the area's main town of Mezcala.
The style emphasizes geometric abstraction to
represent the human figure, a rare format in Mesoamerican art. The only similar sculptural style is
the Valdivia tradition from Ecuador, although those
works are likely at least one thousand years older
(4000–1500 BCE) than the Mezcala pieces. Interestingly, however, archaeologists working in western
Mexico have found evidence for contact with Ecuador from perhaps as early as 700 BCE, which suggests a foreign stimulus for the Mezcala style.

In the 1950s these abstract artworks became
highly desirable among such collectors as the artist
Diego Rivera and the actor Vincent Price. The dating,
function, and meaning of Mezcala sculptures remain
uncertain. Recently, a cache of figurines and incense
burners was found inside a ritual cave, suggesting
a ceremonial function and symbolic connotation.
Unfortunately the cache's date could not be accu-
rately determined because the cave contained burials
and other ritual remains spanning a thousand years
from 700 BCE.

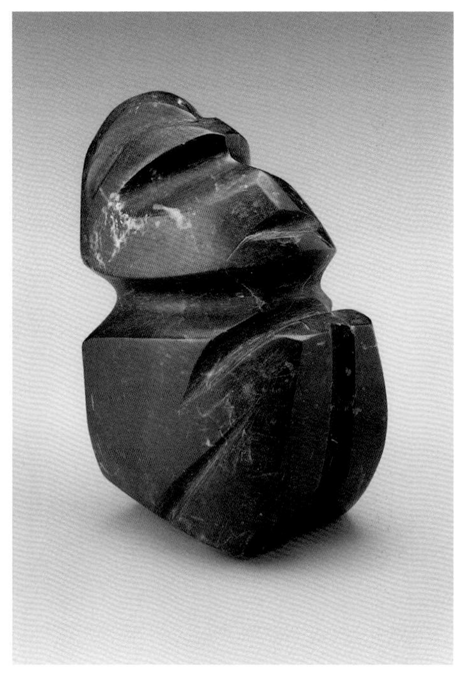

Drinking vessel

**Maya, Late Classic Period, 600–700 CE
Lake Petén Itzá area, Guatemala**

The resurrection of the Maize god is chronicled on
this drinking vessel. For the Maya, the Maize god Juun
Ixim embodied their belief in new life springing from
death, which they witness each spring when the dry,
bone-like maize seed sprouts anew from the earth.

In this version, the artist painted three deities
riding in canoes to the place of the Maize god's
emergence from the underworld, here symbolized
by a split turtle shell from which peer two elderly
earth gods. The canoe deities constitute a version
of the Palenque Triad (GI, GII, and GIII) merged
with the Paddler gods who ferried the dead into the
underworld. The Palenque Triad were patron gods of
Palenque, Mexico, and are related to the four Chan
Tuun Itzam group of deities as aspects of the rain-
storm and lightning god Chahk.

GI leads the group as he raises his lightning axe to crack open the earth. The second deity may be GII, whose name among the sixteenth-century K'iché Maya of Guatemala meant "abundance" and "bounty." He beats on a turtle shell with a deer antler to imitate thunder. The carapace-drum sits atop a water jar that may allude to rain and agricultural bounty. Bringing up the rear is GIII, who shares many features with the Jaguar Paddler. These three deities face Juun Ixim (shown here), who carries a bag of maize seeds and a water gourd as he rises from the earth represented by the split turtle carapace.

Earthenware with dark red, brown, black, and white on red ground slip paint
H. 22.1 cm (8¾ in.), diam. 12.1 cm (4¾ in.)
Gift of Landon T. Clay   1988.1178

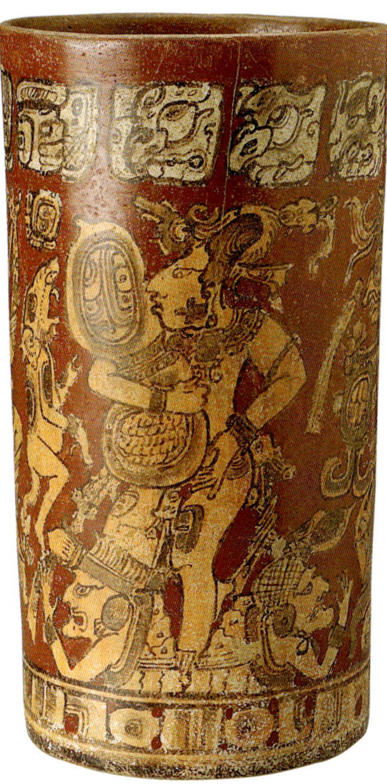

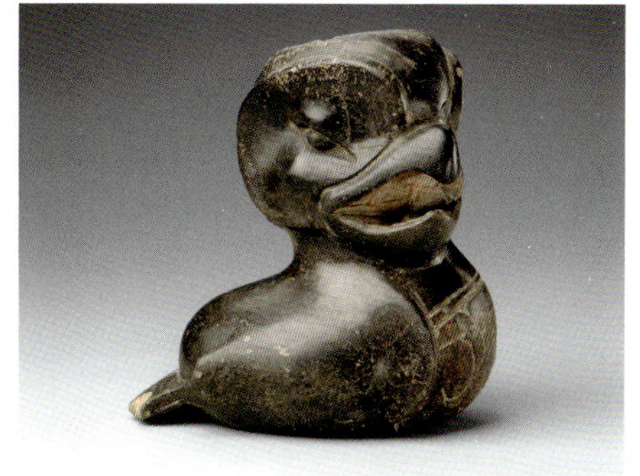

Bird effigy vessel

Olmec, Middle Formative Period, 900–600 BCE
Puebla or Valley of Mexico, Mexico

Naturalistic renderings of birds and aquatic animals typify early ceramic sculpture from highland Mexico. This vessel represents a composite avian rather than a specific species, featuring the rounded eye area and hooked beak of the laughing falcon (*Herpetotheres cachinnans*), and a feather tuft at the back of the head characteristic of hawks. The large head and small body suggest a juvenile bird. Such merged forms are a hallmark of the shamanic undercurrent in Olmec religion with its pantheon of deities and spirit beings. A complex icon on the bird's chest may represent the "composite zoomorph," one of three fundamental themes in Olmec art. This entity symbolizes the boundary between the surface of the earth and the underworld—the transition point between earth-light-life and underworld-darkness-death. The watery Olmec underworld was inhabited by spirit entities and preternatural animals often portrayed as fantastical zoomorphic-anthropomorphic beings.

Earthenware with traces of red pigment
H. 14.5 cm (5¾ in.), w. 9.7 cm (3⅞ in.), d. 14.4 cm (5⅝ in.)
William Francis Warden Fund   1972.422

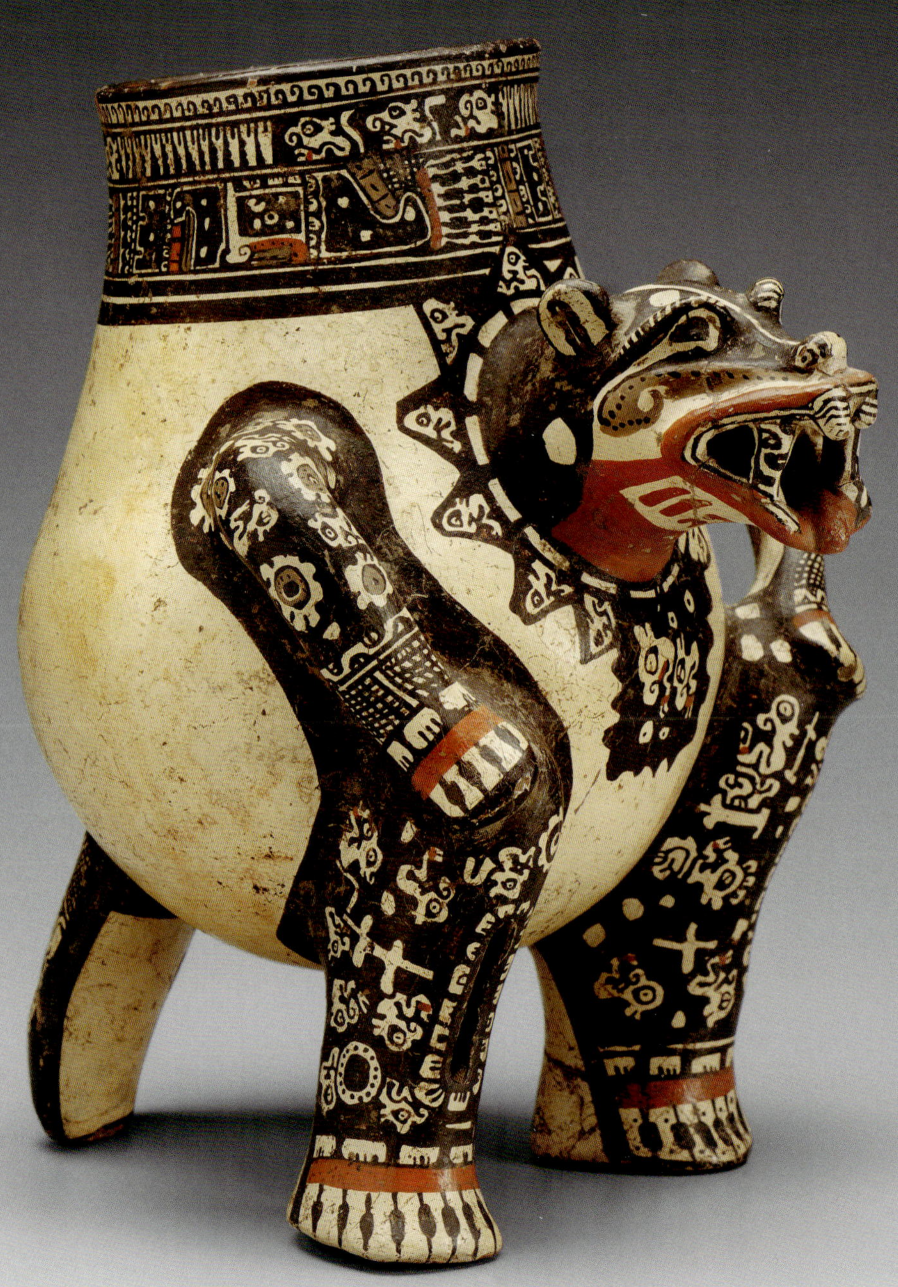

Jaguar effigy vessel

Guanacaste-Nicoya, Period VI, 1000–1350

Rivas region, southern Nicaragua

This bulbous jar depicts a shaman transformed into his/her jaguar spirit form during a visionary quest. The fierce shamanic spirit erupts from the jar, jutting its feline head out through a dark rayed circle, its gaping mouth with bared teeth ready to attack. Small pellets inside the hollow front legs produce a rattling sound when shaken, resembling the jaguar's low grumble as it stalks its prey. Further evoking the jaguar-shaman's combat against preternatural forces is the low-slung head like that of a hunting cat. A successful strike is implied by the blood-red slip paint encircling the mouth and paws.

The shaman is not absent, however. Her/his human form is conveyed by the vertical pose mimicking that of the trance-seeker's conventional seated position on a low, three-legged stool with hands resting on bent knees. The animal's tail serves double duty as the stool's third leg. The verticality of the arms, legs, and tail suspends the jar in space, mirroring the shaman's ascent into the realm of shamanic vision. Tiny profile jaguars adorn the black-painted limbs in contrast to human-like forms seen around the neck opening, which together echo the art-work's theme of the shaman residing within the visionary jaguar.

Earthenware with red and black on white slip paint
H. 29.2 cm (11½ in.), w. 21.1 cm (8¼ in.), d. 24.1 cm (9½ in.)
Museum purchase with funds donated by Leigh B. and Steve Braude   2005.9

Pedestal dish

Macaracas style, Period VI-B, 800–1000
Azuero Peninsula, Panama

The exuberant Macaracas ceramic style reflects the artistic vigor of ninth-century Panama, a time of social, economic, political, and spiritual dynamism. Increasing populations, larger towns, and foreign exchange indicate plentiful food production and complex social networks, regional trade, and political growth. Macaracas painters responded with an innovative style reflecting the spirit of the times (or zeitgeist) with unreserved visual dynamism using simple lines and color. The painted compositions vibrate with visual forms that disavow the two-dimensional surface.

Here the artist masterfully portrayed the shaman's transformation from human to spirit realm, likening this unobservable transition to the agile motion of a crocodile as it slips below the water's surface. Serrated lines fill the background to create visual agitation that shatters the flat surface into an oscillating three-dimensional space. The jagged edges replicate the shaman's pulsating trance-vision and allude to the shaman's penetrating powers and the ephemeral, water-like spirit world through which the human-crocodile glides. The solid red color of the humanoid body contrasts with the willowy lines of the head and claws, fixing the body in space while the head and appendages dematerialize into the visionary world. The spiked rays between the figure's legs point perpendicularly to those of the background, breaking the composition's hypnotic horizontal energy and invoking the multi-directionality of the shamanic journey.

Earthenware with red, purple and black on cream slip paint
H. 16.5 cm (6½ in.), diam. 25.9 cm (10¼ in.)
Promised gift of Timothy Phillips

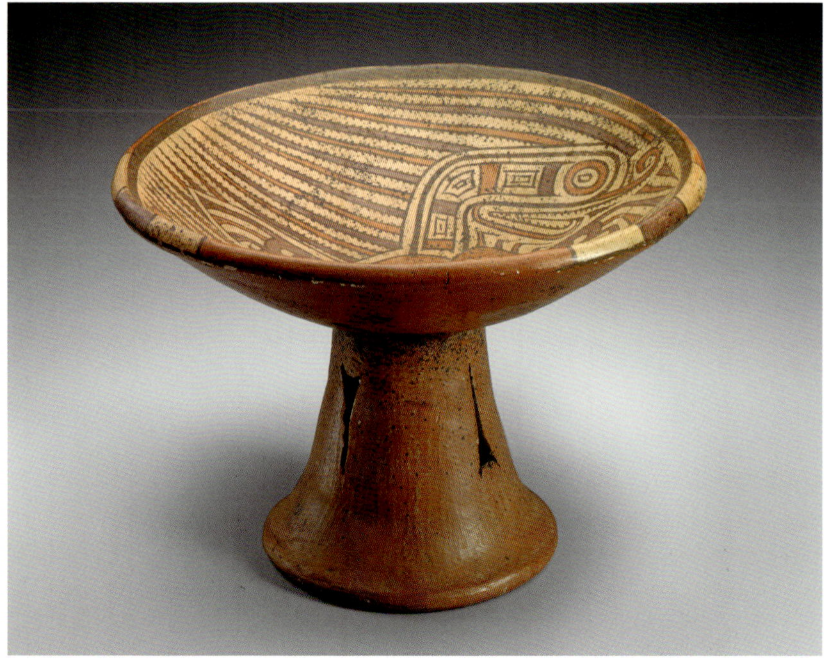

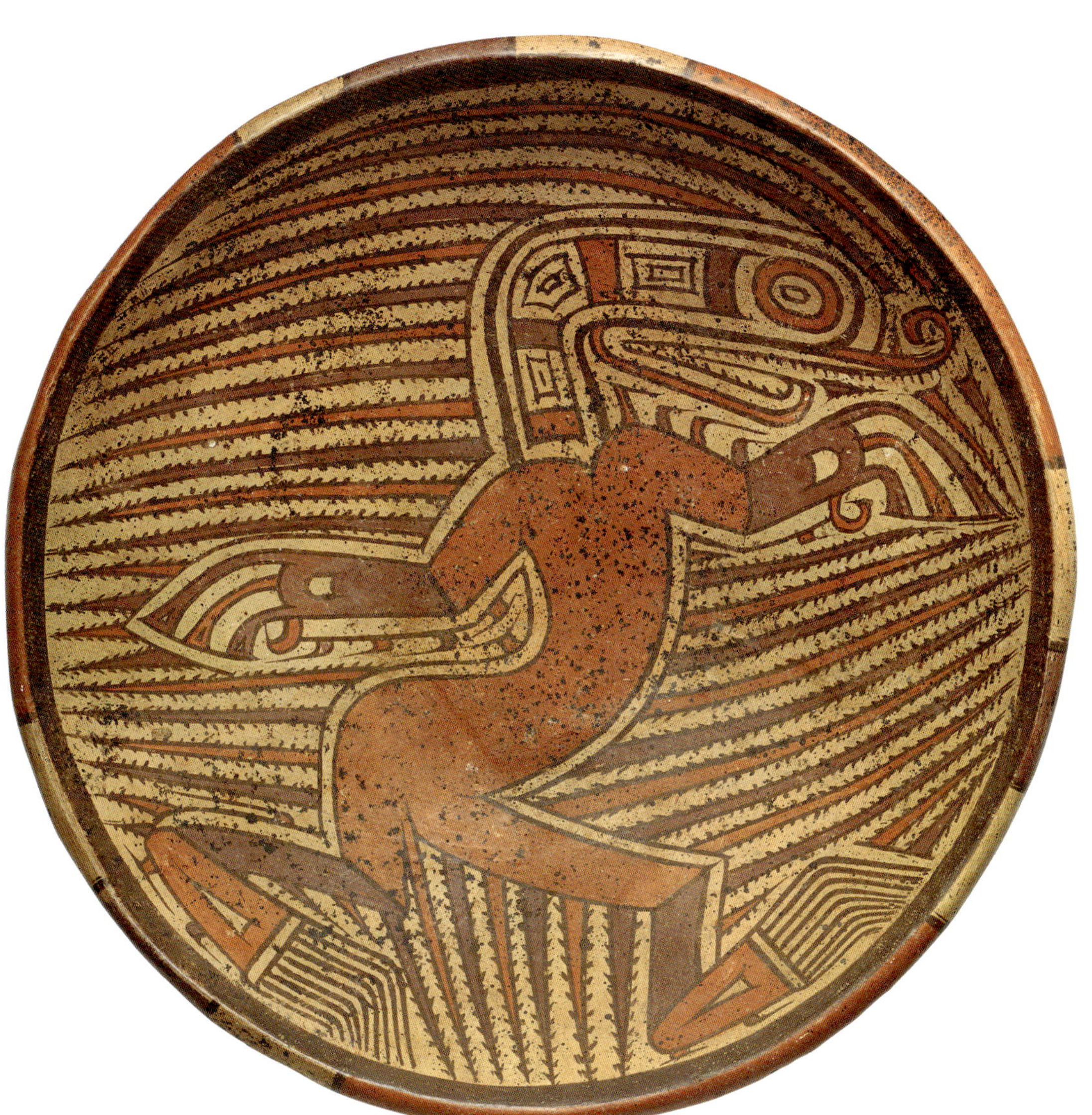

Pectoral

Coclé, Periods V–VI, 700–1520

Sitio Conte area, Coclé Province, Panama

This gold disk evinces the trance state of shamanic transformation. The splayed figure's limbs ending in crocodile claws and the absence of sex indicators portray the ambiguity of the shaman during trance. The pointed ears and serrated bands erupting from the torso evoke the heightened hearing, sharpened sounds, and pulsating visual effects experienced during trance. They also denote spirit energy and supernatural power, and, as an artistic device, negate the separation between foreground and background and form and essence, thereby expressing the here-but-not-here paradox of the shamanic loss-of-body sensation and expansion of consciousness. Two fish-beings float above the figure, no longer governed by earth's gravitational restraints. They share the central figure's large eyes with fixed stare, which denotes the enhanced sight experienced during trance and the shaman's ability to look through earthly boundaries and across the visionary realm.

Gold adornments were commonly worn by peoples in Costa Rica and Panama according to eyewitness accounts by sixteenth-century Spaniards, who observed incredulously that these precious ornaments took the place of other clothing. Spanish witnesses of a Panamanian leader's funeral describe the cloth-wrapped body completely covered in golden plaques, wide bands, and a plethora of other precious metal objects. It is likely that large disks such as this one were among such funerary items.

Gold alloy

H. 10.3 cm (4 in.), diam. 10.8 cm (4 ¼ in.)

Gift of Landon T. Clay   1971.1124

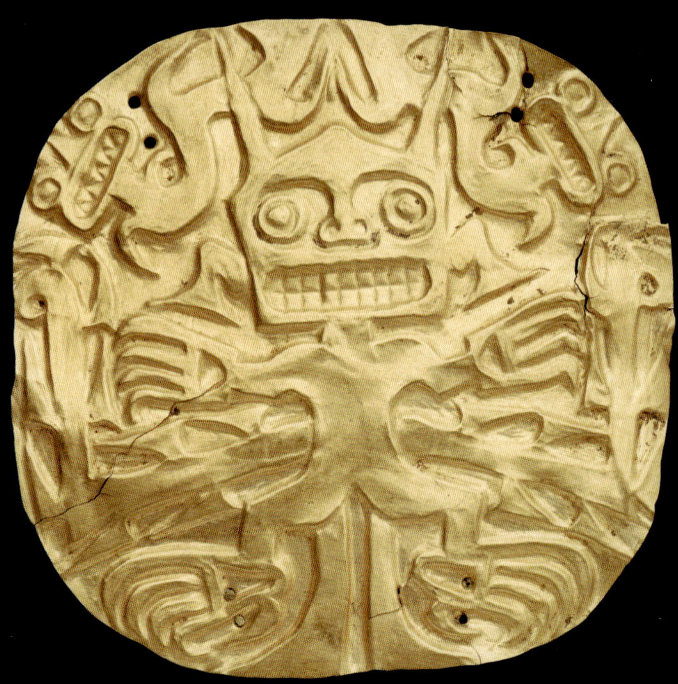

Drinking vessel

Maya, Late Classic Period, 650–750 CE
Upper San Pedro River, northwestern Petén
lowlands, Guatemala

This vessel for drinking chocolate was made for an aristocrat of the Hix Witz polity located in northwestern Guatemala. With painting and hieroglyphic styles typical of this region, its theme is ritual drinking. Hieroglyphic texts divide the scene into three sections, each recounting a different part of the rite. The first part, featuring a seated man with upraised arms, illustrates the preparation of the alcoholic libation. The large jars shown nearby contain the draft, two of which are marked with a hieroglyph indicating the contents' intoxicating nature (*chih*, fermented agave [pulque]). The second section, shown here, portrays the intoxicated participant being helped to his feet by two attendants while a cloaked figure offers a burning roll of tobacco. The third scene presents the intoxicant's ritual dance in the company of a kneeling assistant, both richly attired in garments specific to rites of ritual intoxication and vision quest.

Inebriation facilitated the transcendental event, whose goal was to activate sacred powers on earth. Participants smoked strong tobacco and consumed mind-altering beverages such as balché, a honey-based alcoholic brew, or pulque, both of which continue to be made by Yukatek Maya in Mexico. Hallucinogenic substances also may have been consumed. Maya art frequently depicts rulers and members of the elite participating in such ceremonies because political authority was based, in part, on their conducting these rites. Success was measured by such outcomes as the timely beginning of the rains, bountiful crops, and victories in warfare.

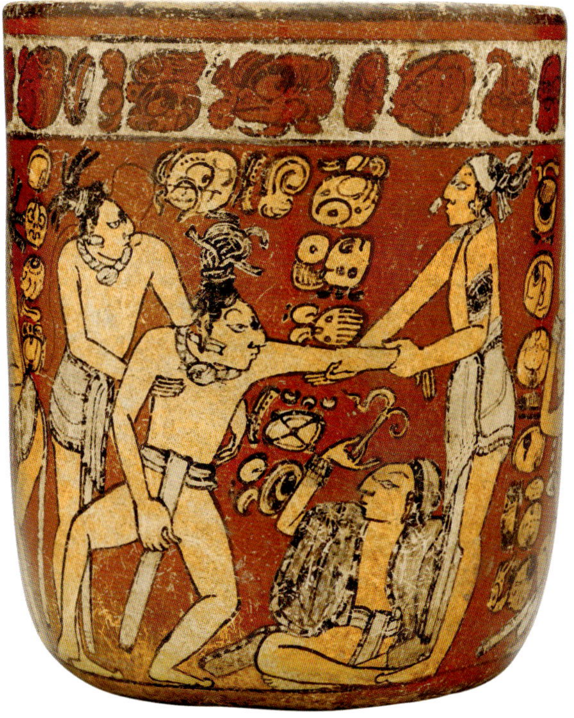

Earthenware with red, orange, black, and white on cream slip decoration
H. 19.1 cm (7 ½ in.), diam. 15.9 cm (6 ¼ in.)
Gift of Lavinia and Landon T. Clay   2003.775

Plate with rattle feet

Maya, Late Classic Period, 650–750 CE

Xultún area, Guatemala

A nobleman performs a dance ritual in front of a throne adorned with celestial symbols. This type of adorned throne is found inside palace buildings throughout the Maya lowlands, with those of Copán, Honduras, featuring the same set of celestial emblems carved onto their front edges. The plate's painting style and clay paste chemistry, however, affirm its production in a workshop in eastern Guatemala near the prominent city of Naranjo.

The nobleman's ritual performance took place during a formal event that included the presentation of tribute or gifts placed on the left edge of the throne. Note the large stack of white cloth, quetzal bird feathers, and *Spondylus shells*—all valuable commodities throughout Mesoamerica. The lord gazes into a divination mirror propped against the stack of cloth, the mirror placed in an ornate basketry frame. Divination mirrors were the symbolic portal to the supernatural realm, which could be opened by those with special abilities. This lord's successful quest is implied by the four "vision serpents" encircling him and the black background evincing the spirit realm's darkness.

Earthenware with pink, black, and orange slip decoration
H. 12.4 cm (4 ⅞ in.), diam. 38.1 cm (15 in.)
Gift of Lavinia and Landon T. Clay
2004.240

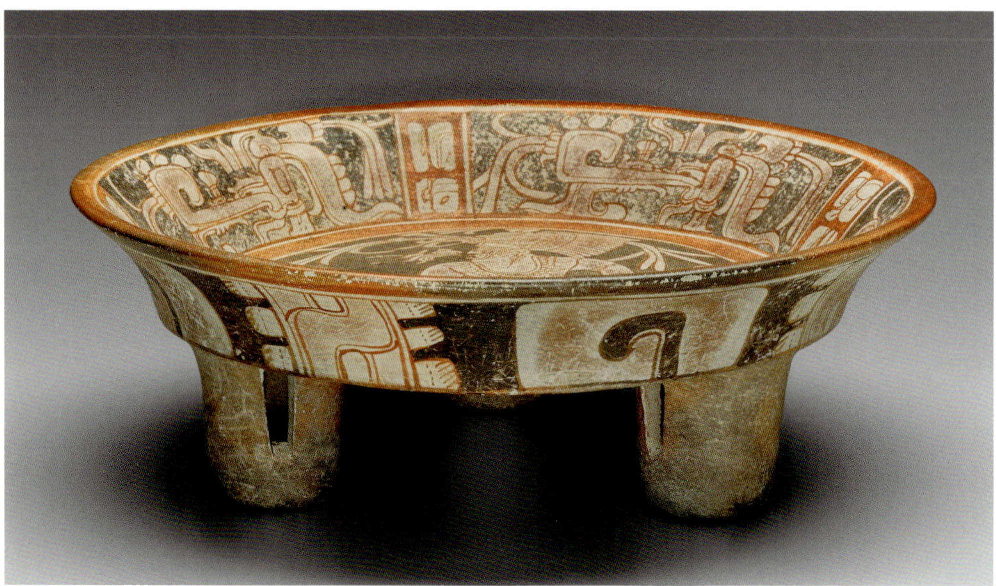

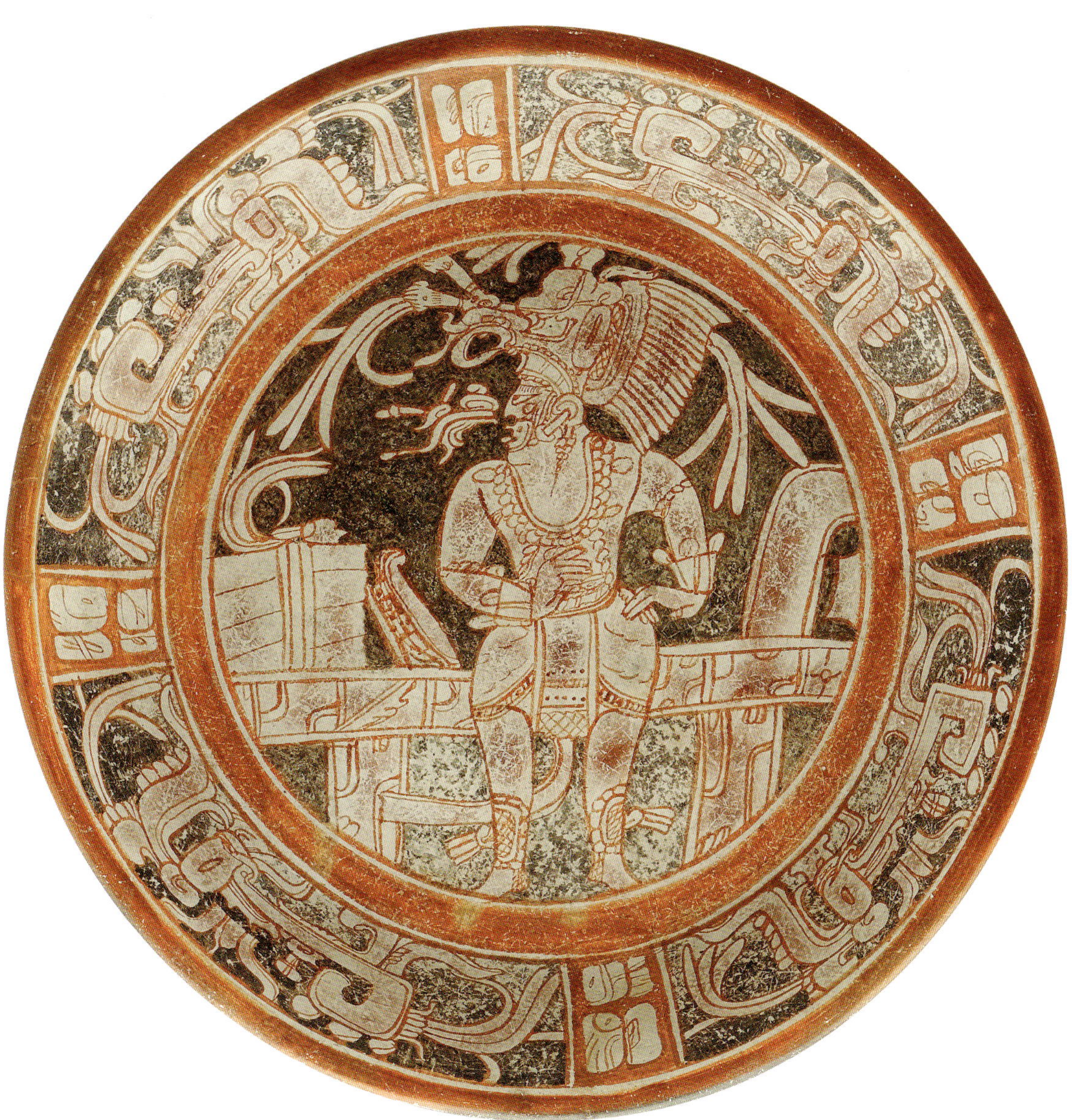

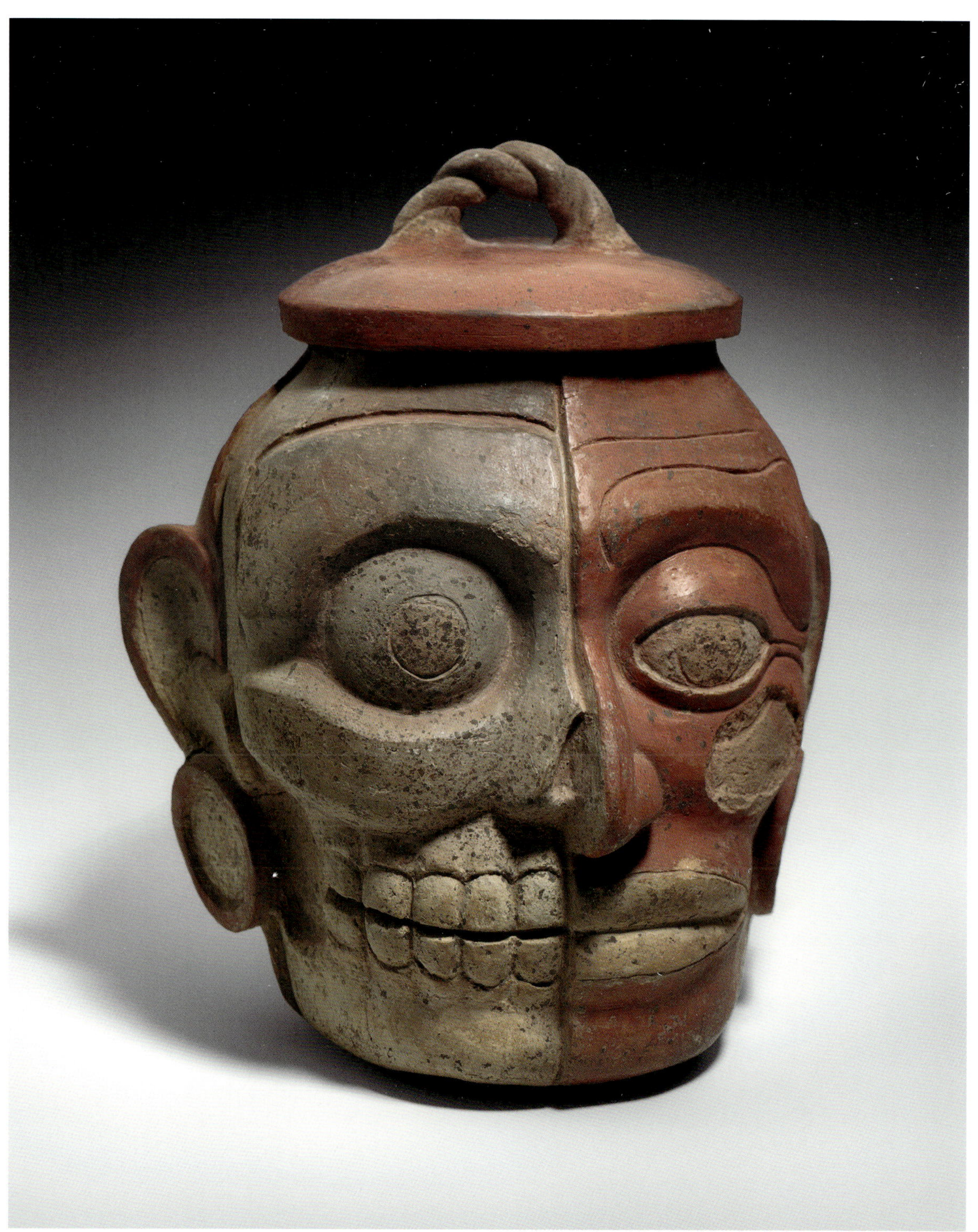

Head effigy jar

Maya, Late Classic Period, 600–850 CE

Southern Highlands, Guatemala

Human head effigy jars, which are typical of Guatemala's Southern Highlands, are simultaneously naturalistic and emblematic. This unique example addresses the universal experience of all living things—the ever-linked duality of life and death and the unanswered question of an afterlife or a rebirth. It also likely makes reference to the shaman's experience of losing her/his physical body upon entering the supernatural realm and the eventual return to earthly form.

The artist pictorially divided the head effigy vessel into two equal halves. One side depicts a fully fleshed, living person, even portraying the person's idiosyncratic forehead wrinkles. An intense red slip paint colors the flesh, sparkling with the iron flecks of hematite. The deep red-hued skin contrasts with the cream-colored lips, which are further emphasized with an incised outline. The other half of the jar depicts the skull within, here painted a whitish color like that of bone. Curiously, both eye orbits contain eyeballs, their pupils accentuated by red pigment to enhance the piercing gaze. The "death" side also includes a fleshed ear complete with ear ornament. Together these anatomical features suggest an alternative interpretation of the jar as a reference to shamanic transformation, which is likened to the "sleep of death" by modern Maya practitioners. From this viewpoint, the jar foretells the "death" of the shaman's earthly self and loss of body as he/she enters the supernatural realm of shamanic experience. The two eyes and fleshed ears signify the shaman's need for vision and hearing to receive the mystical divinatory knowledge as well as his/her eventual return to an earthly existence.

Earthenware with specular hematite slip paint

H. 29.9 cm (9 in.)

Gift from the Collection of Shirley and Hy Zaret

2008.190a-b

Pedestal dish

Gran Coclé, Conte period VI-A, 600–800 CE
Panama

Plates with tall pedestal supports are unique to Panama. They were used as serving dishes and perhaps as jar stands, their distinctive form recalling that of hallucinogenic mushrooms ingested by shamans to assist their spirit journey. The Gran Coclé style features fine-line painted imagery in careful balance between order and chaos, imitating the shaman's experience of being in the unpredictable otherworld yet present in the orderly human realm.

Panamanian pottery artists created a unique pictorial vocabulary to depict that which cannot be seen, heard, or described. Modern-day shamans frequently state that words simply are inadequate to articulate their interaction with the otherworld, because the linearity of speech defies the multiplicity of the visionary experience. Art is especially equipped to represent such experiences because imagery can be many-layered and simultaneously make multiple references. Here the main figural form combines features of a stingray, boa constrictor, lizard, and hammerhead shark to convey the idea of a transformed, spirit-world form. The strong undulating outlines with jagged spiked edges cause the image to expand and contract against the plate's rim. They also visually dissolve the distinction between form and space, and thereby capture the visionary experience. The artist rendered the creature in an upside-down position to further denote the shamanic world's alternate orientations.

Earthenware with red, purple, and black on white slip paint
H. 14.1 cm (5½ in.), diam. 28.6 cm (11¼ in.)
Gift of Timothy Phillips in honor of Thomas F. Phillips, Jr.
2015.3299

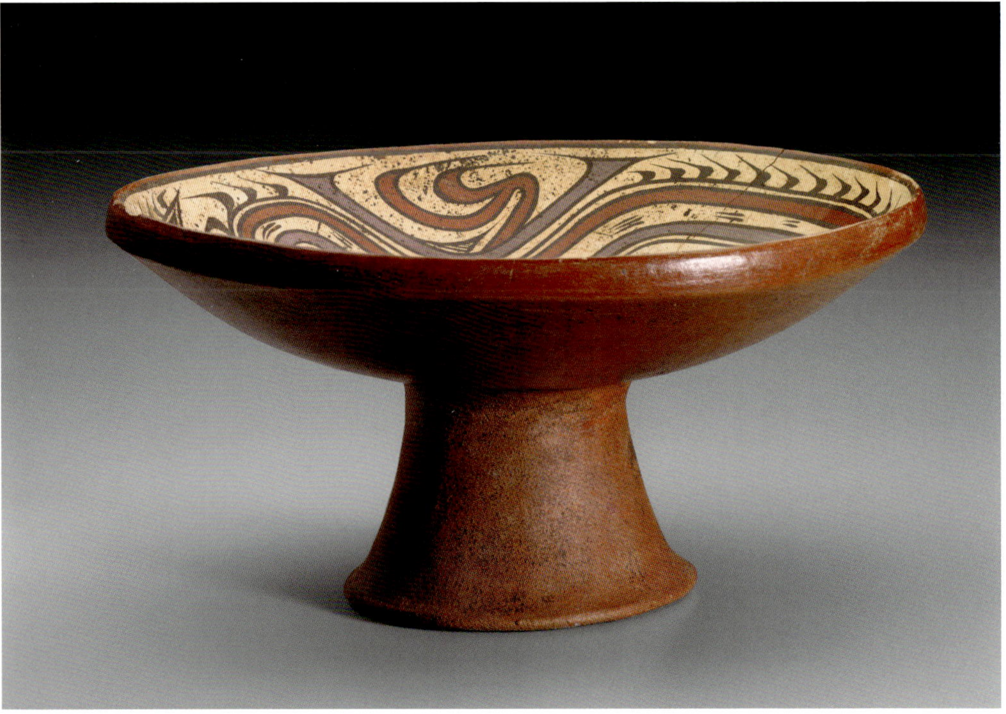

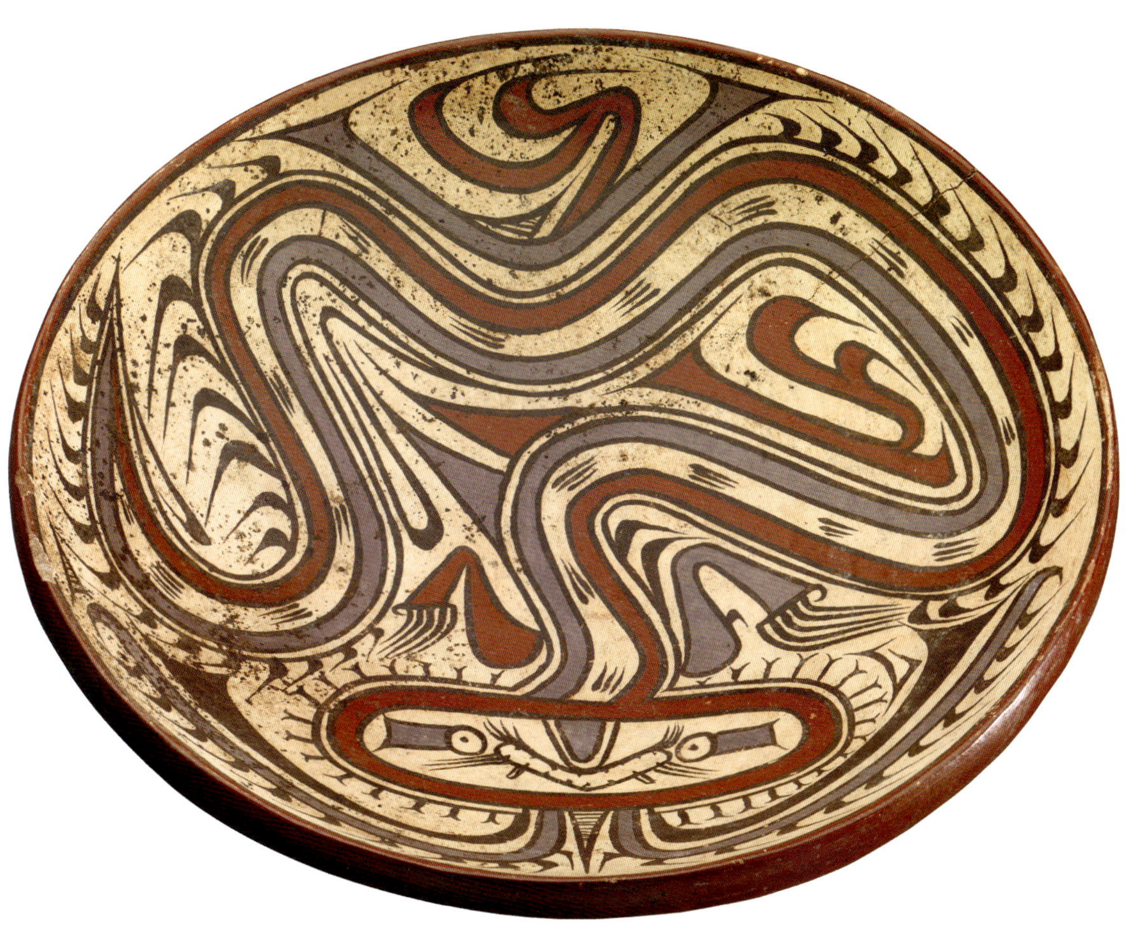

Burial urn

K'iché Maya, Late Classic Period, 700–850 CE
Southern Highlands, Guatemala

This impressive burial urn is among the finest expressions of Late Classic period K'iché Maya ceramic sculpture, one of eight such urns in the MFA's collection. Here the Maize god sits atop the urn's lid, cradling a maize plant with two ripe ears. This deity symbolized resurrection based on the metaphor of the maize plant emerging in the fields at the beginning of each rainy season. The shark-head-like lid symbolizes the entrance to the watery underworld, its mouth open to receive offerings. This same shark-like creature is modeled with a gaping maw on the urn's base, and an aged supernatural peers out from the netherworld.

Large burial urns are unique to Guatemala's southern highlands. None has been scientifically excavated, but twentieth-century accounts by itinerant explorers confirm that these urns were found buried inside temple platforms and concealed in caves. The cave urns were said to contain human bones, plain pottery vessels, shell and jadeite adornments, small animal bones, bits of charcoal, and the blackened remains of decayed organic matter. They were surrounded by intentionally broken objects and small piles of charcoal, ash, and melted candle wax. These are the remains of offerings made by the living to their honored dead. The offerings were intended to ensure the ancestors' wellbeing in the afterlife and to seek their divine advice; some offerings were made by Christian Mayas, who embrace their ancestors as sacred figures similar to the saints.

Earthenware with white, black, yellow, blue-green, and red paint
H. 132 cm (52 in.), w. 64 cm (25¼ in.)
Gift of Landon T. Clay   1988.1290a-b

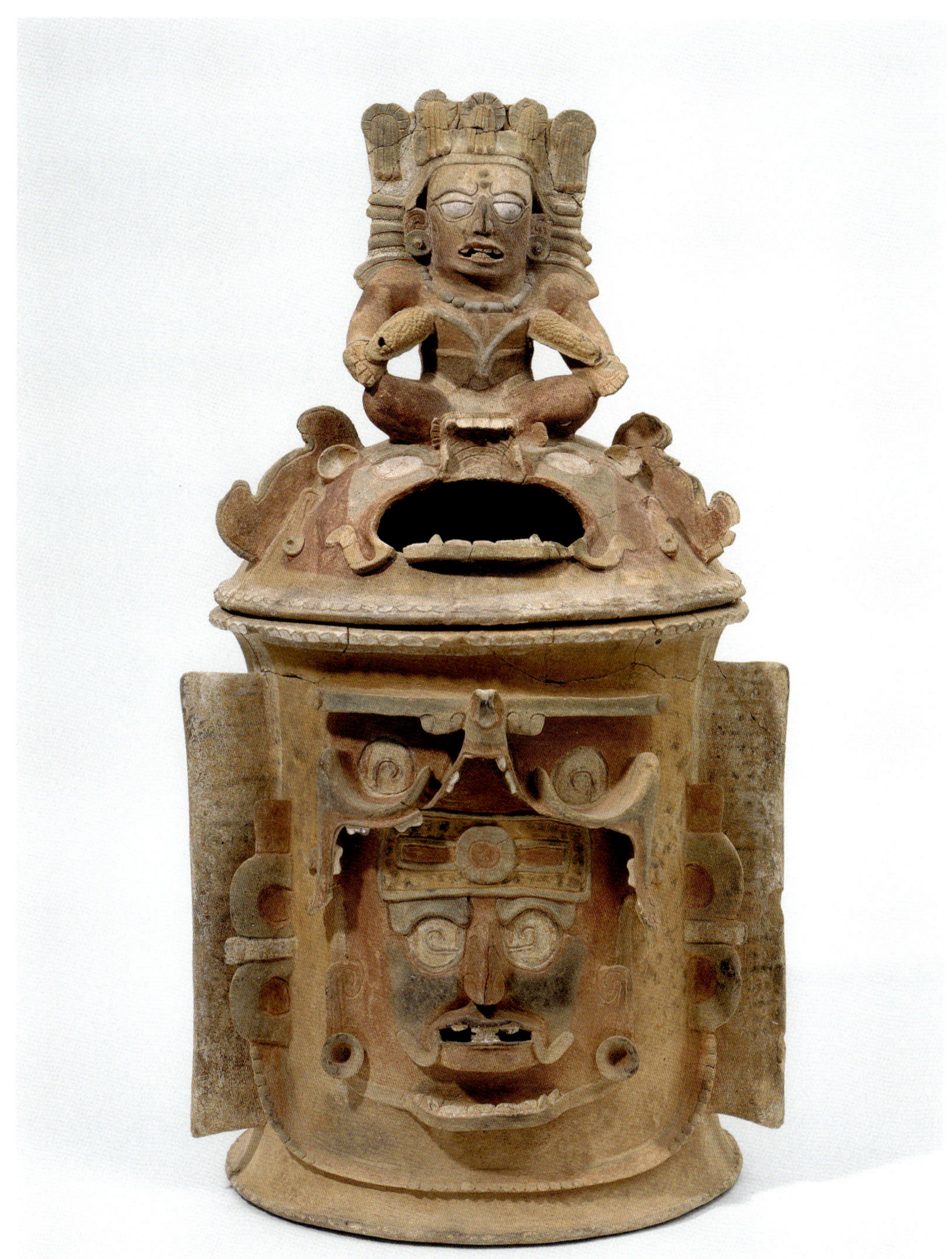

Burial urn

Tairona, Chimila style, 1000–1500
Lower Magdalena River, Colombia

Rounded jars modeled to evoke the human form and used as burial urns are characteristic of funerary practices in northern Colombia. These distinctive jars were placed inside shaft tombs, whose vertical entrances led to burial chambers. The urns contained human bones, de-fleshed either by cremation or burial in the ground where flesh quickly decays in the wet, warm soil.

Shaft tomb burials were believed to be a vital link between life and death because the bones were viewed as seeds from which new life would emerge. By preserving a person's bones (seeds) in urns that were "planted" inside womb-like chambers in the ground (mother earth), it was understood that new life would spring forth. A related belief has been recorded among the modern-day Desana people of northern Colombia who describe the grave as a uterus to which the physical bodies of all humans return at death.

The Chimila burial urn style is distinguished by a rounded main body with a small ring base. The urn's lid comprises an inverted bowl-like form modeled with human facial features to denote the person's head. Arms and legs are indicated by thin rolls of clay attached to the body of the jar, and the figure is adorned with earrings, a nose ring, and necklaces, the latter implied by three rows of tiny indentations representing beads. The figure's closed eyes and lack of expression suggest a meditative or sleep-like state, perhaps reflecting the belief in new life awakening from death.

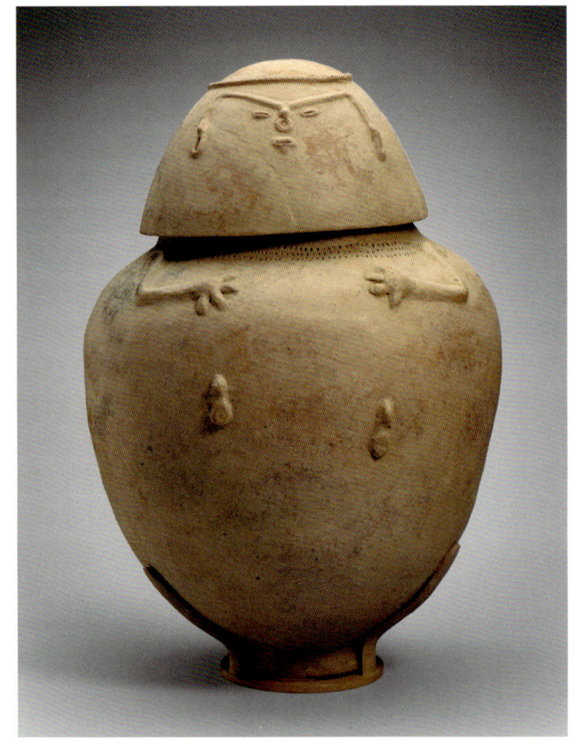

Earthenware
H. 51.1 cm (20⅛ in.), w. 35 cm (13¾ in.), d. 35 cm (13¾ in.)
Gift of June Blanco   2005.1120a-b

Female effigy jar

Paracas, Late Early Horizon Period,
perhaps Phase 10, 100 BCE–1 CE
South Coast, Peru

A mummy bundle is implied by this rare, oval-shaped ceramic jar, which is among the largest of the few surviving examples. The head is bent backwards and peers upward, the circular mouth forming the jar's opening. The bundle is that of a woman, with tiny nipples on her chest and two hair braids falling down her back. Her mantle is implied by the ocher-colored body of the vessel in contrast to her red-painted arms. The garment is decorated with an undulating serpent motif, probably a local evolution of Chavín symbolic imagery pertaining to metaphorical substitution (called "kenning"). The woman's diamond-shaped eyes with round pupils, gaping mouth, and unnatural position of arms rigidly hugging her back suggest a figure frozen in trance.

The exceptionally thin-walled vessel was formed and incised, and then fired in a reduction atmosphere to create a black surface. Resin-based paints then were applied to color the areas defined by the incised outlines. This technique recalls pyro-engraved gourds, an ancient artistic tradition in Peru from before 2200 BCE.

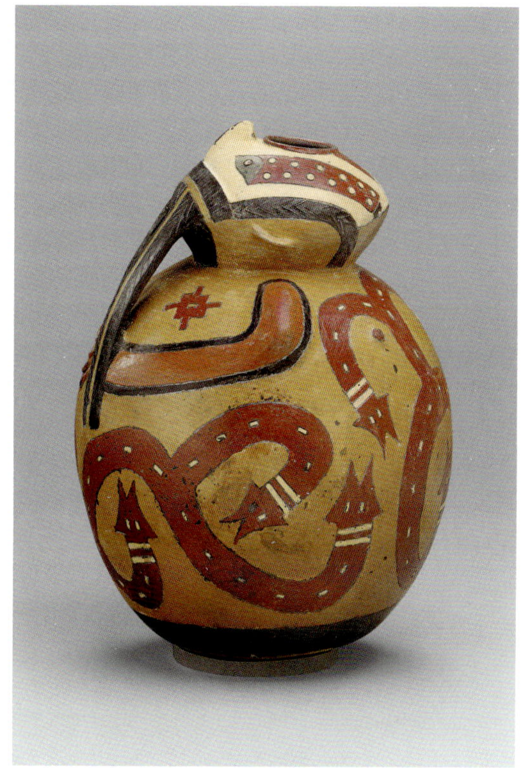

Earthenware with red, ocher, black, and white post-fire resin paint
H. 40 cm (15¾ in.), diam. 28 cm (11 in.)
Gift of Landon T. Clay   2004.2205

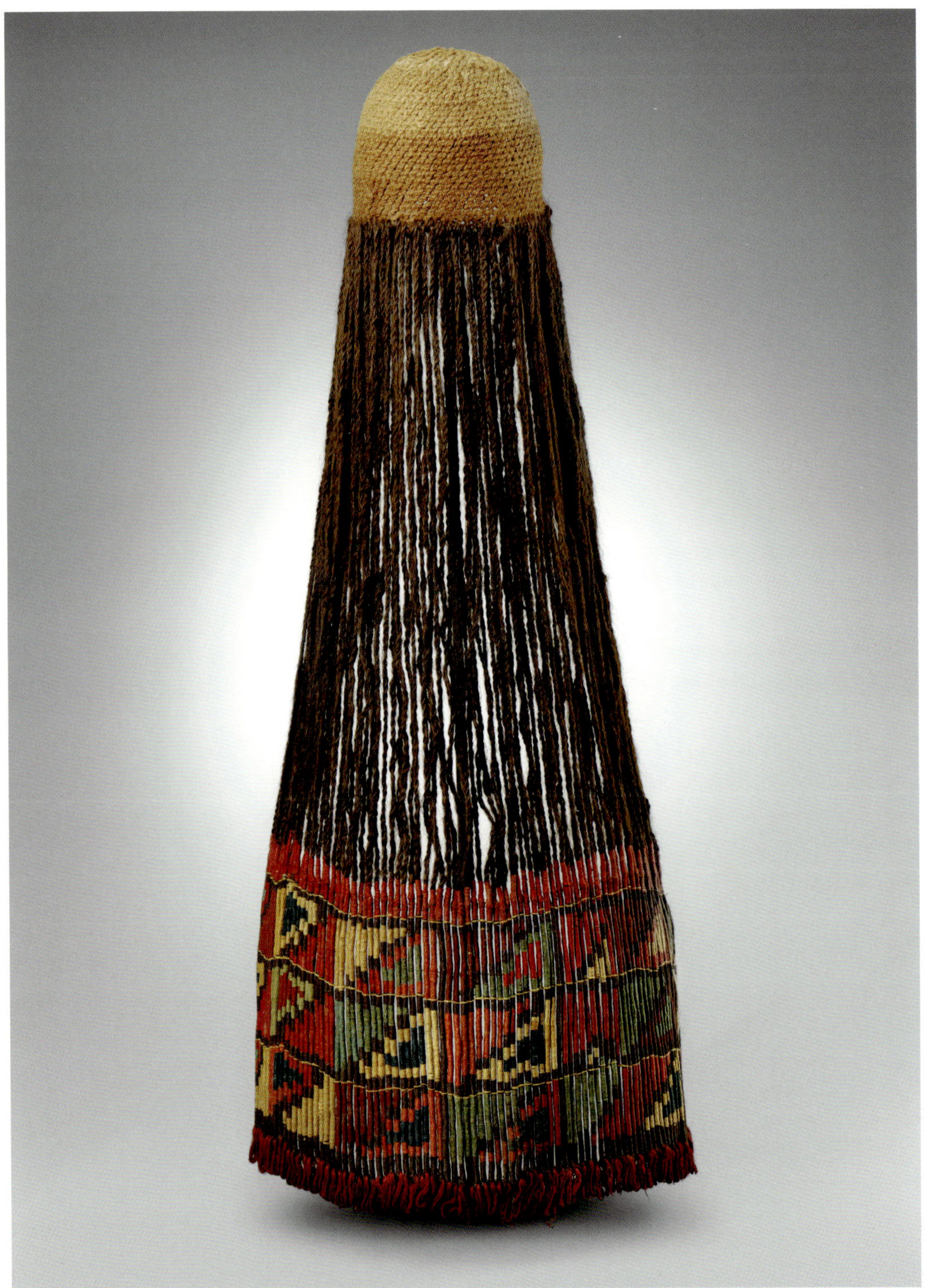

Cap with human-hair braids
Wari, Middle Horizon Period, 600–900 CE
South Coast, Peru

Human hair wigs adorned mummy bundles, a practice that began among peoples on Peru's South Coast.
The bundled, tightly flexed body was clothed in
fine garments, and a stuffed and embroidered false
head was sewn atop the bundle. The false head was
garlanded with human hair to complete the bundled
remains as a proper illustration of the person. Many
Andean societies reverently cared for the bundled
remains of ancestors who continued to play active
roles after death. For example, among the Inkas,
funerary bundles were brought out during important
social and state events for the purpose of feting the
honored ancestors. Their presence sanctioned the
occasion and endorsed its participants.

The ancestors' vital role among the living decreed
that they be arrayed properly, including intricate
wigs representing substantial skill and labor. Here
more than ninety thin braids were meticulously
wrapped in delicate threads of dyed camelid fiber.
The sequence of colored bands reflects Wari aesthetics that include hierarchies of dye colors, repetitions
of established patterns, and requisite variations
thereof. Each braid's wrapping begins with a red
band and ends with the red-then-gold sequence, the
asymmetry of one combination (blue, white, brown)
breaking the otherwise static composition of repetitive stepped motifs.

Wool (camelid), human hair, plant material
H. 97 cm (38¼ in.), w. 60.5 cm (23⅞ in.)
Morris and Louise Rosenthal Fund, John Wheelock Elliot
and John Morse Elliot Fund, Seth K. Sweetser Fund, Samuel
Putnam Avery Fund, Arthur Mason Knapp Fund, Mary L.
Smith Fund, and Susan Cornelia Warren Fund   1996.8

Mantle

Paracas-Nasca, Early Horizon Period, 450–175 BCE
South Coast, Peru

The unsurpassed textile traditions of ancient Peru
display an astonishing array of sophisticated dyeing, weaving, and decorative techniques, aesthetic
creativity, and symbolic content. Those of the South
Coast, including the Paracas embroidered fabrics and
the later Nasca woven textiles, are among the world's
finest examples of technical and narrative expertise
in the fiber arts. Paracas artists pioneered the embel-
lishment of plain-weave fabrics with delicately
embroidered images that float across the woven "picture plane." They used both locally grown cotton and
camelid wool fibers imported from higher elevations
in the Andes Mountains.

Paracas textile imagery illustrates three main
themes: blood (and blood sacrifice), fertility, and
spiritual transformation. This mantle (and skirt, not
shown) feature the latter, the surface flickering with
ephemeral shamanic figures as they abandon their
earthly bodies and take spirit form. The shaman's animal spirit form is evoked by the nearly nude figures
(note the rib lines on their torsos), because nudity was
antithetical to Andean social norms of human behav-
ior. Spirit conversion also is signified by the bent-back
pose, sinuous limbs, and lack of horizontal ground
lines as the figures are freed from the earth's gravity.
Supernatural flight is further implied by the unbound
hair, a characteristic of Peruvian shamans noted by
sixteenth-century Spanish chroniclers.

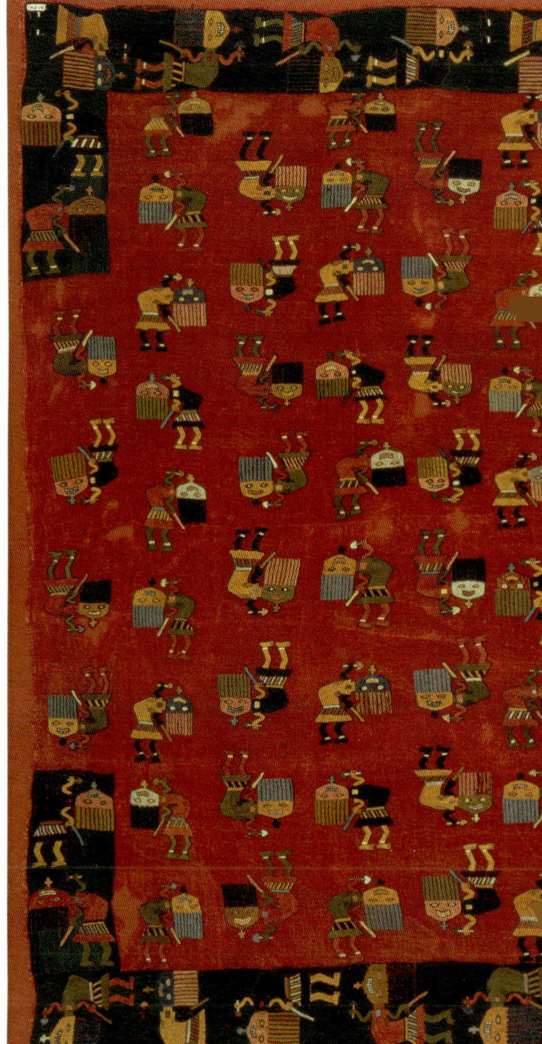

Wool plain weave embroidered with wool (camelid)
H. 142 cm (55⅞ in.), w. 241 cm (94⅞ in.)
William Alfred Paine Fund 31.501

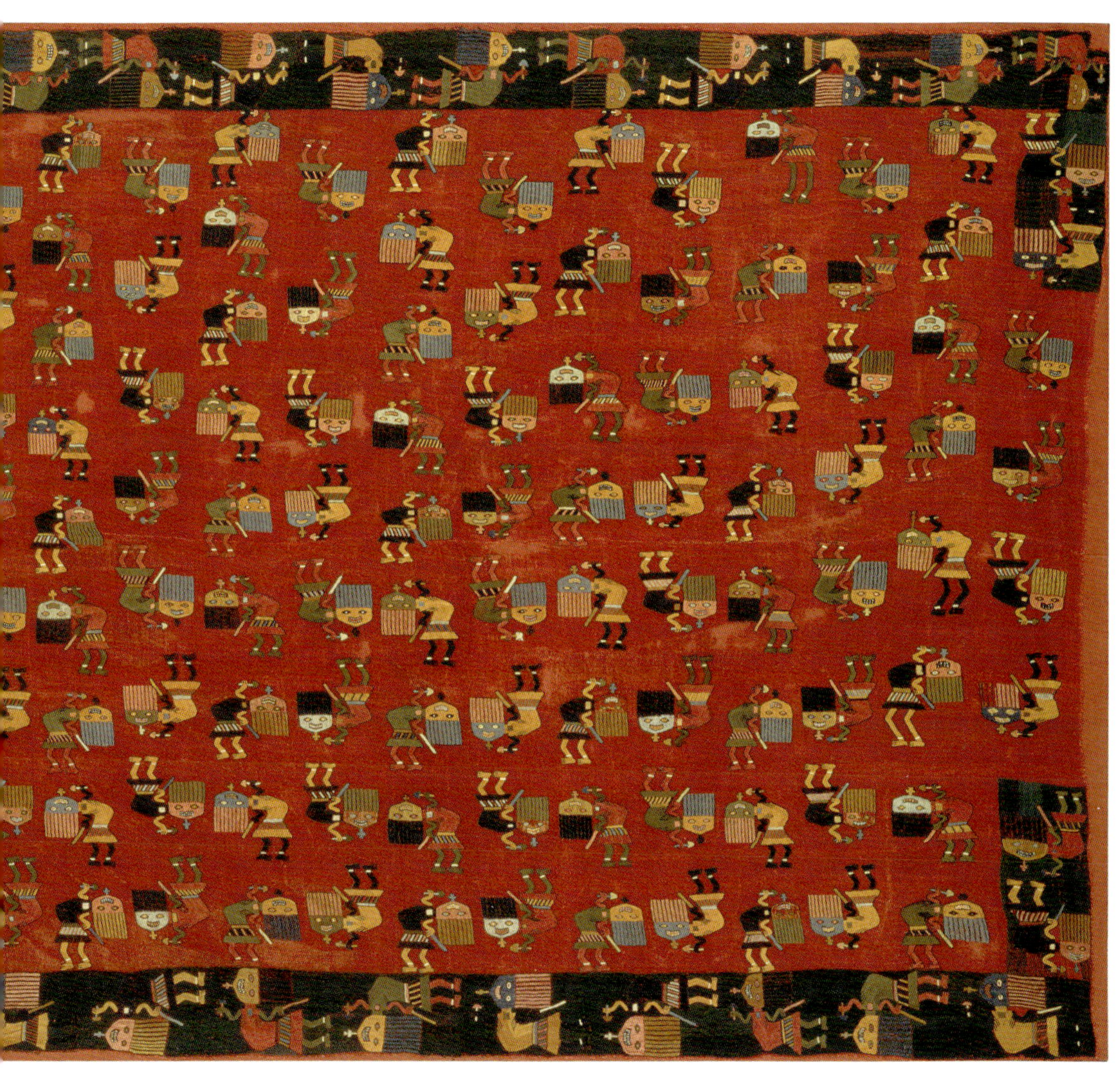

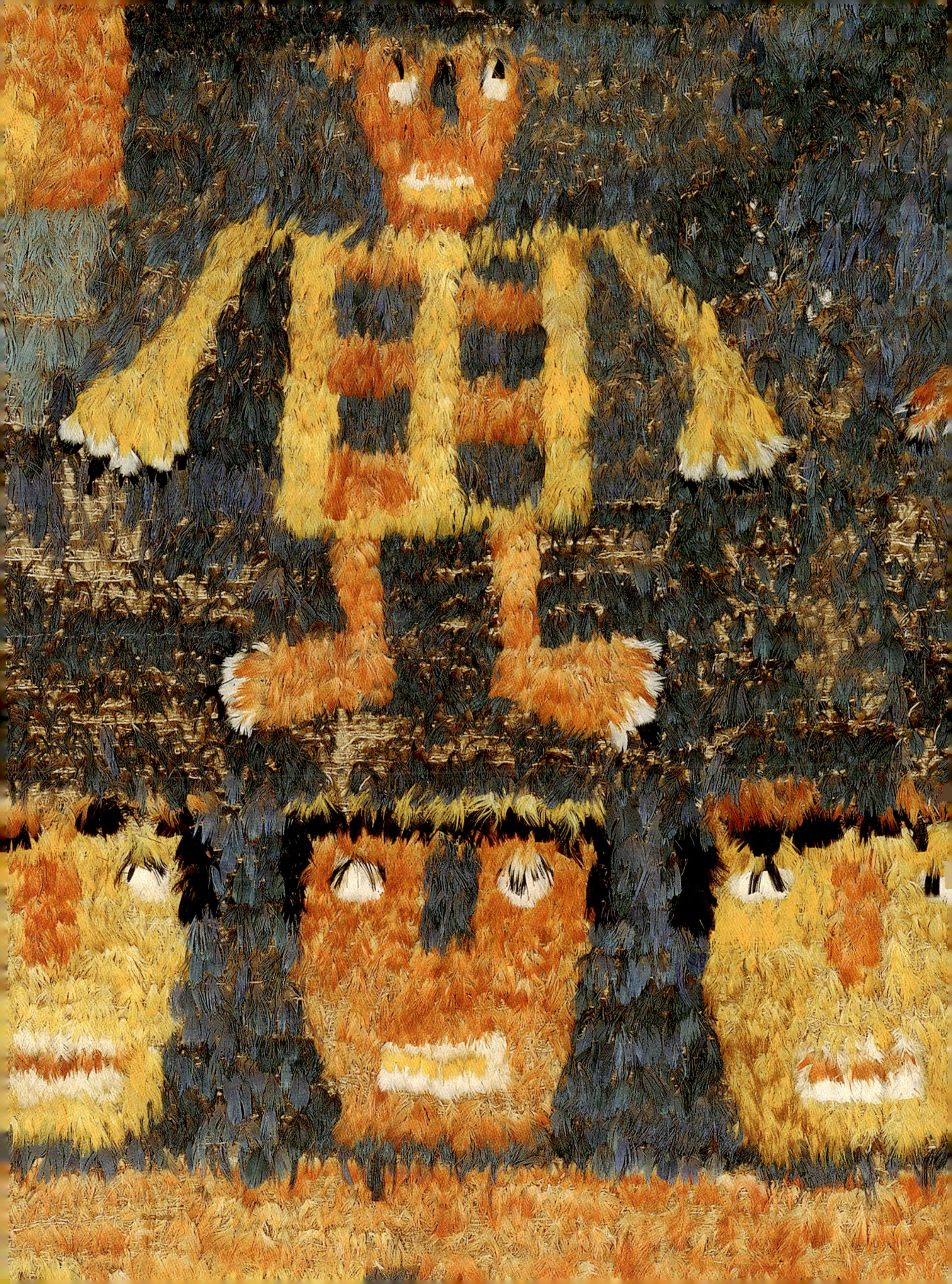

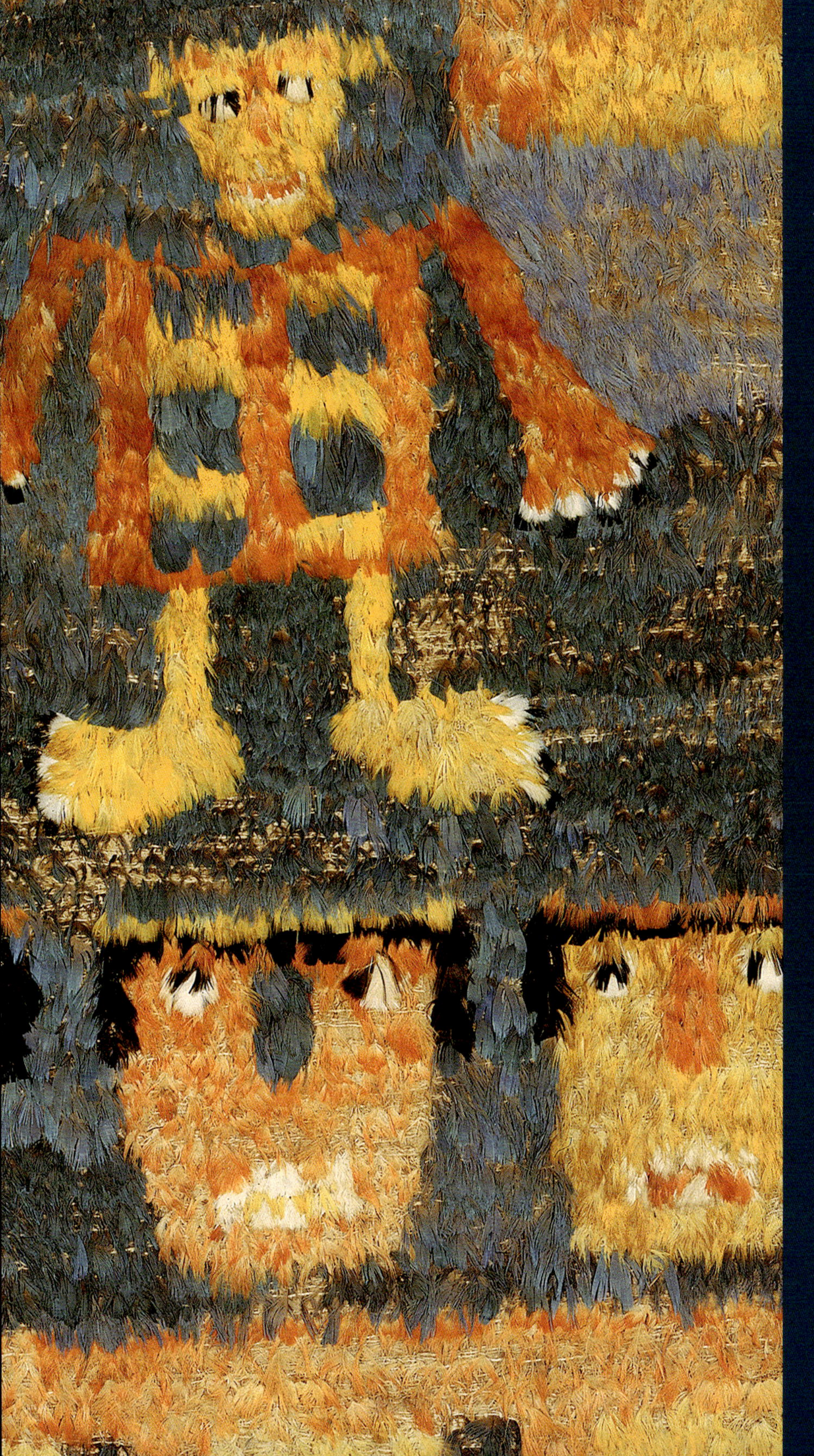

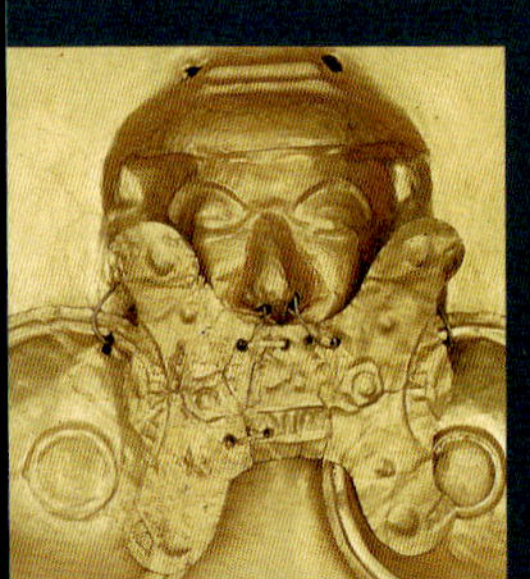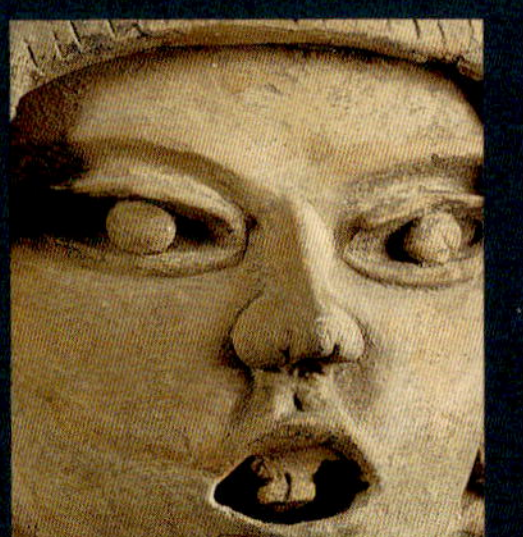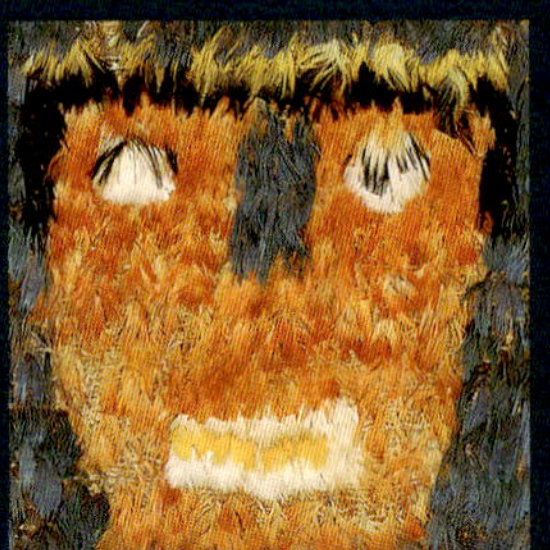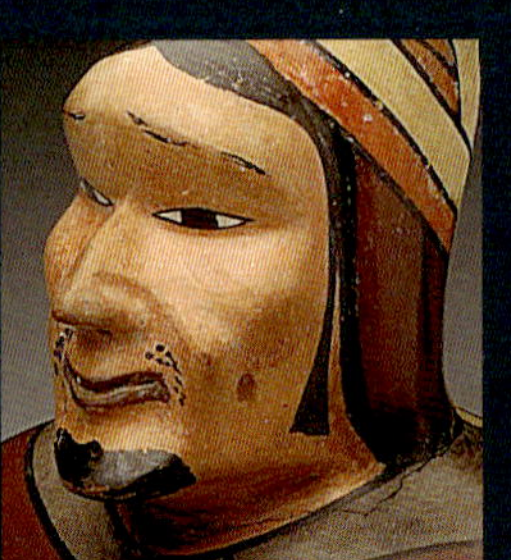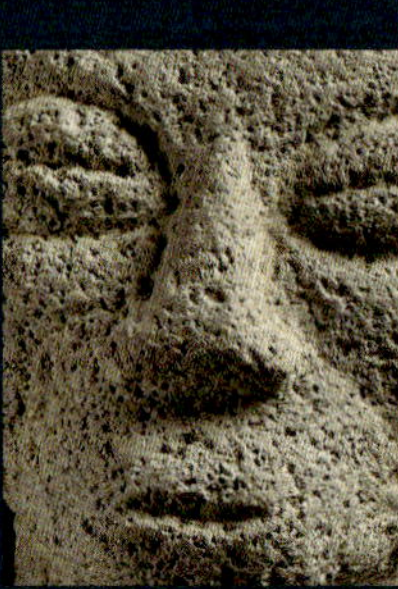

Portraiture

Simply stated, a portrait is a graphic representation of likeness—whether it replicates a person's physical features or is a conceptual, abstract study of the person. Artists throughout the ancient Americas interpreted the portrait in many ways. They realistically represented physical likeness when the artwork's function and context required such a depiction. Yet ancient American portraiture rarely depends on physical likeness as a remembrance of the physical person. Instead, memory and veneration were aided by a variety of other celebratory customs—from preserving bones or mummified bodies to creating talismans as "houses" for the deceased's spirit. Those portraits intended for public spaces, especially of political and religious leaders, often incorporate standardized forms and emblems to create the socially appropriate illustration. Here artists focused on tradition-bound poses, formal attire, official adornments, and hieroglyphic writing to produce the rendering. Such codified imagery was especially useful for illustrating what cannot be seen, such as the divine nature of kingship and the person's spiritual powers.

In this light, portraits from the ancient Americas recall Modernist and post-Modernist traditions in which the portrait simultaneously comprises a unique image while adhering to customary parameters of the society's artistic genres. They also share the objective of depicting the sitter's psychological condition and social milieu, encompassing not only an interpretive transaction between sitter and artist but also addressing the civic context of both the sitter and his/her image. The multilayered information embedded in such renderings provides an avenue for the viewer to examine the individual behind the image as well as the fundamental traits of the sitter's (and artist's) society. As such, the portrayals explored in this chapter shed light on the social and political systems and religious philosophies of the ancient Americas and the individuals who peopled them.

Mask

Olmec, Middle Formative Period, 900–600 BCE

Río Pesquero-Los Choapas area, Veracruz, Mexico

Olmec artists are renowned for both monumental and miniature portrayals of
what are assumed to be persons of authority—from six-ton head sculptures to
life-size masks. This is one of the finest Olmec portrait masks, celebrated for its
high degree of naturalism rendering the fleshy characteristics of the nobleman's
face. The mask may have been a symbol of state authority or a funerary item, perhaps tied to a mummy bundle. It is carved from jadeite, an extremely hard stone
which Olmec sculptors worked without the benefit of metal tools. String-sawing
and abrasion-carving were the carver's main tools, which required high-level skill
and great patience to work this difficult but beautiful fine-grained translucent
stone. Jadeite artworks were highly valued because their green to blue-green
color was symbolically linked to the Maize god and the ideology of fertility and
life. This mask's gray color, black splotches, matte finish, and fractured nose are
the result of its having been thrown into a fire during a solemn ritual.

    This is one of approximately twenty-seven life-size masks that were among the
hundreds of jadeite and serpentine objects found in 1969 in a freshwater spring
in the Río Pesquero where it meets the Gulf of Mexico in southern Veracruz. The
spring may have been a shrine to a water deity for nearby La Venta, the center of
Olmec power during the Middle Formative period. Many of the jadeite artworks
found in the spring were ritually burned, all having the same ashy gray color and
dull surface.

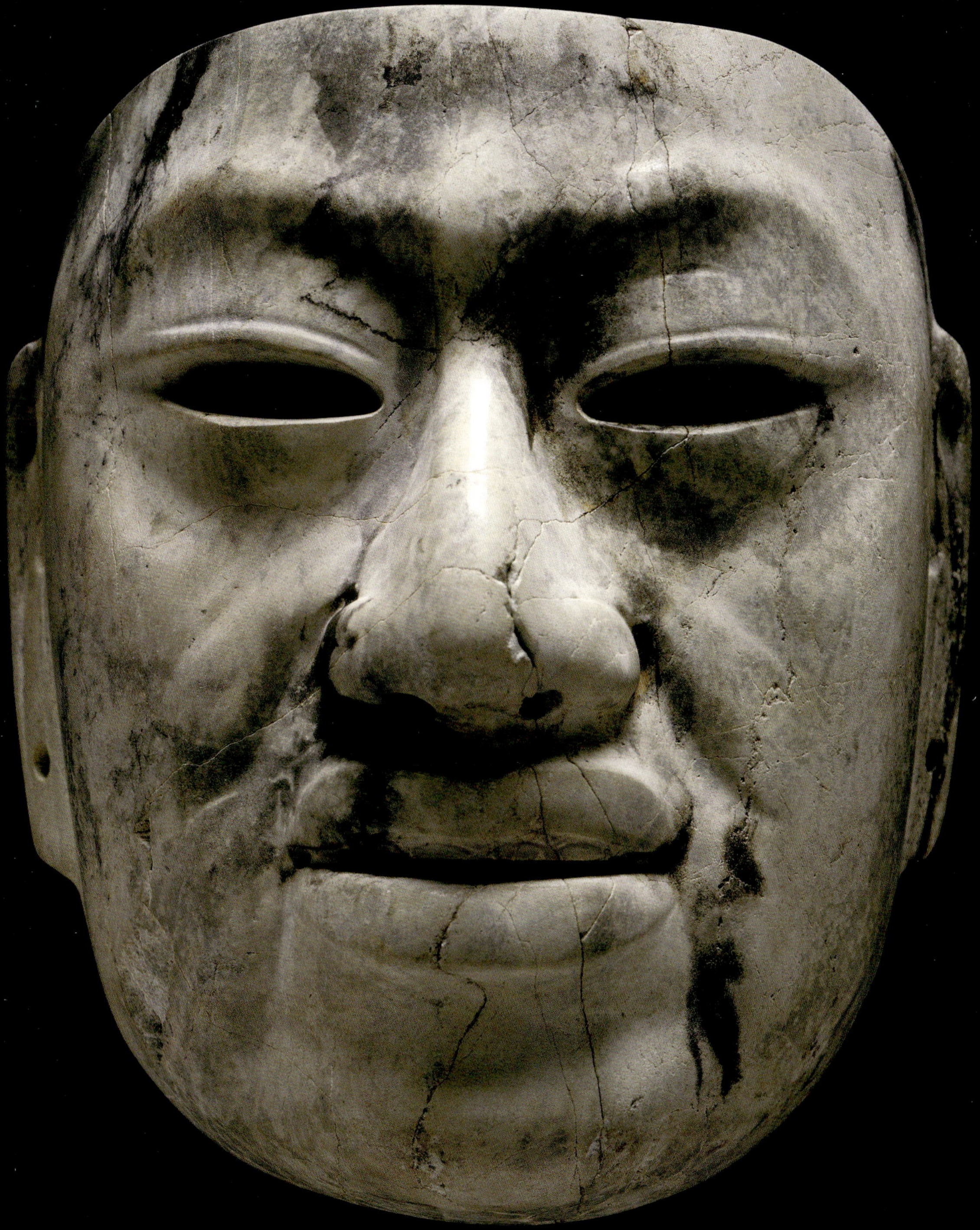

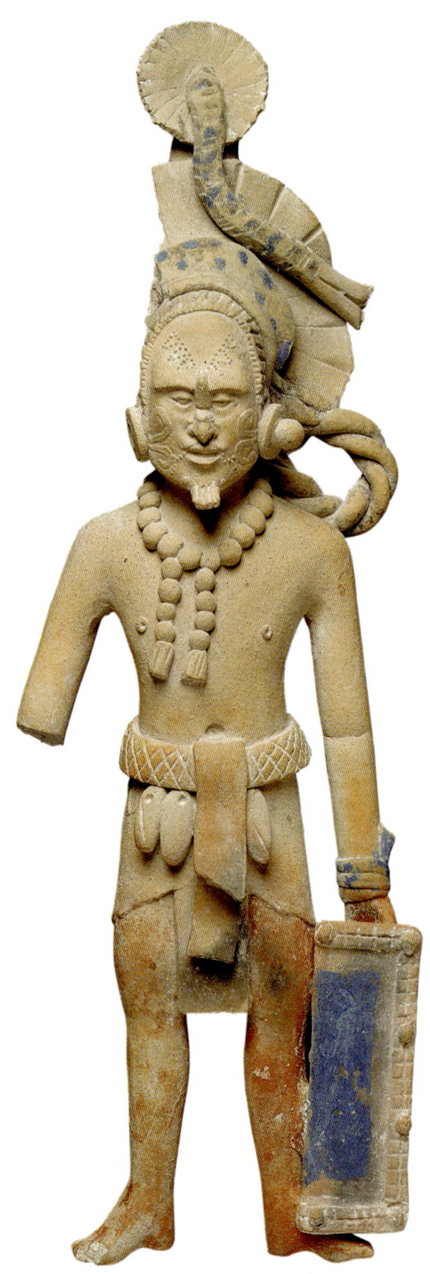

Warrior effigy figurine

Maya, Late Classic Period, 600–750 CE
Jaina Island area, Campeche, Mexico

Figurines are common in Mesoamerica, although perhaps the greatest variety of styles belongs to the Classic Maya (250–900 CE). Maya figurines were both hand-modeled and mold-made, and they depict a diversity of persons both human and divine. Many have been found in burials, the most famous being those on Jaina Island, off the Campeche coast, where figurines were placed in the arms of the deceased, and then wrapped using cotton cloth and fiber mats. The wrapped corpse was buried in dirt or stone-lined cysts (small chambers) accompanied by more figurines, pottery vessels, and personal adornments of stone and shell, whistles, and flutes. Figurines, often in fragmentary condition, also are commonly found in household debris and the construction fill of ceremonial structures, which confirms their additional use during household and formal rites of a non-funerary nature.

The curious shape of this warrior figurine's nose suggests a combat injury, and his face is patterned with intentional scarification. He carries the warrior's rectangular flexible shield and perhaps once gripped a spear in his now-lost right hand. Yet he stands as a nobleman, expressed by his towering headdress, opulent jadeite necklace and earflares, and a fancy belt with pendant *Oliva* shells. It is possible that the loss of his right forearm and the right side of his headdress is the result of ancient ritual killing of the piece, a practice noted on other figurines.

Earthenware with orange and white slip paint,
post-fire blue pigment
H. 33 cm (13 in.), w. 10.8 cm (4¼ in.), d. 7.3 cm (2⅞ in.)
Gift of Landon T. Clay   1973.14

Female effigy figurine

Maya, Late Classic Period, 600–750 CE

Jaina Island area, Campeche, Mexico

Naturalistic portrayals are typical of Classic Maya figurines. Here a seated woman wears a wrap dress whose fabric is adorned with wide vertical stripes. Her face is marked by what may be beauty scarifications, and her stylish stepped haircut is often seen on painted and carved images of Maya women in other artworks. Her jewelry includes large earflares and an unusual double-strand, choker-style necklace. Typically, Classic Maya women wore long necklaces with a few large beads or a strand of small beads. This example more closely resembles the rope bindings of captives as portrayed in Maya art.

The artist rendered the woman seemingly in mid-sentence as she interacts with an unseen companion; note the tilted head and forward-leaning body, slightly opened mouth, and arms (now fragmentary) reaching forward. Her fine attire and gracious demeanor intimate the portrait of a noblewoman, although the rope-like binding around her neck suggests another interpretation. Regardless of her correct identification, the figurine may be viewed as more than a simple depiction. Classic Maya hieroglyphic inscriptions and modern-day beliefs hold that an image is far more than a picture. As summarized by the hieroglyph introducing name phrases, *u-bah* ("his/her image") encapsulates the belief that a representation reaches beyond the physical body and embraces the spirit of the person. Therefore, this figurine may be interpreted as the embodiment of the essence of noble womanhood in spite of her captive circumstances.

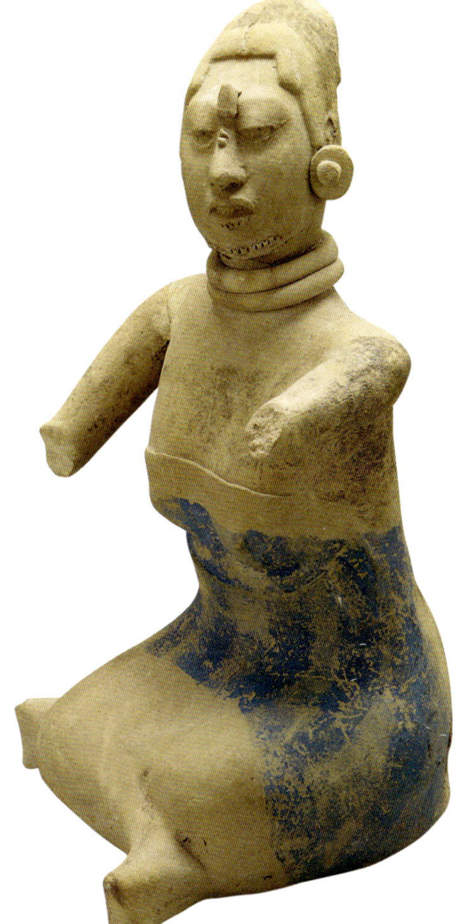

Earthenware with traces of black and red slip paint
and post-fire blue pigment
H. 22.1 cm (8¾ in.), w. 12.5 cm (4⅞ in.)
John H. and Ernestine A. Payne Fund   1972.876

Cylinder vessel

Maya, Late Classic Period, 757–67 CE
Ik' Polity, Motul de San José area,
Department of El Petén, Guatemala

The scene on this vase is one of the rare instances where a Classic Maya painter faithfully reproduced the unique physical characteristics of the sitter. The artist, who signed his works with the phrase "it is his painting for his lord," created at least seven vessels for the rotund ruler Yajawte' K'inich, who governed the Ik' polity from about 738 to 768 CE. Yajawte' K'inich is renowned not only for his substantial physique but also for his name phrase's ample list of royal titles proclaiming both his earthly authority and his association with an allegorical geopolitical order tied to the mythical Chan Te' Chan ("Four-Tree-Sky") locale.

On this small drinking vessel, the artist faithfully reproduced Yajawte' K'inich's delicate hands and feet, while his corpulence dominates the picture plane. His bulk, stern gaze, and ostentatious titles paint a picture of a fearsome and confident individual—just the type of leader needed to guide the Ik' polity through the contentious politics of the eighth century. Yajawte' K'inich advanced his political ambitions by featuring this formidable portrait on feasting vessels that served as relentless reminders of his power among those who received them as gifts. Compare his assertive image here with that from another vase painted by the same master artist (see p. 164).

The scene on this vase depicts Yajawte' K'inich and his successor K'inich Lamaw Ek' (reigned about 756–79) during a *joyaj* ceremony in either 757 or 765. This accession-related ritual involved donning royal regalia and participating in a vision-quest rite, although its full meaning remains unclear. A divination mirror is held by the courtier Chahk Tok' Bahlam kneeling behind the ruler.

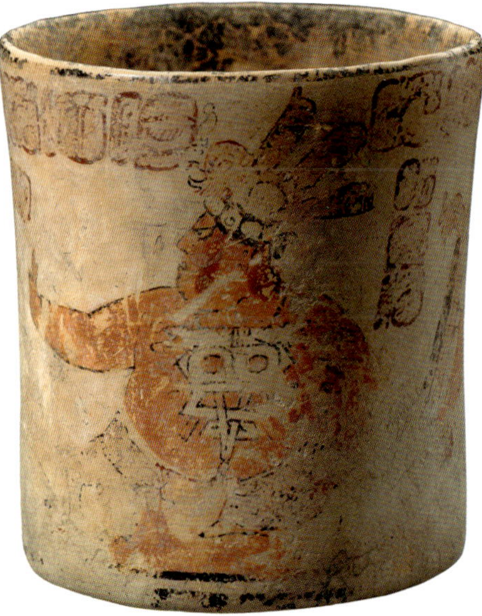

Earthenware with polychrome slip paint
on white slip ground
H. 10.5 cm (4⅛ in.), diam. 10.2 cm (4 in.)
Gift of Timothy Phillips   2009.318

Human effigy vessel

Coclé, Cubitá style, 550–700 CE
Central Panama

Red and black painted designs cover the head and body of this ceramic effigy jar portraying a seated woman. Her closed eyes and lax mouth signal introspection, and the dynamic decorative motifs dissolve her physical form into abstract space. These characteristics evoke the shamanic experience of simultaneously existing "inside" and "outside" the body as it de-materializes in the spirit realm and re-materializes in earthly space.

The use of design to negate solid form is especially notable on the lower torso where energetic patterns dance across the orange-colored background, the interlocking swirls of orange and black shifting position between foreground and background. Her legs tucked under her body are suggested by the two black-painted, rounded forms, and her slightly rounded arms are vaguely implied by a solid red outline. Her crocodile claw hands are a common allegorical device in Central American art to represent the shaman's spirit animal form.

Earthenware with red and black on orange slip paint
H. 24.8 cm (9¾ in.), w. 24 cm (9½ in.), d. 21.1 cm (8¼ in.)
Promised gift of Timothy Phillips

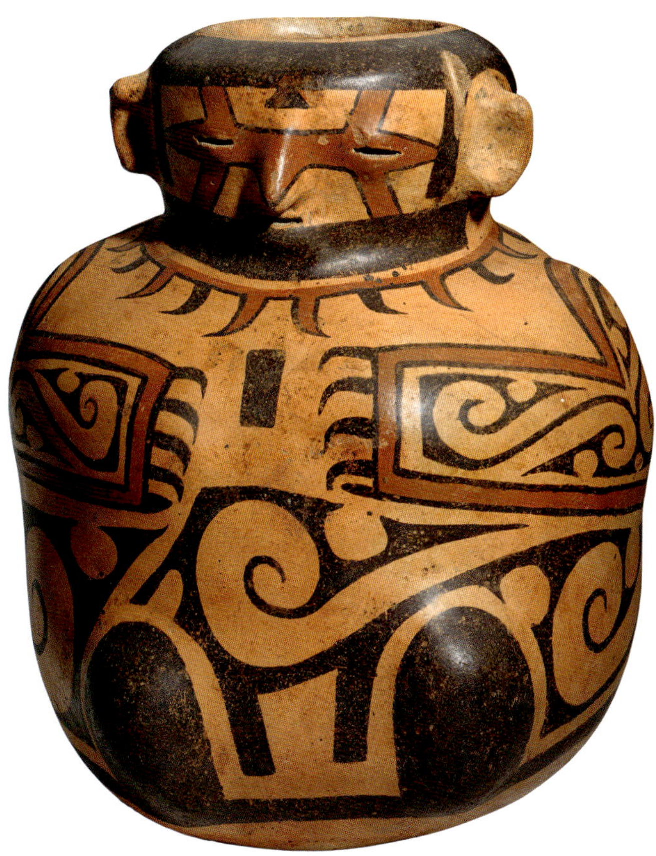

Seated female effigy

Nayarit, Lagunillas Type B, Proto-Classic Period,
200 BCE–200 CE
Nayarit, Mexico

The Lagunillas style, formerly called "Chinesco"
(Spanish for "Chinese-like") because of its supposed
Asiatic facial traits, features introspective portraits
of young women. Their standard seated pose—with
bare breasts, exposed genitalia, and hands on the
abdomen—focuses attention on women's procreative
potential and role as child-bearers. This young woman's meditative demeanor calls to mind the mystical
power underlying the miracle of childbirth. As is usually seen in Lagunillas-style sculptures, she is seated
on the ground in contact with the earth, evoking the
archetypal Mesoamerican belief in the earth as primordial mother and thus the necessity for childbirth
to take place in close proximity to the earth. Her
nudity and youthfulness suggest formal presentation
as a young adult ready to assume her maternal tasks.

In spite of the small size of this sculpture, the
artist skillfully represented intricate details of clothing and jewelry. Slip paint renders a wide band of
ornately woven cloth around her hips and the elegant
jewelry encircling her upper arms and neck. Her nose
ring and ear disks are both modeled and painted.
Their cream-white color suggests shell jewelry,
which commonly is found in West Mexican tombs.
The patterns on her face, torso, and legs are produced
by resist slip painting, a technique in which a resis-
tive material (such as wax) was used to paint the
designs, and then the piece was covered with a different colored slip or fired in a reduction atmosphere.
The resist material disappears to reveal the designs
in the underlying color. The bold geometric patterns
on the legs, arms, and face may denote body painting
while also artistically accentuating the body's essential forms.

Warrior effigy vessel

Nasca, Phase 5, Early Intermediate Period,
400–500 CE
South Coast, Peru

Throughout the Andes, garments functioned as more
than coverings to shield the body. Clothing revealed
the wearer's status and position, communicating
rank, official duties, political alliance, community
membership, and family association. This effigy
bottle represents a warrior, indicated by the thin
spear-thrower (atlatl) in his left hand, the sling-stone
weapon wrapped around his head, and the finely
woven tunic typical of successful warriors' garb.

Like most Andean cultures, the Nasca state
engaged in warfare for the purpose of controlling
land and resources, especially water sources, which
were all-important to this desert-dwelling culture.
The warrior's goatee and sparse mustache are a relatively rare feature among indigenous Andean men,
although both are common in Nasca male portraits.

Earthenware with slip paint and negative-resist painting
H. 21.6 cm (8½ in.), w. 13.2 cm (5¼ in.), d. 18.4 cm (7¼ in.)
Frank B. Bemis Fund   2015.2220

Earthenware with orange, dark red, white, and black on slip
paint
H. 16 cm (6¼ in.), w. 12.4 cm (4⅞ in.), d. 15.9 cm (6¼ in.)
Gift of Philip Ainsworth Means   20.1604

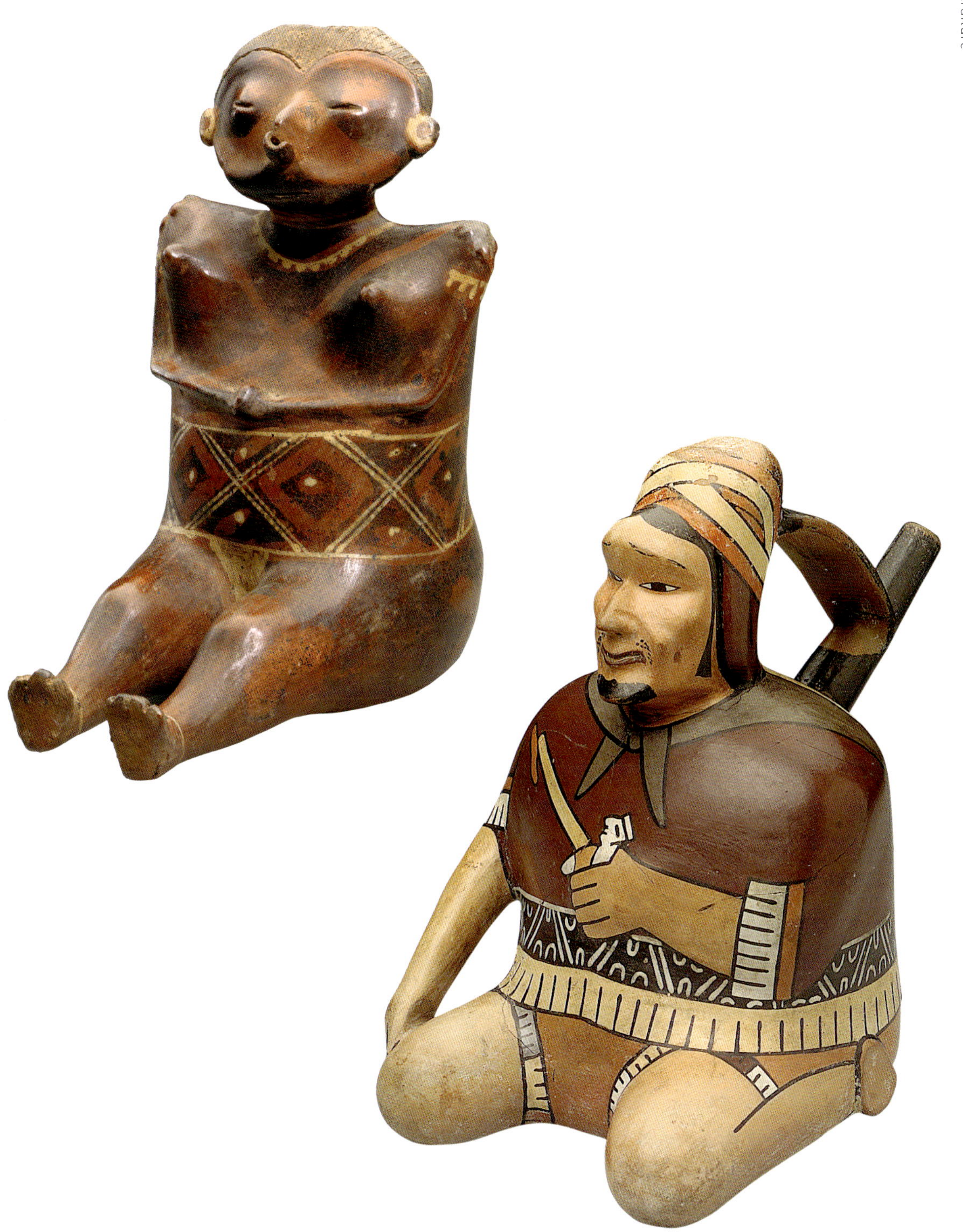

Tunic

Wari-related, Middle Horizon (?) Period, 500–800 CE

Peru

Tunics woven with feathers were among the most valued textiles in the Andes. This fine tunic, richly decorated with prized tropical bird feathers, hails the wearer as a successful, high-ranking warrior. Its motifs feature two men in patterned tunics like those of Inka warriors and nobility as described by the Spanish. The five human heads may be war trophies, and the stepped motifs below them recall ceremonial platforms.

Feathered garments were highly prized because the materials came from the far distant Amazon Basin, an area accessible only by negotiating the world's second-highest mountain range and a linear distance of nearly a thousand miles. The feathers' iridescence creates a dramatic, shimmering effect as vibrant today as when the tunic was made more than 1,200 years ago. This tunic incorporates the especially vivid feathers of the Scarlet and/or Red-and-green Macaw (*Ara macao* and *Ara chloroptera*, respectively), the Blue-and-yellow Macaw (*Ara ararauna*), the Razor-billed Curassow (*Mitu tuberosa*) or Slavin's Curassow (*Mitu salvini*), and the Great Egret (*Egretta alba*) or Snowy Egret (*Egretta thula*).

Cotton plain weave, feathers
H. 99.5 cm (39⅛ in.), w. 98.5 cm (38¾ in.)
John H. and Ernestine A. Payne Fund   60.253

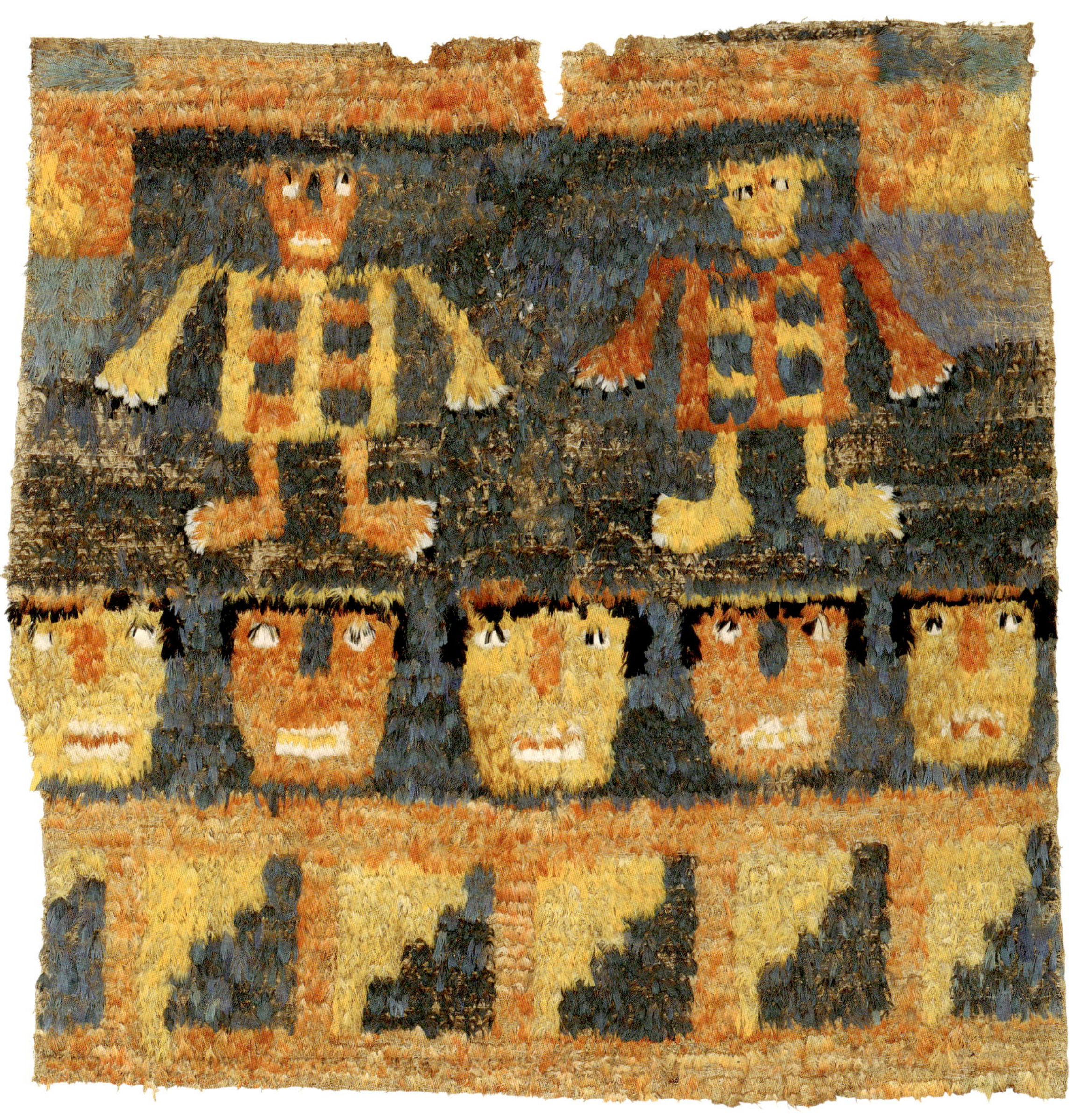

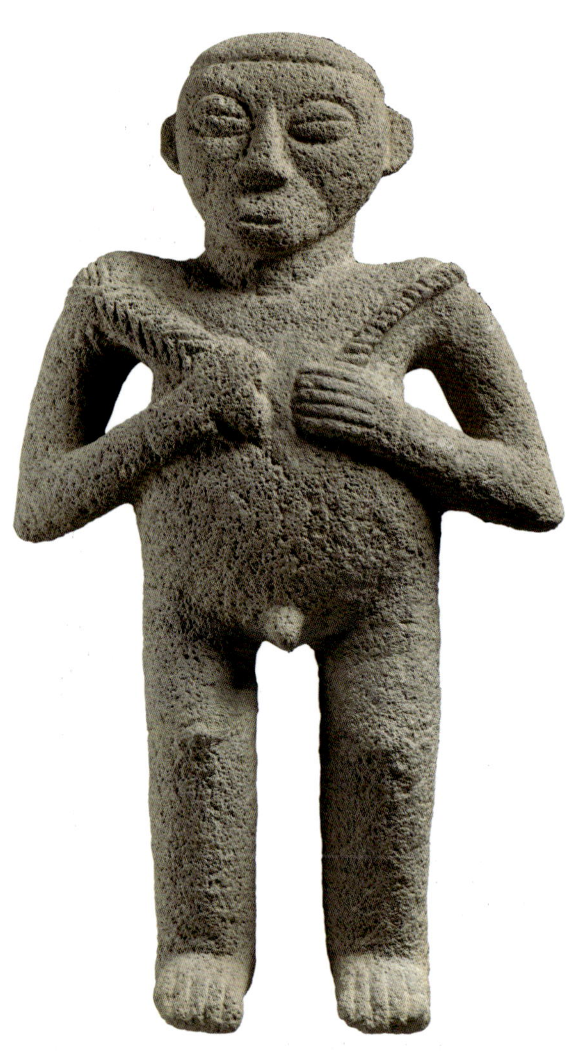

Standing male figure

Late Period V–Period VI, 800–1550
Atlantic Watershed, Costa Rica

The sculptors of eastern Costa Rica developed a standard format for warriors' portrayals that emphasized their political and ritual expectations rather than the individual's likeness. These sculptures are concerned with the belief in a direct linkage between sacrifice and fertility: the capture and ritual decapitation of warriors express this ideology. Ranging from small to large, warrior sculptures were likely displayed in households and along ceremonial avenues leading to civic buildings. This orthodox depiction features a nude male clutching a club weapon in his right hand and a rope in his left hand; the rope is tied to a severed human head hanging on his back. The figure's closed eyes recall renderings of a shaman in trance. Modern-day practitioners in Costa Rica and Panama, who ingest ayahuasca (*Virola*) to aid in their spiritual journey, often close their eyes to reduce the dizziness and nausea caused by the hallucinogen. Shamans refer to their spiritual labors as fighting the destructive forces that cause illness and other earthly woes, thereby correlating shamans and warriors.

Volcanic stone
H. 42.6 cm (16⅞ in.), w. 23.7 cm (9⅜ in.), d. 10.7 cm (4⅛ in.)
Gift from the Collection of Shirley and Hy Zaret
2008.196

Effigy head

Late Period V–Period VI, 800–1550
Atlantic Watershed, Costa Rica

Sculptures of a vanquished warrior's detached head often have unique hair patterns suggestive of an individual's exclusive braiding style. At the same time, this standardized type of sculpture serves as an official emblem of the triumphant warrior's prowess. Therefore, this head may be interpreted as a dual portrait—first, of a historical warrior and, second, as a symbol of the victorious combatant's prowess.

Severed head sculptures are typical of the Atlantic Watershed zone of eastern Costa Rica. Their typically small size likely was an intentional artistic choice to emphasize the combatant's loss of power. Some have been found in burials, which suggests a belief in the transference of the warrior's earthly powers to the afterlife. A desire for longevity is expressed by the volcanic stone medium, which preserves the victorious warrior's accomplishment far into the future, unlike an actual—but perishable—trophy head.

This sculpture was excavated from a burial discovered about 1905 on the Lindo Brothers' coffee plantation in Juan Viñas, a small town in the agriculturally and archaeologically rich Cartago province of Costa Rica's Atlantic Watershed. The burial contained domestic and ritual objects including three vessel flutes, a small jaguar-effigy grinding stone (see p. 102) for preparing ritual substances such as hallucinogens, two incense burners, and a *sukia* sculpture thought to depict a shamanic practitioner.

Volcanic stone
H. 8.3 cm (3¼ in.), w. 10.2 cm (4 in.), d. 10.5 cm (4⅛ in.)
Gift of J. Denis Glover and Sydney L. Glover   2011.2094

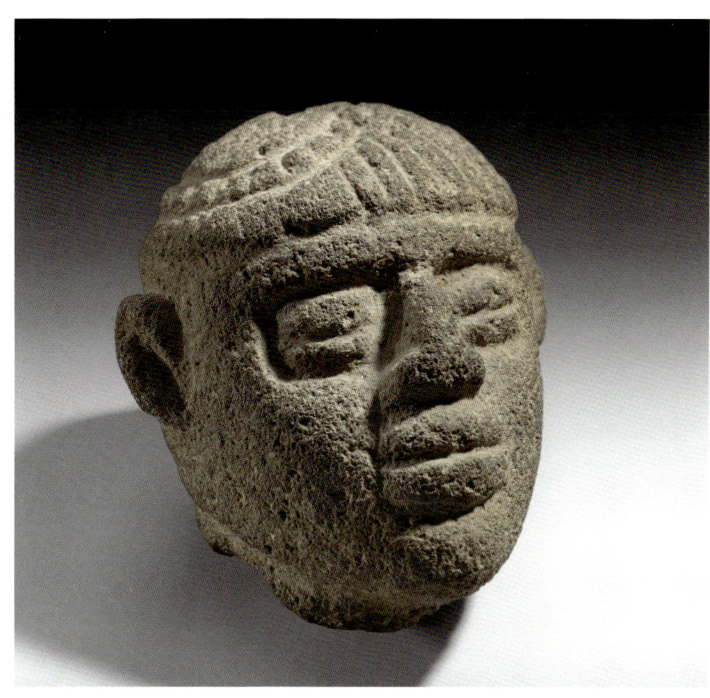

Funerary mask

Calima, Early Yotoco Period, 50–550 CE
Cauca and Calima River Valleys, Colombia
Gold
H. 15.6 cm (6 ⅛ in.), w. 16.8 cm (6 ⅝ in.)
Gift of Lavinia and Landon T. Clay
2004.2206

Pectoral

Calima, Yotoco Period, 100–1000
Cauca and Calima River Valleys, Colombia
Gold
H. 35.2 cm (13 ⅞ in.), w. 28.9 cm (11 ⅜ in.), d. 4.1 cm (1 ⅝ in.)
Gift of Landon T. Clay
1982.387

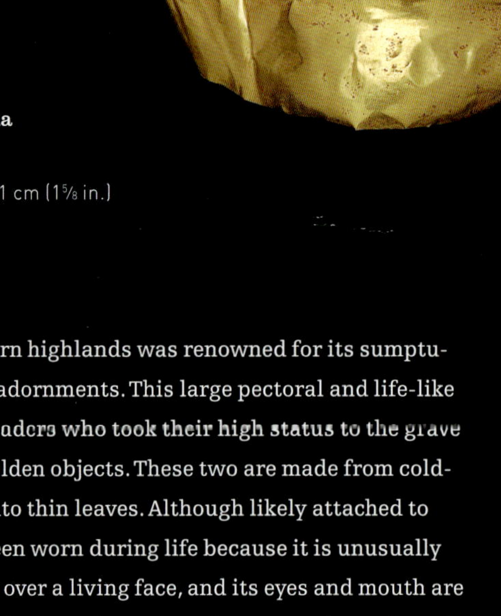

The Calima culture of Colombia's southern highlands was renowned for its sumptuous use of nearly pure gold for personal adornments. This large pectoral and life-like mask were articles of dress for Calima leaders who took their high status to the grave as cloth-wrapped corpses gilded with golden objects. These two are made from cold-hammered sheet gold expertly worked into thin leaves. Although likely attached to a funerary bundle, the mask may have been worn during life because it is unusually naturalistic and three-dimensional to fit over a living face, and its eyes and mouth are pierced. Most funerary masks are flat, lack pierced openings for eyes and mouth, and have tabs for attachment to bundled remains.

Flamboyant pectorals were quintessential elite attire, made to show prestige and supernatural power by bathing the wearer in shimmering, golden light. The central image is a three-dimensional illustration, perhaps of the owner. He is adorned with large gold disks hanging from the ears and an ostentatious nose ornament featuring a feline motif symbolizing the sun's spiritual energy and its powers of fertility. The pectoral's lower edge is rimmed with a geometric border reminiscent of textile patterns, textiles being a common symbol of elite authority throughout ancient Colombia.

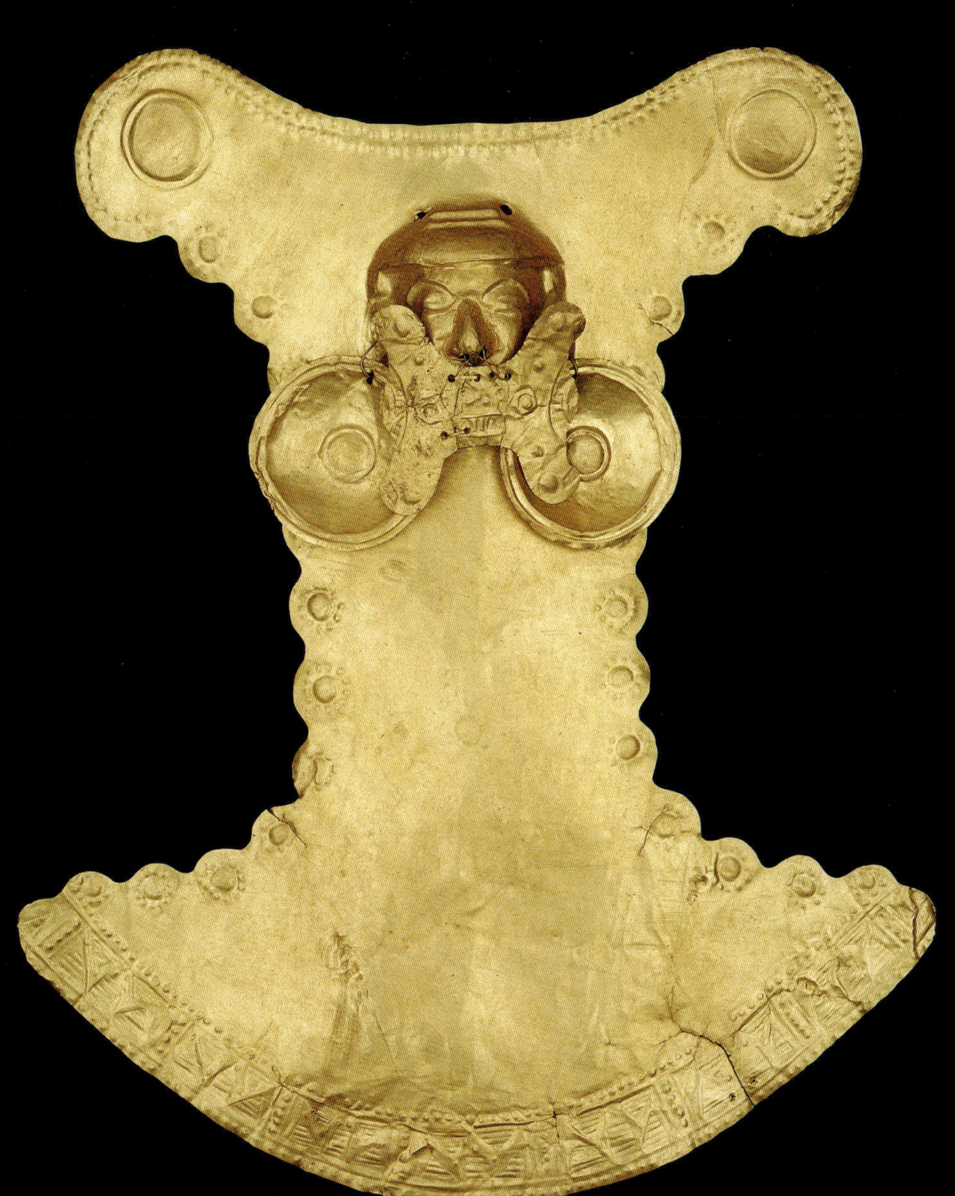

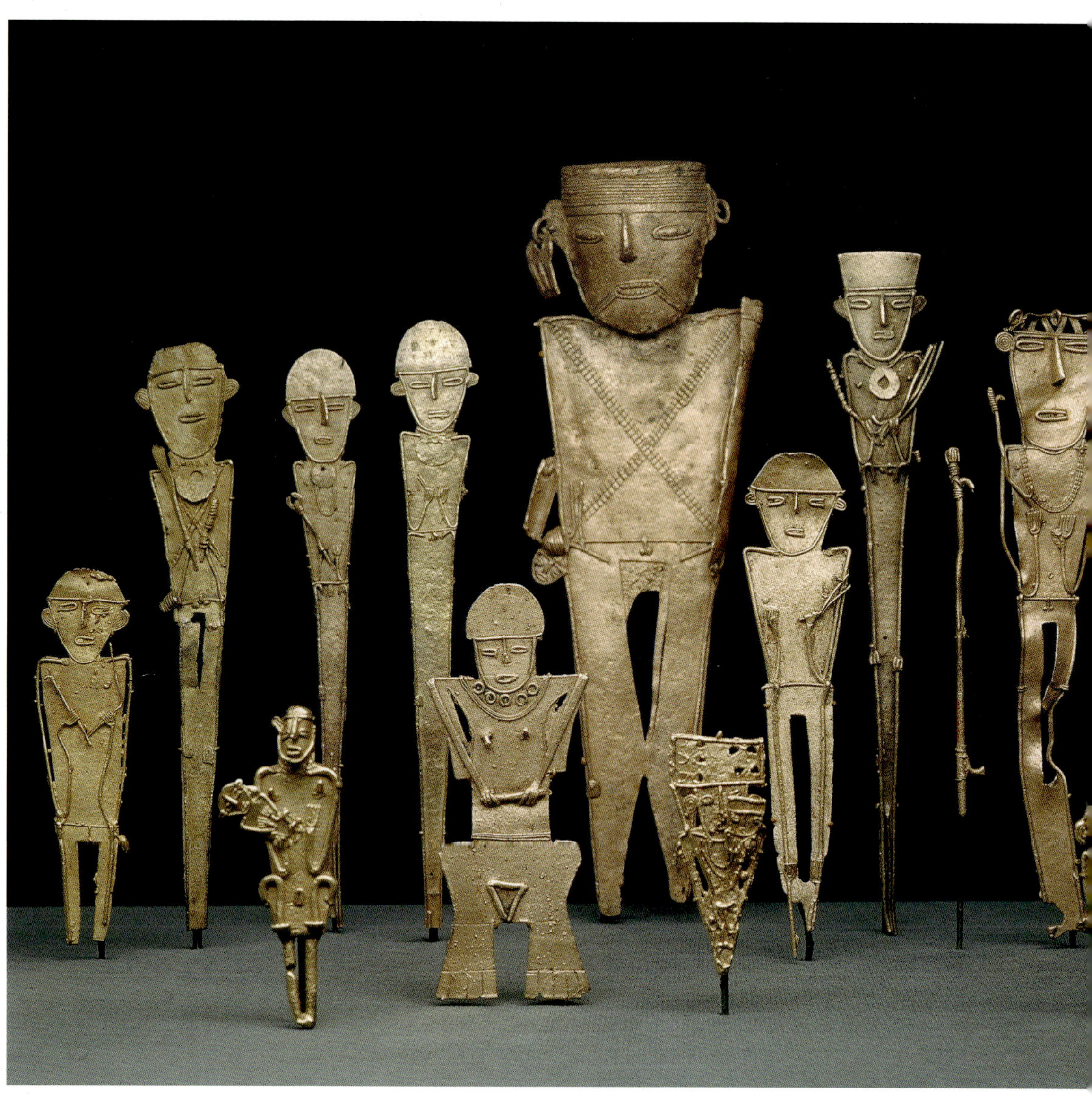

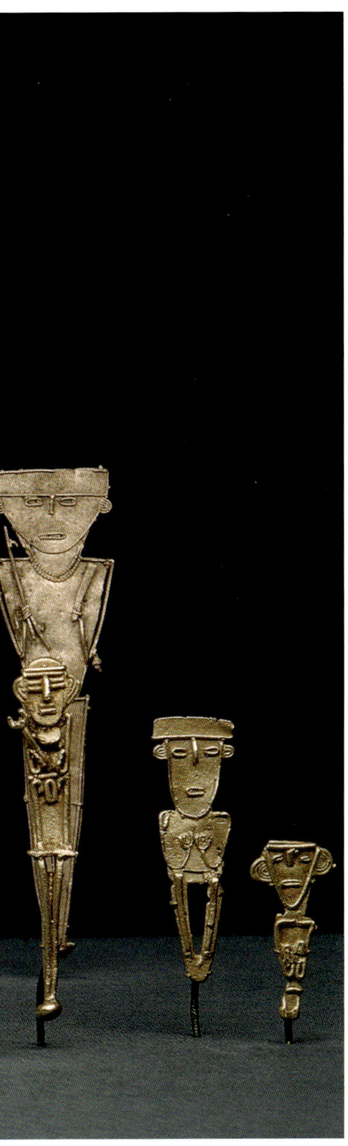

Votive effigy figures

Muisca, 1100–1550
Departments of Cundinamarca and Boyacá, Colombia

Votive offerings, known as *tunjos* after the modern city of Tunja (Colombia) near where many were found, are unique to the Muisca (or Muexa, meaning "the people") of Colombia's Eastern Cordillera. The figurines were used during religious rites, often grouped and placed in ceramic containers that were deposited as offerings in caves, lagoons, and temples. Their diversity of portrayals also indicates their use during various social and political rites. Tunjo themes relate to common subject matter, the most common being male warriors carrying spear-throwers, darts, and trophy heads. Some may depict leaders (political and religious) adorned with ornate headdresses and carrying official staffs and weapons. Others portray women in ritual attire or tending children. A few rare tunjos depict rulers seated on a litter carried by retainers (fig. 6).

Tunjos are made of an alloy of copper and gold, and were cast using the lost-wax process which requires a new mold for each figure. After the figure cools, it was coated with acid to dissolve impurities in the alloy, leaving a nearly pure layer of gold on the surface.

Gold and copper alloy
Tallest figure: h. 21 cm (8¼ in.)
Gift of Landon T. Clay
Back row: 1975.65, 1975.39, 1975.37, 1975.38, 1975.51, 1975.44, 1975.41, 1975.115, 1975.48, 1975.43; front row: 1975.76, 1975.67, 1975.79, 1975.88, 1975.78, 1975.81, 1975.86

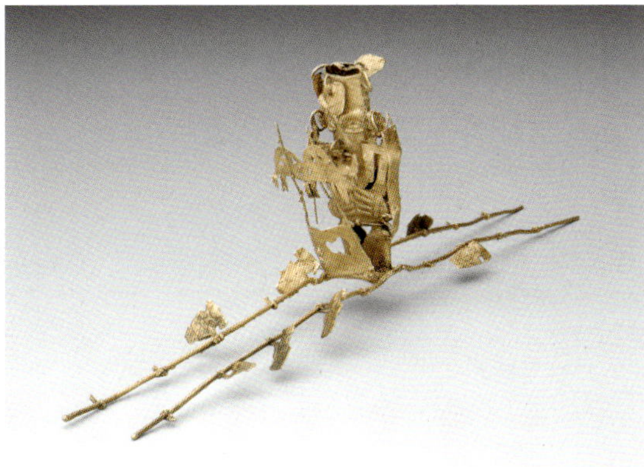

fig. 6. **Man on litter effigy, Muisca, 1100–1550**

Standing woman

Veracruz, Classic Period, 400–800 CE

Veracruz, Mexico

A female performer raises her arms and stands with open mouth, her pose implying song and dance. Her front teeth are filed into a T-shape, a Mesoamerican custom denoting status. Bell-like appendages hanging from her wide cloth belt may be shells or dried seed pods, both of which are worn today by traditional dancers throughout Mexico. She is dressed in typical ancient Veracruz fashion, with a wrap skirt and bare breasts. Her large crocodile-like headdress, adorned with a panache of cropped feathers, recalls the iguana-crocodile supernatural being unique to Gulf Coast cosmology and religion.

This sculpture's style relates to both the Remojades and El Zapotal traditions of central Veracruz. El Zapotal art is famous for narrative groupings of life-size figures representing deities and human celebrants, this sculpture perhaps coming from one such narrative montage. The tableaux were intentionally buried under earthen platforms along with vast numbers of human bones, smaller clay sculptures of humans and animals, and musical instruments.

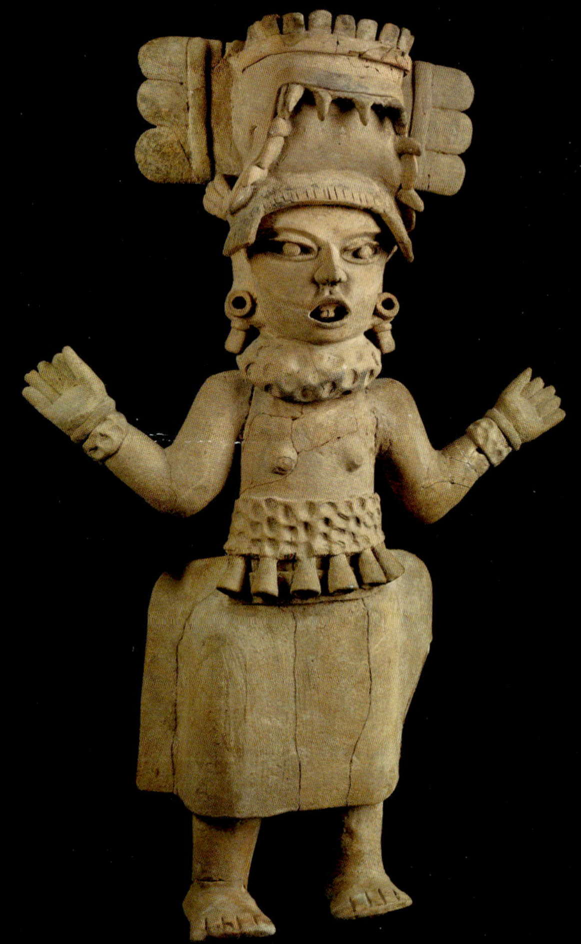

Earthenware with traces of blue paint
H. 69.2 cm (27¼ in.), w. 43.2 cm (17 in.), d. 12.1 cm (4¾ in.)
Gift of Marla S. and Bertram Perkel   2014.541

Nobleman effigy incense burner

Maya, Early Classic Period, 375–550 CE
Tikal area, Department of El Petén, Guatemala

Two-part, seated figural incense burners are a hallmark of Early Classic Maya ritual containers. The relatively plain base held burning coals into which copal incense was tossed. A tall effigy lid was placed on the base, and the narrow chimney attached at the rear of the effigy allowed the aromatic smoke to exit at the top. Many depict deities, although some are rulers who occasionally are portrayed in the guise of supernatural beings. This burner is one of three that likely were a set found together in a tomb. All three male figures wear royal jewelry, including a large pectoral with the visage of the Maize god—a patron deity of Maya kings. Sacrifice and vision-quest, prime duties of kings, are implied by the human heart offered by each figure and the divination mirror surmounting the head-dresses. The one surviving base features the face of the underworld sun with an avian headdress.

Similar incense burners have been found at Tikal, Guatemala, in building dedication offerings, including one inside a bench-throne in a temple constructed atop the tomb of Tikal's 22nd ruler (K'inich Waaw, nicknamed "Animal Skull"), who died sometime around 593. The most celebrated example portrays Tikal ruler Chahk Tok Ich'aak I (reigned about 360–78), whose name glyph is painted in the divination mirror in his headdress. Unfortunately, this same area on the three MFA examples is now blank, although their close resemblance to the Chahk Tok Ich'aak censer suggests a similar royal portrait and place of origin.

Earthenware with red, orange, white, and black slip paint
Base: h. 16.7 cm (6⅝ in.), w. 20.1 cm (7⅞ in.); top: h. 56 cm (22 in.)
Gift of Landon T. Clay   1988.1228a–b

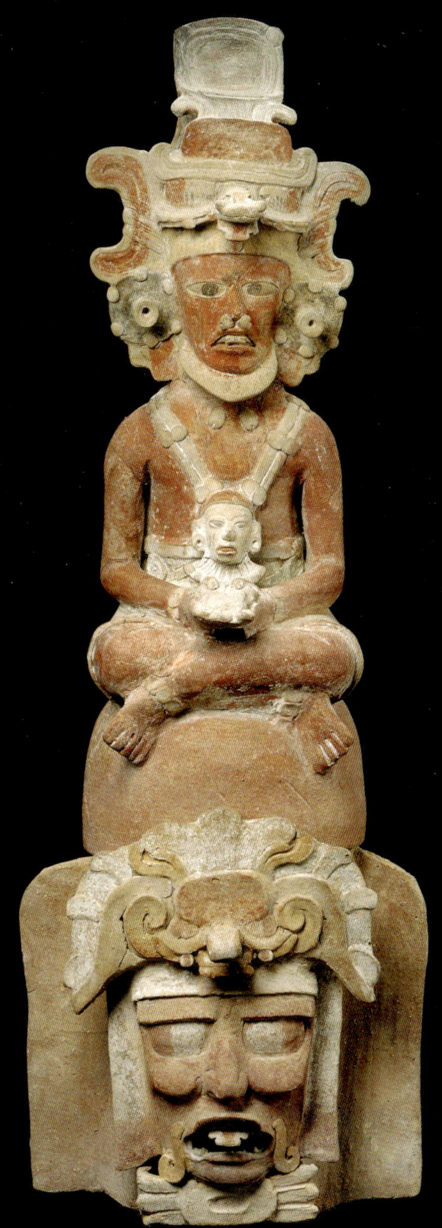

Artist's paint palette

Maya, Late Classic Period, 550–850 CE
Guatemala, Mexico, or Belize

Here the quintessential Maya painter's palette, made from a halved conch shell (*Strombidae* family), symbolically represents an artist by replicating the formal gesture of courtly painters with curled fingers and one extended digit. The elongated form, carved from a conch shell and retaining its original contours, follows the shape of the artist's hand as he/she cradles the palette, its elongated end resting on the inner wrist. This is one of only two known examples of a shell paint pot replicating an artist's hand, although halved shell palettes are pictured in scenes of artists at work. A drinking vessel depicts a masked painter (lower right) seated in front of a conch shell palette that rests atop a jaguar-pelt-covered book (fig. 7).

Shell paint pots have been found in elite Maya tombs and palaces, implying the occupants were engaged in artistic activities. Confirming their use as paint palettes is the rare presence of dried paint in the chambers of a few examples, such as one excavated at the site of Cahal Pech, Belize, which held red and black pigments. Traces of red pigment are found on this palette. An unusual version, made of earthenware but modeled in the form of a halved conch shell, was found in the tomb of Hasaw Chan K'awiil, ruler of Tikal, who died in 734. Its main chamber is painted with the hieroglyph for "storage place" or "place for liquid," a fitting label for a painter's palette.

Conch shell (*Strombidae* family) with traces of red pigment
H. 4.2 cm (1⅝ in.), w. 20.9 cm (8¼ in.), d. 8.6 cm (3⅜ in.)
Elizabeth M. and John F. Paramino Fund in memory of John F. Paramino, Boston Sculptor, John H. and Ernestine A. Payne Fund, Helen and Alice Colburn Fund, William Francis Warden Fund, Seth K. Sweetser Fund, Helen B. Sweeney Fund, and Harriet Otis Cruft Fund   2017.849

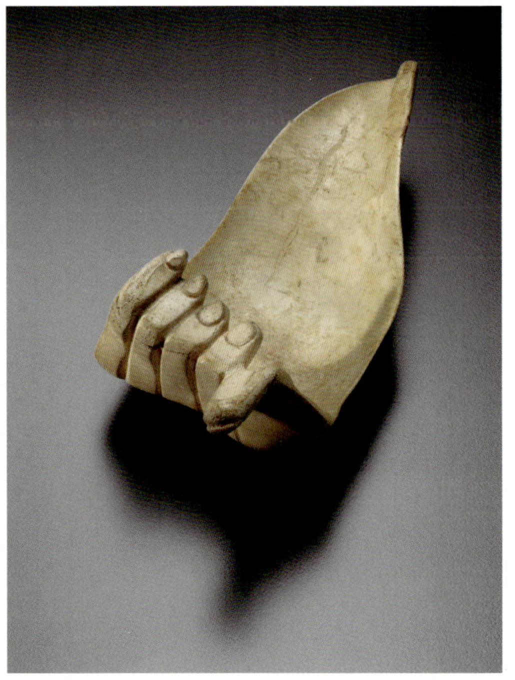

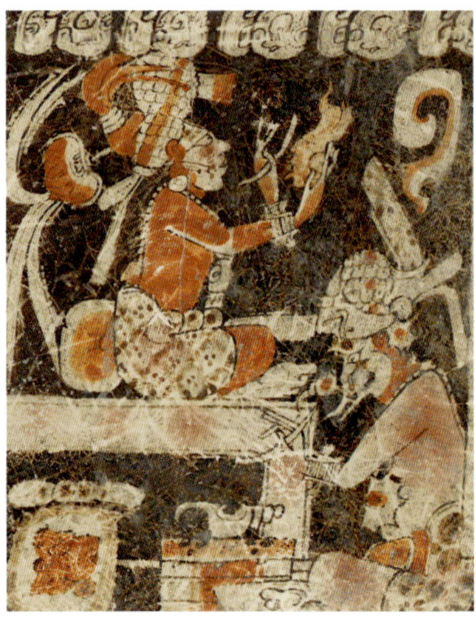

fig. 7. **Detail of drinking vessel, Maya, 675–750 CE**

Drinking vessel

Maya, Late Classic Period, 600–750 CE

Campeche, Mexico

Classic Maya artists used many pictorial devices to make a portrait, including hieroglyphic writing as featured on this vase. All Mayan languages have only a single term for writing and painting—*ts'ib*—revealing the fusion of what most cultures view as separate graphic endeavors. This union goes beyond the fact that the Maya "wrote" with the paintbrush and extends to the fundamental characteristics of Maya hieroglyphic writing, which merges writing and picture-making.

Maya hieroglyphs constitute true writing—meaning the graphic representation of spoken language. But the graphic system encompasses more than recording speech by embracing the word and image potential of the system to assemble layers of expression. Maya writing can be described as both linguistic (spoken word) and graphic poetry unified as a single art form.

The hieroglyphic system uses three types of signs—phonetic, logographic, and pictographic; and three graphic formats—geometric, head-variant, and full-figure hieroglyphs. Artist-scribes combined these to create a textual and visual poetic narrative. The interplay of text and image is exemplified by this vase, whose scene illustrates a key episode in the *Popol Wuuj*, a seventeenth-century K'iché Maya manuscript with Classic period origins. Here the Hero Twins Juun Ajaw and Yax B'ahlam confront the deity Itzamnaaj in his underworld palace. The upper hieroglyphic text names the Twins using head-variant signs; that of Yax B'ahlam combines the logograph for "precious" (*yax*) and a pictograph of a jaguar (*b'ahlam*) head superimposed over a human one, thereby merging language and image into a single portrayal of Yax B'ahlam.

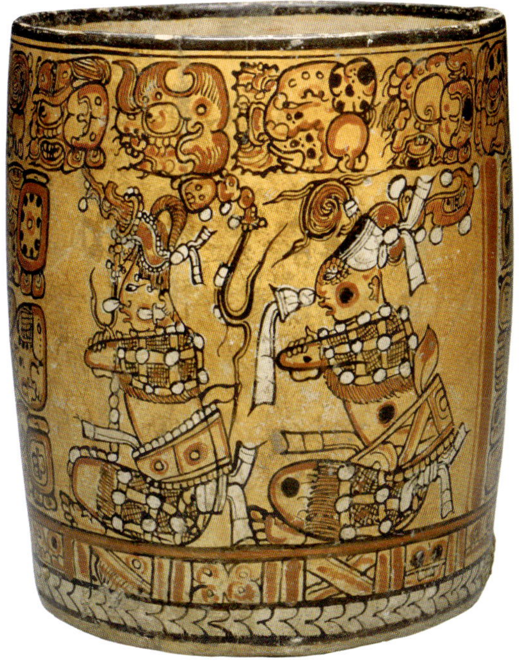

Earthenware with red, white, and black on yellow-cream slip

H. 19.8 cm (7¾ in.), diam. 17.2 cm (6¾ in.)

Gift of Landon T. Clay   1988.1169

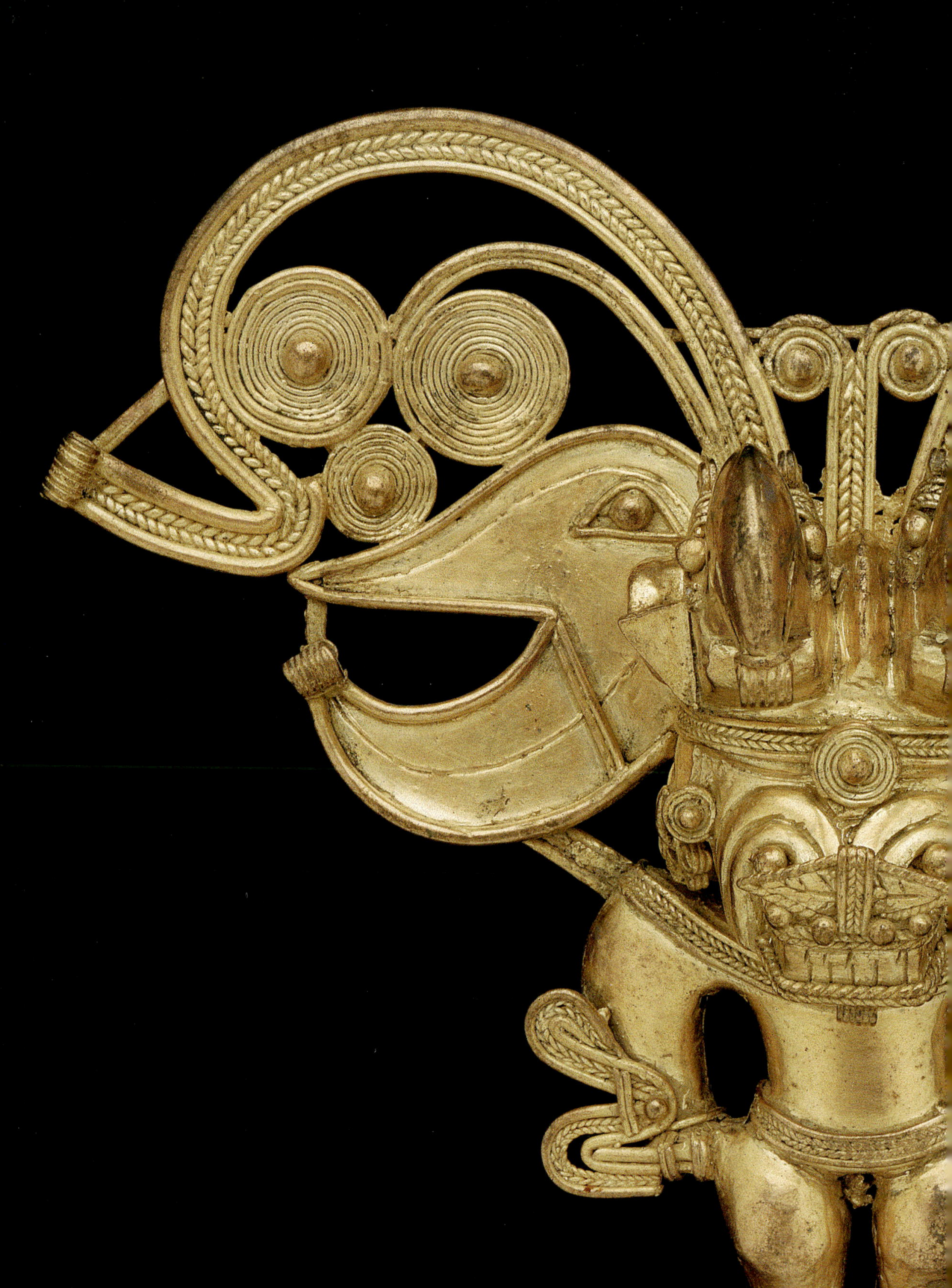

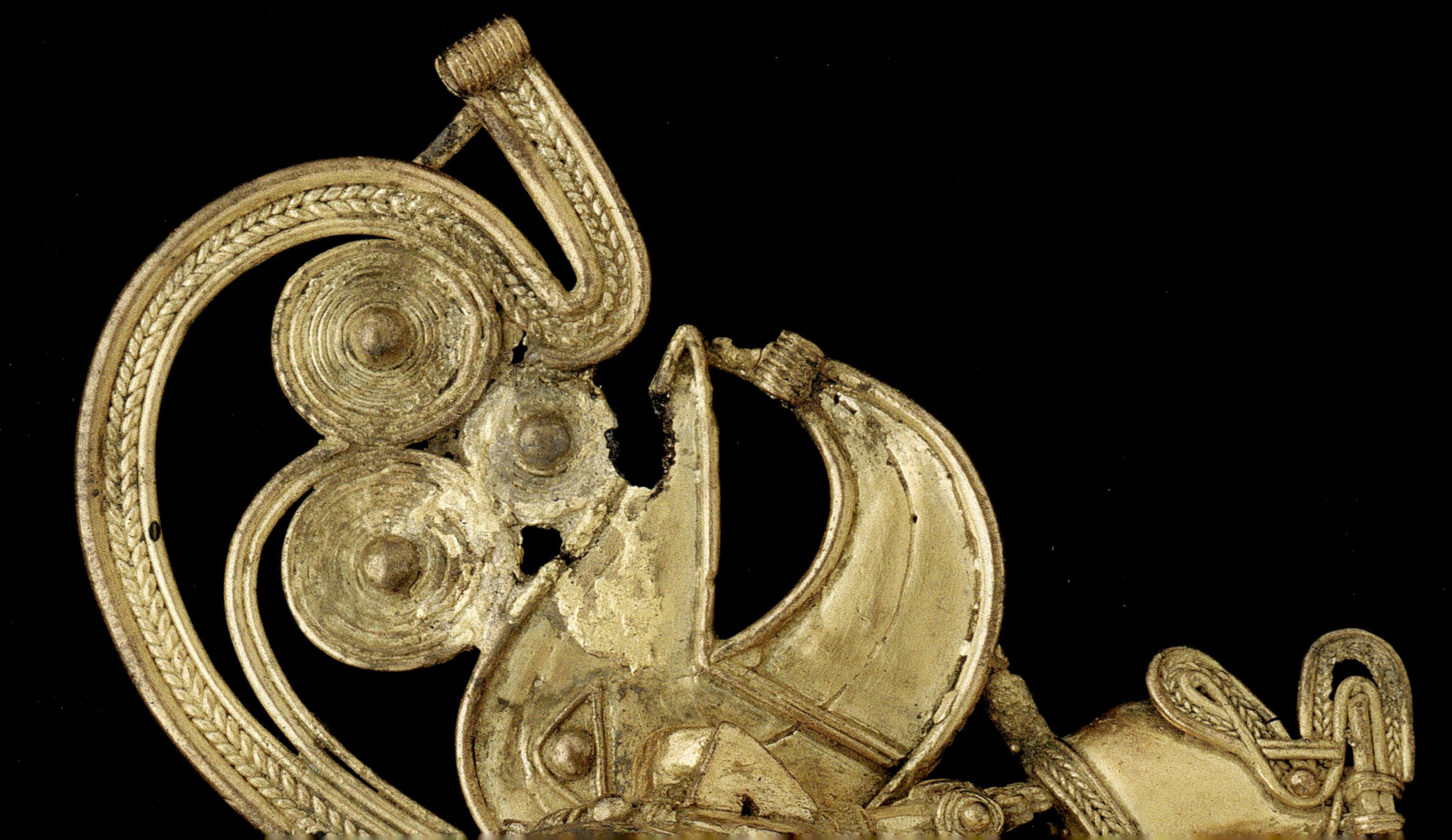

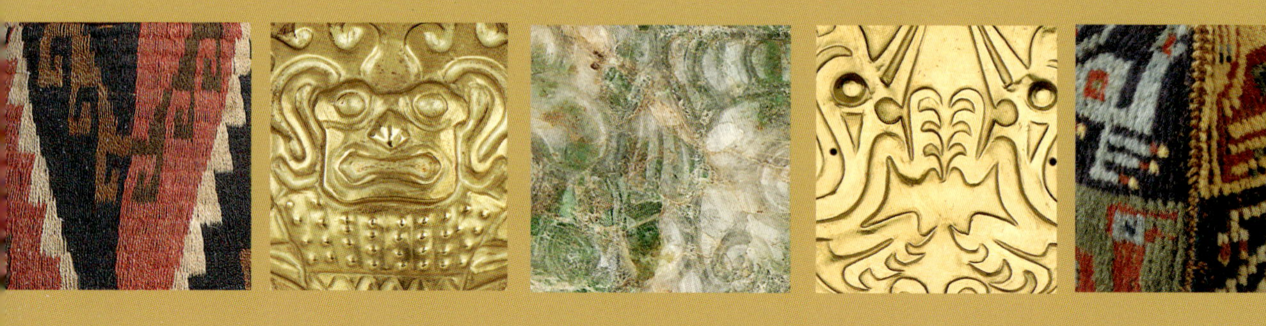

Beyond the simple need for clothing, peoples throughout history have used regalia as decoration to beautify, denote wealth and accomplishments, and signal confederation and community. From the finest dress of the nobility to the ceremonial trappings of the religious elite, regalia personified status and deeply held values. In the ancient Americas, regalia affirmed social position and prestige, and the raw materials from which it was made were prime tribute and gift items fundamental to political and economic interaction. Surviving artworks from throughout the ancient Americas express the importance of bestowing regalia, illustrating offerings and exchanges between persons of high status.

Among ancient cultures of the Americas, regalia also had powerful associations with the divine. Not only did its special insignias identify sacred beings and deified individuals, but the precious materials from which it was made were believed to possess sacred properties. Such beliefs, which often differ from Western conceptions of value, varied from culture to culture. For example, the most precious material in Mesoamerica was jadeite due to its fine-grained green-to-bluish color, which symbolized water, fertility, and healthy maize plants—the primary food that nourished Mesoamerican societies. Jadeite was transported over long distances, brought from quarries in southern Guatemala and carried to all corners of Mesoamerica to be transformed in the workshops of skilled artisans. Notably scarce and difficult to carve because of its hardness, jadeite was worked into a wide range of elite adornments, including earflares, necklaces with royal diadems, and funerary masks. Jadeite mosaics embellished feasting vessels, scepters, divination mirrors, and even human teeth. Delicate jadeite figurines portrayed sacred beings, especially the Maize god, and served as precious votive offerings; some were treasured possessions for centuries.

Central American peoples also prized jadeite, although beginning around the seventh century gold replaced it as the highest valued material. Ancient artisans mastered a variety of complex metalworking techniques, from cold-hammering to lost-wax casting. An alloy of gold and copper became the dominant metal for regalia, and metalsmiths developed the technique of depletion gilding—coating the alloy with acid to dissolve base metals and leave a shiny layer of nearly pure gold on the artwork's surface. During his fourth voyage in 1502, Christopher Columbus named the region Costa Rica (Rich Coast) because the people he encountered wore prodigious amounts of golden adornments, including large gold disks and wide bands of gold, often without other clothing.

Sixteenth-century Spanish writers in Peru chronicle the extensive use of regalia among the Inkas, its rulers dressed head-to-toe in golden pectorals, wide earflares, necklaces, headdresses, arm and leg cuffs, and even sandals so that onlookers had to shield their eyes from the metal's glaring reflections in the intense Andean sunlight. Only Inka nobility were allowed to possess gold because of its sacred association with the sun, which reinforced their special connection to the solar divinity. In spite of the extensive use of gold, silver, and copper to denote status, the Inkas readily surrendered these objects to the astounded Spanish because textiles—not precious metals—were the most highly valued material among Andean peoples. Textiles had been the prime status material in the Andean world from before the development of metalworking during the third millennium BCE. The earliest surviving fragments of cloth reveal mastery of sophisticated dyeing and weaving techniques to create spectacular woven regalia using both animal and vegetal fibers.

Regalia also ornamented administrative and ceremonial buildings, adding to the spectacle of ritual performance and providing markers of identity and station for the structures and their users. Elaborate displays of cloth, decorated with painted or woven insignia and pictorial narratives, adorned walls. Impressive incense burners ornamented the exteriors of buildings, their smoldering incense and modeled imagery activating sacred forces to sanctify the structures and the rites held there. Classic Maya incense burners are especially ornate architectural regalia, often embellished with depictions of deities and sacred locales made manifest during ceremonies. Those from Guatemala's Pacific Coast frequently take the form of miniature temples themselves, with figures arrayed in fine regalia, such as flamboyant feather headdresses, circular earflares and broad nose ornaments, intricate shields, and other symbols of elite status (see p. 98).

Throughout the ancient Americas, regalia was a potent marker of identity, rank, and distinction, and its form and imagery manifested complex belief systems—from the creation of the universe to the divine basis of authority. Regalia also was the conduit through which sacred power flowed between the divine and human worlds. In spite of its widespread use, our interpretations of regalia's multifaceted meanings are limited by the scarcity of ancient written records, the incomplete inventory of surviving objects, and the near extinction of many indigenous societies and their beliefs. Nevertheless, ancient American regalia captivates the modern viewer with its artistry and intricacy, and offers a window into the complex social, religious, and intellectual lives of the indigenous peoples of the Americas.

The regalia of the Maize god takes center stage on this two-scene vase. In one scene, the Maize god's twin sons Yax B'ahlam and Juun Ajaw retrieve their father's regalia from the underworld. Yax B'ahlam holds aloft a large dish containing his jadeite jewelry—strings of beads, a maskette pectoral, earflares, and belt and headdress ornaments. Juun Ajaw totes a large bundle on his back that may contain his father's bones, recalling the opened bundle pictured on another vessel (see p. 164).

The second scene features a rare depiction of the death of the Maize god, in a grief-stricken pose and stripped of his regalia. He is surrounded by the underworld's waters, symbolized by skeletal heads and waterbirds. A finely arrayed woman, seated in front of the skeletal centipede-maw entrance to the netherworld, offers up the god's insignia—a *Spondylus* shell jewel and shark-head belt adornment. The accompanying hieroglyphic text recounts the Maize god's death on 13 Ok 8 Sip, which corresponds to October 19, 3110 BCE, in mythological time and just four years before the current creation and advent of humans. The death phrase is expressed by the metaphor "enter water" as depicted in the scene. The text ends with the rare naming of the agent of his death using a title for the gods of Creation. Evidence from other artworks identifies the deity as Itzamnaaj (God D).

The rim text dedicates the vase as a cacao-drinking vessel, and concludes with the name and titles of its patron Yajawte' K'inich, divine ruler of the Ik' polity (reigned 738–about 768). This confederacy was located near the modern-day town of Motul de San José on the western edge of Lake Petén-Itzá, Guatemala.

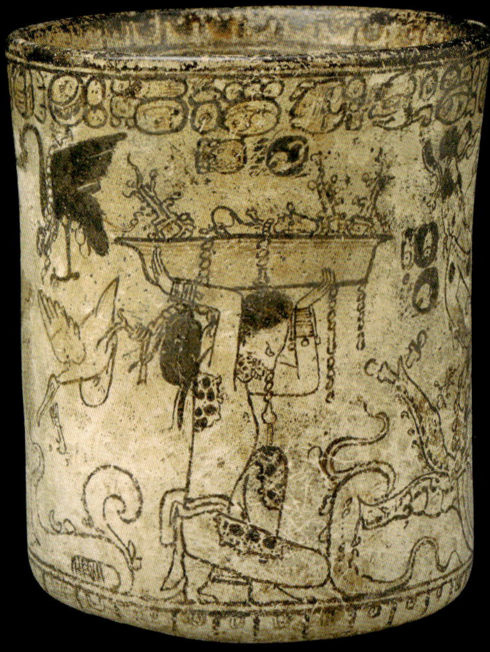

Earthenware with brown-black on cream slip
and traces of orange slip
H. 14.8 cm (5⅞ in.), diam. 13.3 cm (5¼ in.)
Gift of Landon T. Clay   1988.1175

Incised plaque

Maya, Late Classic Period, 550–800 CE
Guatemala or Honduras

Jadeite was among the most precious and sacred materials in Mesoamerica. Found in the mountains and swift rivers of southern Guatemala, jadeite was traded over long distances and worked by skilled craftsmen who created intricate jewelry for the elite. To the Maya, jadeite was associated with water and maize due to its green to blue-green hues resembling those of healthy maize plants and life-giving water. Other green-to-blue-tinted materials, such as the radiant feathers of macaws and quetzal birds, similarly were linked and thus were equally prized for aristocratic accoutrements. Arrayed in a plethora of bright and shiny green ornaments, Maya royalty stood as earthly apparitions of the Maize god and the embodiment of his divine powers of creation and fertility.

The main image on this plaque is a back-to-back rendering of a quetzal bird (*k'uk'*) and a macaw (*mo'*), which together signify K'uk'-mo', a supernatural locale of mythological events and sacred authority. Here K'uk'-mo' is placed at the center of the universe, the heavens symbolized by a double-headed feathered serpent above and entwined underworld serpents below. A suspension hole drilled horizontally through the plaque allowed it to be worn around the neck, perhaps as the central jewel of a large royal pectoral.

Jadeite
H. 9.4 cm (3¾ in.), w. 10.5 cm (4⅛ in.), d. 1.2 cm (½ in.)
Gift of Landon T. Clay   1988.1191

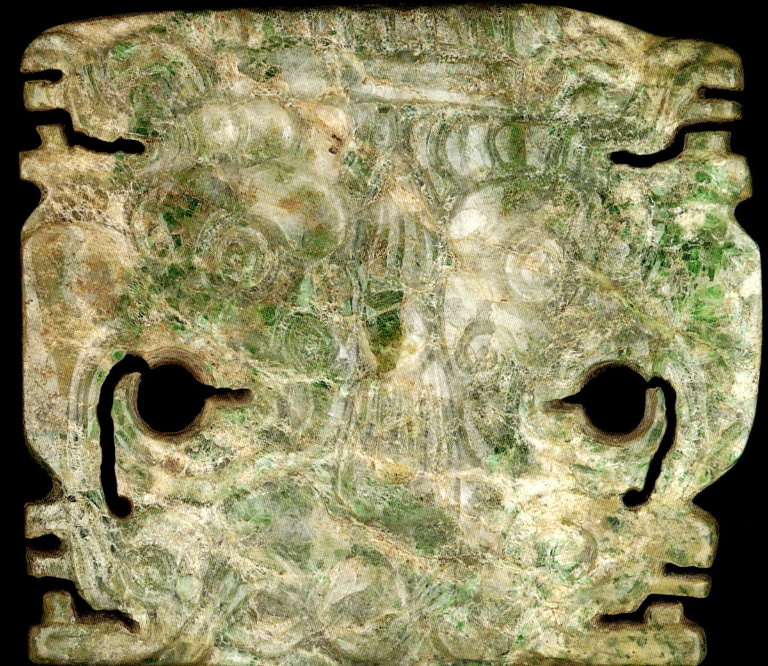

Necklace bead

Moche, Early Intermediate Period, 200–600 CE
North Coast, Peru

The Moche were among the most accomplished goldsmiths of ancient Peru, and some of the richest funerary chambers ever discovered in the Americas are located in the Moche region. These lavish tombs were filled with ornate gold works and other metal regalia of the finest craftsmanship. The gold and silver objects and their decorative motifs identified the individuals' political roles, including those of paramount ruler, war chiefs, and religious leaders.

This large hollow bead, made of two hammered gold sheets, was likely one of many that made up a sumptuous necklace. A pair of drilled holes allowed it to be strung. The image on the front recalls the Decapitator deity, so called because he is depicted on other artworks holding a severed head and a large blade. Here serpent-headed creatures flank the deity, emerging from his midsection. The back side is divided into eight pie-shaped wedges, alternately left plain or stippled using a repoussé technique. Loose particles inside the hollow bead produce a bright rattling sound that would have enhanced the wearer's movements.

Gold alloy
H. 6.7 cm (2⅝ in.), w. 6.7 cm (2⅝ in.), d. 3.8 cm (1½ in.)
Gift of Landon T. Clay   1970.590

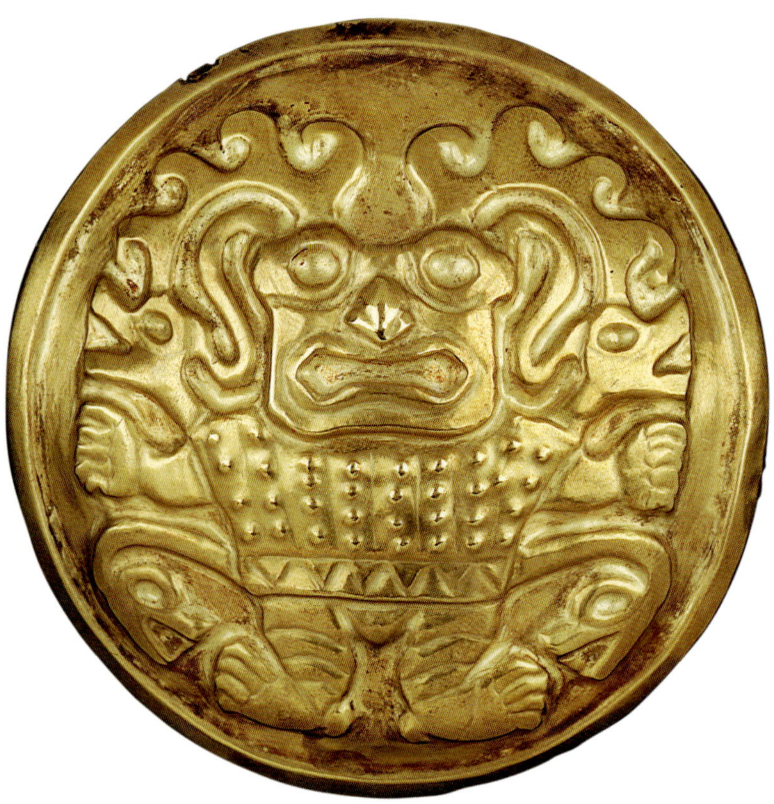

Effigy pendant

Olmec, Middle Formative Period, 1150–550 BCE
Tabasco or Veracruz, Mexico

This jadeite pendant depicts a raptor that may be a harpy eagle, the largest and most powerful of all American birds of prey. The fierce hunter is distinguished by its deadly talons, here poised open and ready to grasp its kill. The artist implies the bird's form using subtle cuts for the feathers and claws, and accentuates its opened beak with tongue extended as it cries out. Two small holes drilled along the wing allow for suspension in a position suggesting the prey's-eye view of the moment of capture.

Finely made jadeite artifacts such as this pendant first appear in Mesoamerica among the Olmecs of Mexico's Gulf Coast region. Recently a major ancient source of this esteemed mineral was located in Guatemala's southern highlands, hundreds of miles away from the Olmec heartland. Lacking metal tools, Olmec artisans painstakingly worked this exceptionally hard stone using simple string-saws, leather strops, reeds, and powdered quartz and jadeite abrasives. After sawing out the main form and abrasive-carving the subtle details, the artisan meticulously polished the piece to produce its shiny surface.

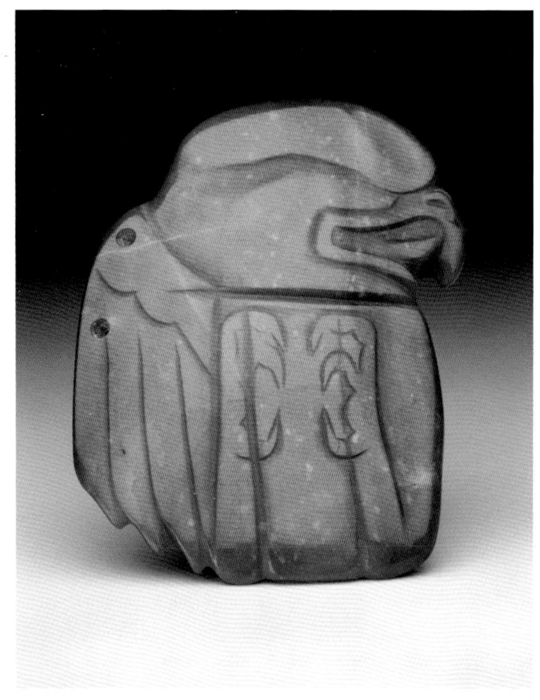

Jadeite
H. 9.4 cm (3¾ in.), w. 7.1 cm (2¾ in.), d. 0.4 cm (⅛ in.)
Gift of Lavinia De Nood   1982.763

Effigy pendant

Tairona, 900–1600
Sierra Nevada de Santa Marta region,
Magdalena Department, Colombia

The Tairona of Colombia's North Coast fashioned
a wide variety of gold alloy objects, from personal
adornments to everyday tools. Metalsmiths mastered
the lost-wax casting technique in which a wax model
is enveloped in a material such as clay. The wax is
melted away when heated, leaving a hollow mold into
which the molten metal is poured.

The showy Tairona figural ornaments are often
called "cacique" ("chief") pendants. They likely represent a high-ranking male figure transformed into his
animal spirit form, here indicated by the leaf-nosed
bat mask covering the lower half of the man's face.
Two raptor-like birds perch atop his forehead, and
curvilinear emanations erupt from his head. Bats
and raptors are especially common motifs in Tairona
shamanic pendants, perhaps referring to the practitioner's hunt for spiritual power to combat earthly
ills. The serpents emerging from his thighs may also
represent shamanic strength.

Among the modern Kogi, descendants of the
ancient Tairona, such transformed humans act as
intermediaries between the community and the
spirit world of ancestors and supernatural beings.
In ancient times, these pendants may have reinforced
the wearers' earthly status by an implied special connection to the supernatural realm.

Gold alloy
H. 16 cm (6¼ in.), w. 12.5 cm (4⅞ in.), d. 2 cm (¾ in.)
Gift of Landon T. Clay   2000.813

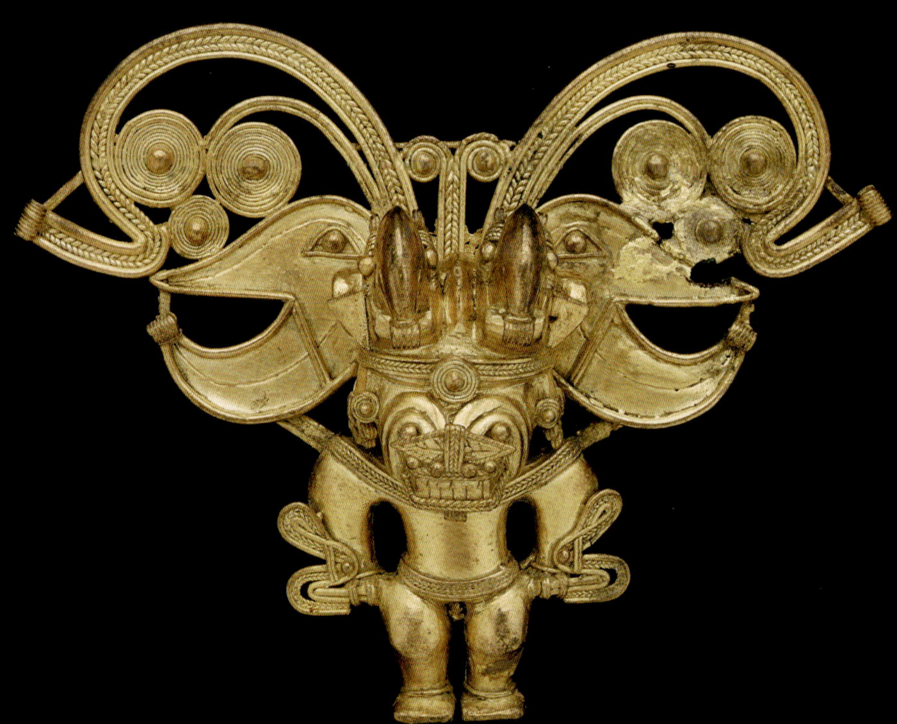

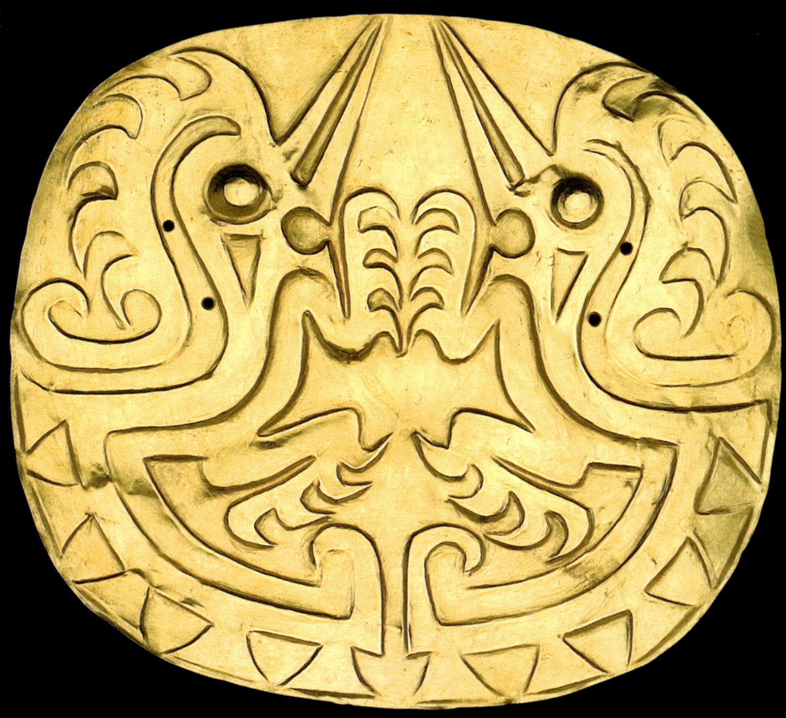

Embossed disk pectoral

Coclé, 700–1520

Sitio Conte area, Panama

According to sixteenth-century Spanish sources, chieftains in Panama wore elaborate golden pectorals, the finest examples reserved for the paramount leader (*quevi*) and secondary chieftains (*sacos*). Pectorals were displayed during public rituals and in battle, ending their ancient lives ornamenting the deceased. This disk features two composite animal beings facing each other. They have a lizard-like body, a long-beaked bird head topped by an iguana's spikey crest, and fearsome crocodile claws and tail. Such composite beings symbolize the transformed shaman whose special powers stem from his/her mystical association with these natural creatures. Crocodiles are particularly compelling shamanic associates because they inhabit both land and water and are formidable hunters.

Among the objects discovered at Sitio Conte in Panama, golden pectorals such as this example symbolically conveyed the special powers of the wearer. Some may be family emblems identifying the wearer's social affiliation whereas others may comprise petitions for supernatural protection. Panamanian artisans hammered gold into thin sheets and then used the repoussé technique to produce imagery by hammering the raised details from both sides. Tiny perforated holes allowed for attachment to clothing or suspension on cords.

Gold alloy
H. 21.6 cm (8½ in.), w. 23.5 cm (9¼ in.), d. 0.2 cm (¹⁄₁₆ in.)
Gift of Landon T. Clay   1972.940

Offering or pendant

Tolima, 1–550 CE
Magdalena River Valley,
Department of Tolima, Colombia

Home to the legendary El Dorado—the gold-covered
man—ancient Colombia is renowned for its extraordinary golden regalia. Artisans mastered many techniques—cold-hammering, depletion gilding, and, in
the case of this pendant, lost-wax casting. This Tolima
adornment, cast in the shape of a human-bird form,
represents a shaman during "soul flight." The visionary
journey is signified by the avian wings, head plum-
age, and bifurcated tail. Abstract, geometric tracery
along the sides of the head and body denotes feathers.
Lines stream from the eyes, perhaps referring to the
shaman's divine sight, and bared teeth evoke his/her
spiritual labors. Modern Colombian shamans believe
that during soul flight their human body remains in
a motionless state, suggested here by the rigid, elongated torso.

Ancient Colombian metalworks also expressed
cosmological concepts. This pendant is cast from tum-
baga, an alloy of gold and copper, which embodied the
belief in a universe composed of paired oppositions
(light-dark, male-female, gold-copper). Gold was linked
to the life-giving energy of the sun while copper was
allied to life-giving blood and the moon. The wearers
of such adornments were believed to absorb the metals' inherent powers.

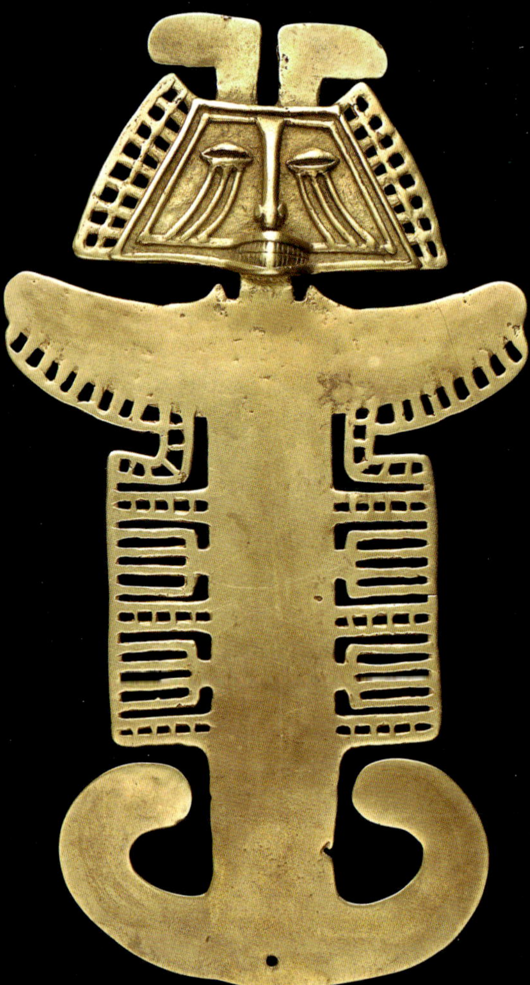

Gold alloy
H. 18.4 cm (7¼ in.), w. 10.2 cm (4 in.), d. 1.6 cm (⅝ in.)
John H. and Ernestine Payne Fund   1975.35

Pectoral

San Jacinto style, probably Zenú (Sinú), 1–900 CE
San Jacinto Mountains, northwestern Colombia

San Jacinto-style gold pendants are renowned for their high level of abstraction, many of which are interpreted as depicting the transformation of a human into his/her animal-spirit or a deity intermediary. Typical of the style is the reduction of the human body to a flat, rectangular form with slab-like legs, feet implied by zigzag lines, and a torso reduced to a narrow rectangle. Stylized hands grasp two staff-like objects emerging from the mouth, sometimes interpreted as flutes. Eclipsing the tiny torso is a large head covered with soldered filigree details. The wide, upturned nose elicits the leaf-nosed bat, a common shamanic spirit form in Colombia. Wing-like appendages, composed of stacked spirals, flank the head. Delicate filigree braids on the face accentuate the piercing spherical eyes. The head is topped by two large half-spheres that may represent hallucinogenic mushrooms, still ingested by modern-day shamans to assist their spiritual journey.

This style of adornment is typical of the Darién region linking Central and South America. Traded widely, Darién gold pectorals are found as far away as Chichén Itzá on the Yucatan Peninsula in Mexico, and some remained in use as late as the seventeenth century. In both ancient and colonial times, figural pendants typically ended up in burials—including urn burials and shaft-and-chamber graves.

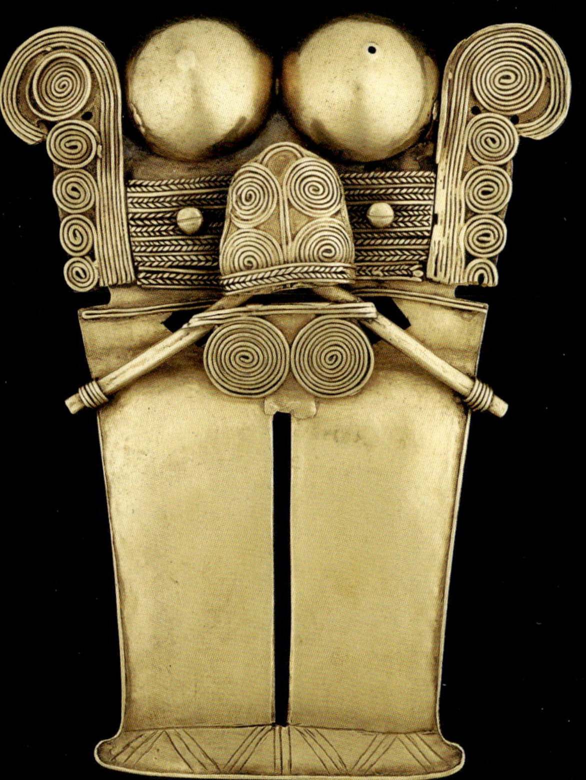

Gold and copper alloy
H. 18.4 cm (7¼ in.), w. 13.8 cm (5⅜ in), d. 2.2 cm (⅞ in.)
Gift of Landon T. Clay   1973.145

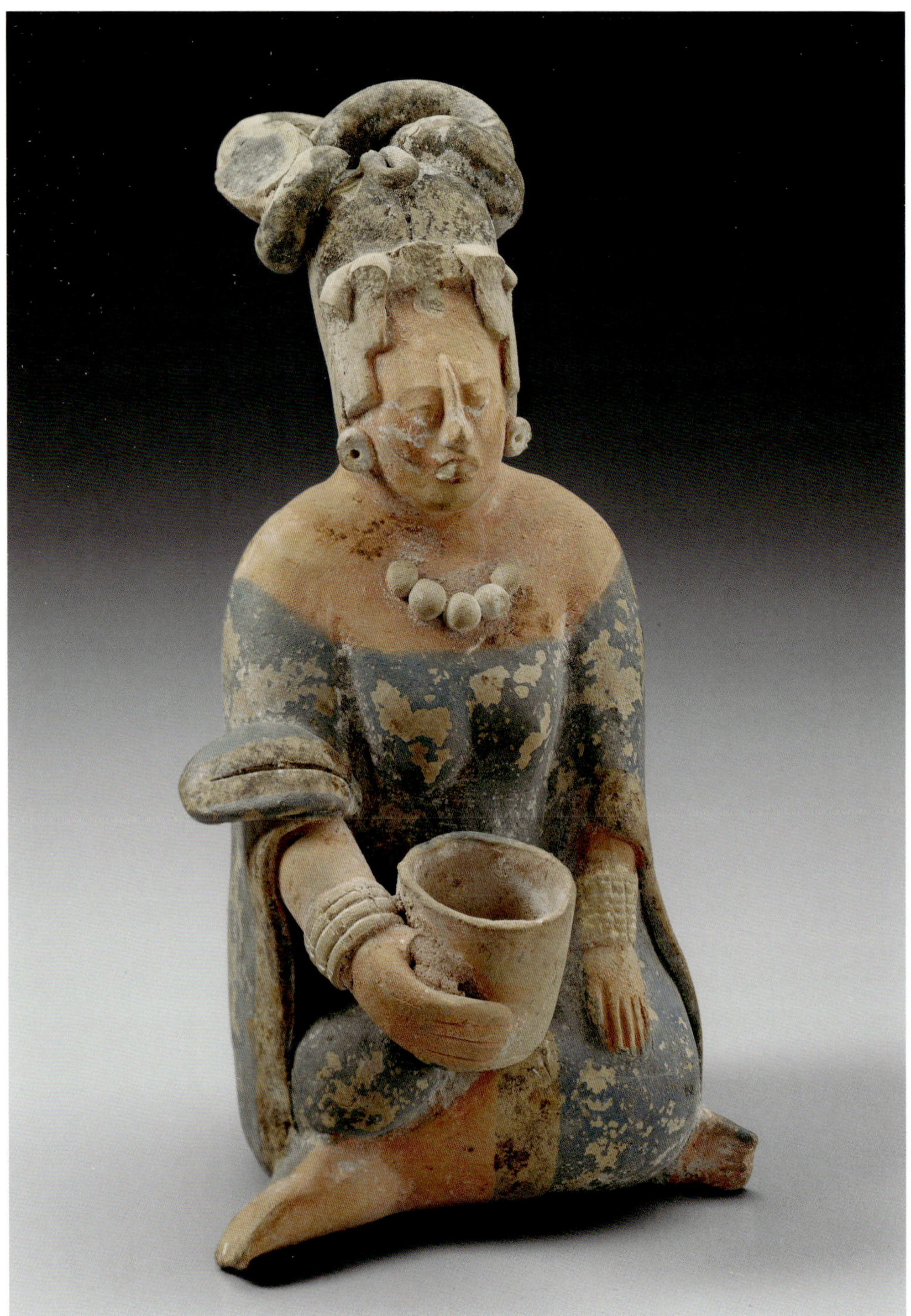

Figurine of a seated woman

Maya, Late Classic Period, 650–800 CE
Jaina Island area, Campeche, Mexico

Elaborate head wraps and stylish accessories were essential to the well-dressed Maya lady. This noblewoman's long tresses are entwined with cloth bands, and the front is cut in the stepped bangs fashionable during the Classic period. This distinctive hairstyle exaggerates her artificially elongated cranium, a measure of beauty that refers to the youthful Maize god. She also wears a prestigious blue wrap dress (*huipil*), large earflares, bead necklace, and white-painted wrist cuffs perhaps meant to indicate shell.

The vessel balanced on her knee alludes to women's vital responsibilities of official hospitality. High-status women were essential to successful aristocratic feasts and thus were influential members of the royal court. Palace feasting scenes frequently picture noblewomen presenting the esteemed cacao beverages and directing the gathering's activities. Further, they were crucial to the longevity of royal dynasties as influential marriage partners who ensured royal bloodlines and thereby affected political and economic matters.

Earthenware with orange, black, and white slip paint, post-fire blue pigment
H. 15.2 cm (6 in.), w. 7.9 cm (3⅛ in.), d. 10.2 cm (4 in.)
Museum purchase with funds donated by Lavinia and Landon T. Clay 2007.48

Four-cornered hat

Wari, Middle Horizon Period, 500–800 CE
Peru

Knotted four-cornered hats were part of elite men's formal attire among the Wari culture of southern Peru and northern Bolivia. Ceramic and stone figurines show four-cornered caps worn with decorated tunics and other high-status paraphernalia. In some cases, face painting continues the lively geometric patterning of the hats. Square hats also adorned the false heads of high-status male mummy bundles.

Wari four-cornered hats were made using a labor-intensive technique reserved only for luxury objects. Knotted cotton threads form the basic structure of the hat. Along the sides and peaks, wool threads dyed in different colors were looped into this structure as it was built up to make pile and create the geometric pattern of composite animals. The colorful loops then were cut, transforming the individual units into a smooth pile surface that covered the cotton threads holding them in place. The repeating figures on the alternating colored squares appear to be a composite creature composed of the beak and distinctive three-toed feet of a bird and the body of a long-necked llama, alpaca, or other camelid from which the wool fibers came.

Knotted cotton ground with wool (camelid) pile
H. 11.4 cm (4½ in.), w. 12.7 cm (5 in.), d. 12.7 cm (5 in.)
Mrs. Cabot's Special Fund   47.1096

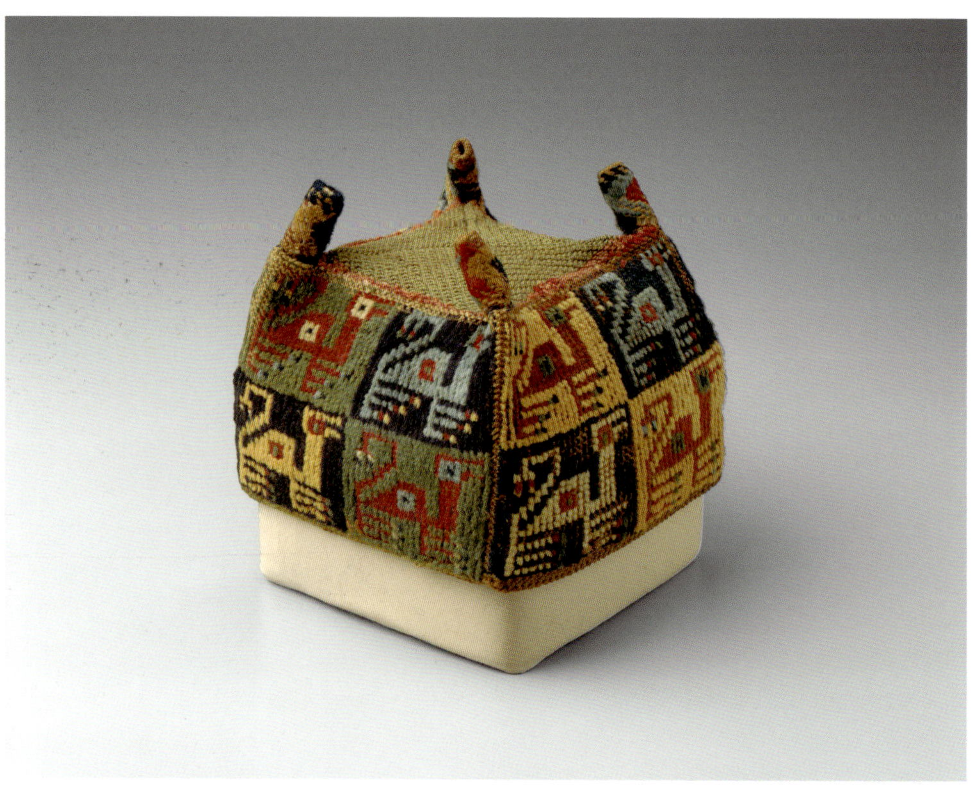

Hat

Aymara, Late Horizon Period, 900–1535
Arica area, Chile, or western Bolivia

In the seventeenth century, the indigenous chronicler Guaman Poma de Ayala illustrated the wide
variety of headgear worn by different societies in
the Inka empire, including feathered headdresses,
headbands with ornaments, and short fez-like hats
with ties around the chin. Similar to other clothing,
headgear proclaimed the wearer's social and political affiliation, a practice that continues today among
indigenous peoples in southern Peru, Bolivia, and
northern Chile. Multicolored headgear was typical
of the Aymara people (including the Carangas, Aul-
lagas, and Quillacas) who came under Inka rule in the
1470s and who continue to live in the coastal plains
of Bolivia and Chile. The region's dry, cold climate has
preserved many ancient fiber creations.

Conical hats with small diameters were worn
high on the head, which explains the need for chin-
straps or ties as depicted in Guaman Poma's draw-
ings of Aymara dress. This hat was crafted using a
coiling technique in which a spiraled bundle of camelid fibers at the center top is held in place by thinner
twisted threads that form the pattern. The colorful,
zigzag design of stylized stepped frets is produced
by alternating the red, blue, brown, and white wrappings around the bundled fibers. Rare examples
of Aymara hats survive with their original feather
panache (or tuft), as seen here, which is composed of
a circular array of green feathers from which project
long red feathers attached to a hole in the top of the
hat.

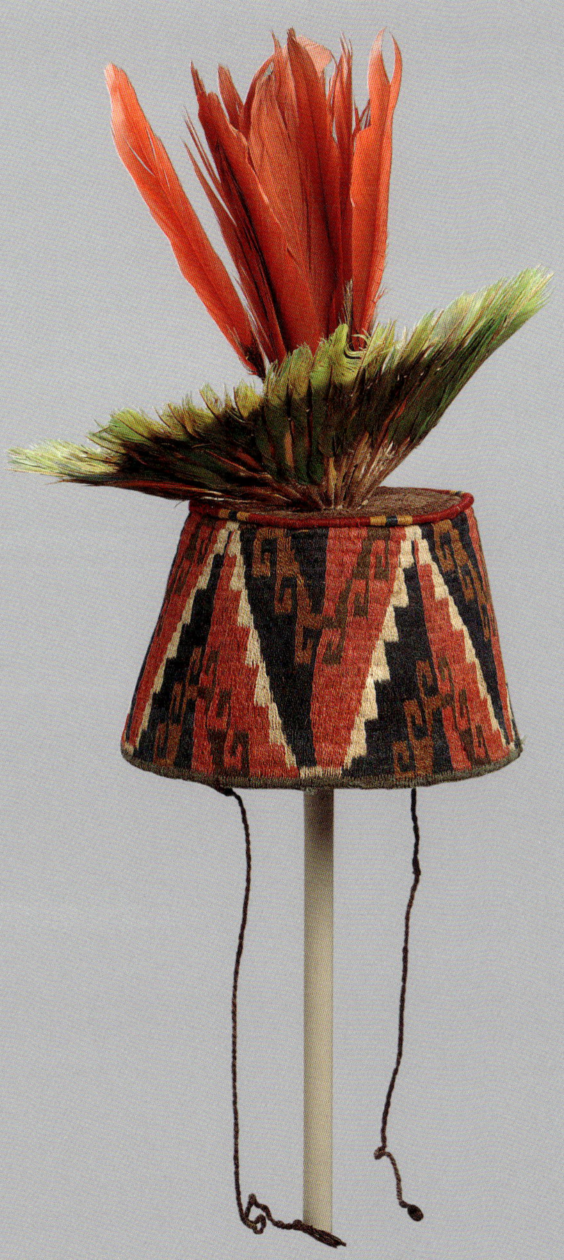

Wool (camelid), feathers, cotton thread
Hat without feathers: h. 11 cm (4⅜ in.), w. 17.5 cm (6⅞ in.),
d. 17.5 cm (6⅞ in.)
Frederick Brown Fund 1996.14

Hanging

Chimú, Late Intermediate Period, 1000–1476
North Coast, Peru

This large textile may have graced an interior wall at Chan Chan, the capital of the Chimú kingdom in northern Peru. Chan Chan was the largest city in ancient South America and remained independent for more than five hundred years until it was conquered by the Inkas in the 1470s. The city featured extensive royal residences with large courtyards, formal meeting spaces, and flat-topped pyramids housing elite tombs. Surrounding the opulent compounds were working-class and artisanal neighborhoods specializing in textile production, metalsmithing, pottery, and the building trades. Chan Chan is famous for its adobe brick walls decorated with painted stucco reliefs of birds, marine creatures, and human and divine figures. Their persistent geometric format recalls that of textiles, suggesting the textile foundation of Chimú architectural aesthetics.

This example belongs to a small number of large-scale cotton textiles from the North Coast that likely had an architectural function. Most have been found as partial fabrics, folded and placed in burials. This example, which represents only four panels from what certainly was a monumental hanging, features two standing male figures with outstretched arms and stepped headdresses. Exceptional skill is demonstrated by the discontinuous warp and weft weaving and paired warp threads. The subtle tan-to-white variations in the background color fully exploit the natural colors inherent to cotton yarns. The brown and blue tones were achieved by dyeing the cotton fibers; the impressive blue was produced by indigo dye. The strong blue shade was the paramount prestige color throughout the Andean world.

Cotton plain weave with discontinuous warps and wefts
H. 147 cm (57⅞ in.), w. 214 cm (84¼ in.)
Textile Income Purchase Fund   65.599

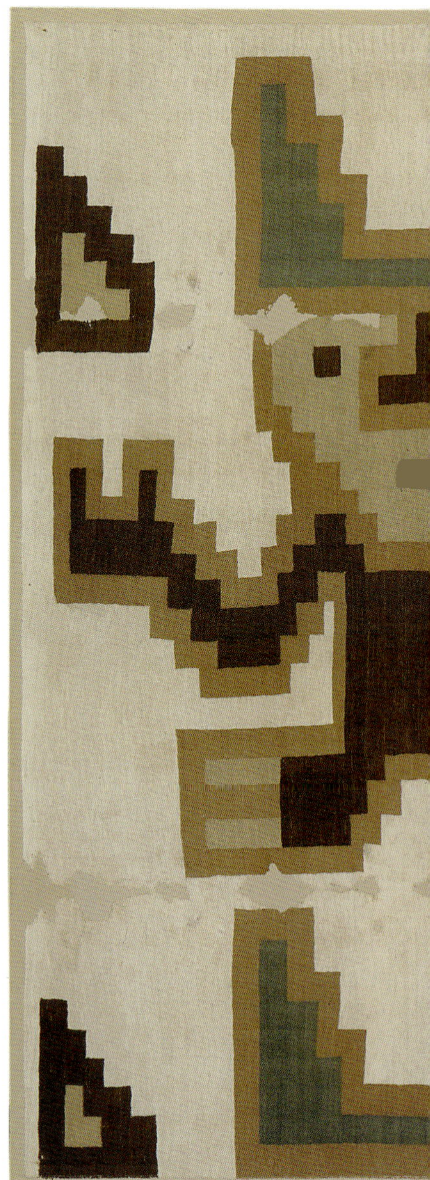

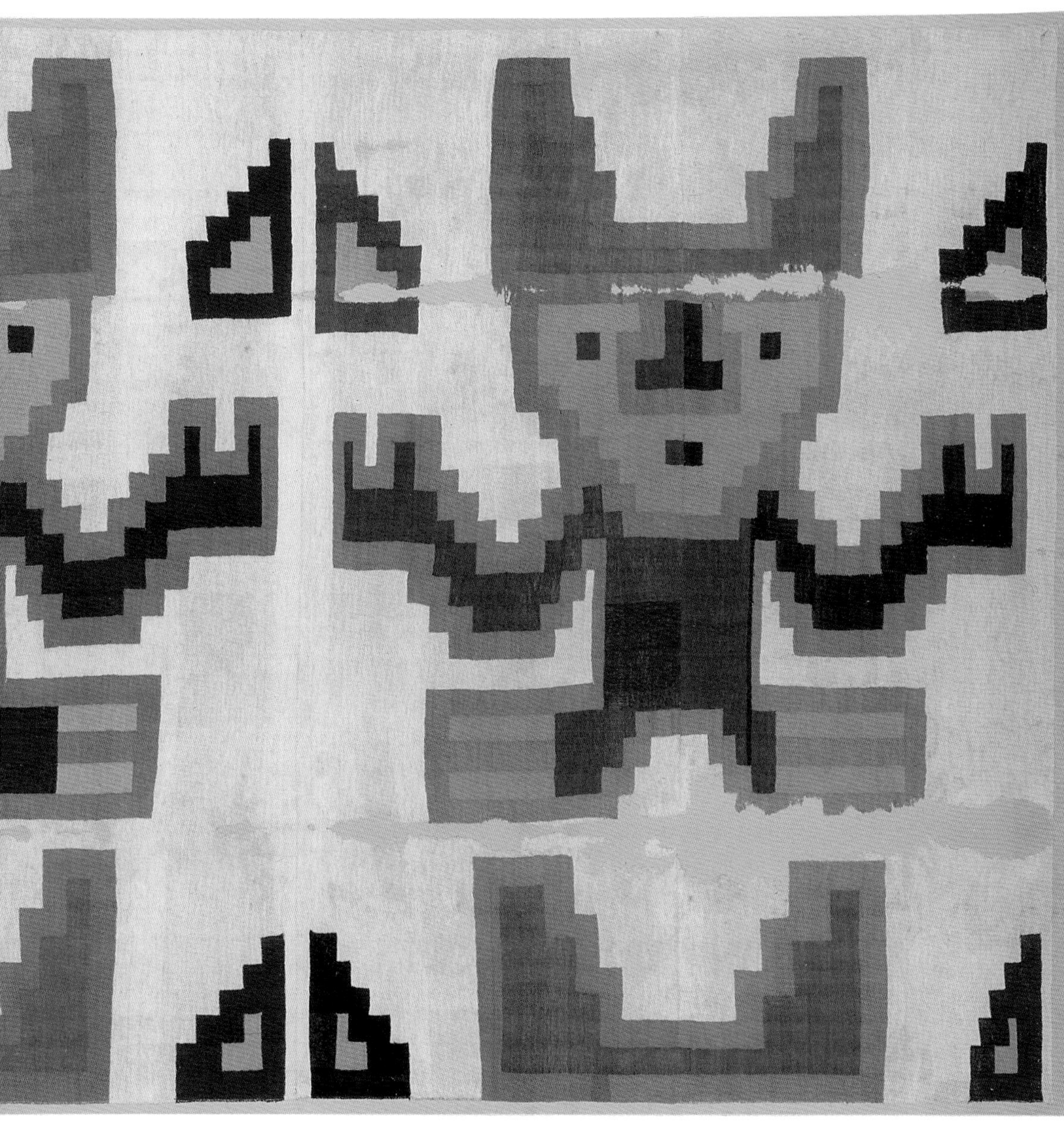

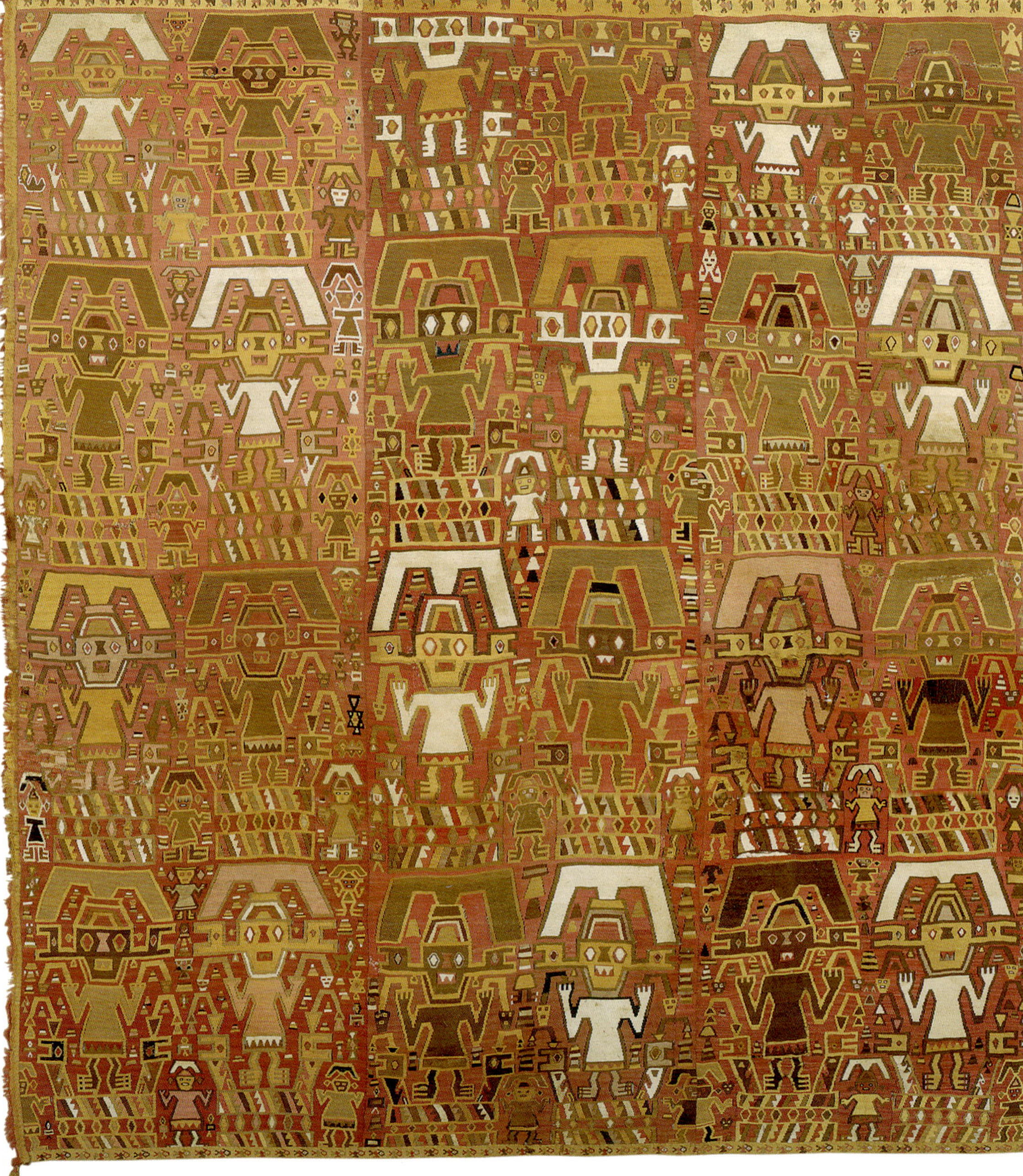

Mantle

Chimú-Inka, Late Horizon Period, 1476–1534
North Coast (?), Peru

Even among the Inkas, Chimú textiles were prized for their high quality and complex designs. The Inkas, who conquered the Chimú state in the 1470s, demanded fine cloth as tribute and even brought Chimú fiber artists to work in Cuzco, the Inka capital city in the distant southern highlands. The woven textiles produced during this period often exhibit the blending of Chimú and Inka styles, and are found both along the North Coast as well as in Inka strongholds to the south. The long arm of the Inka empire is noted particularly in this mantle's unusually high thread count. Yet, it retains Chimú aesthetics and techniques, including the slit tapestry method, wherein different colored weft threads are turned back on themselves to create slits in the direction of the warp threads, thereby producing the illusion of line and shadow.

The complex imagery features male figures dressed in Chimú-style elite regalia, most notably the crescent-shaped headdress denoting rulership and authority throughout the North Coast. The larger figures also wear complex masks and hold aloft trophy heads as they stand on decorated platforms like those found in public places at many North Coast sites. Smaller figures flank the platforms and are dressed in the less ornate attire of lower-status nobles and attendants.

The fiber artist who wove this mantle displayed expertise through the single instance of color anomaly, an artistic element at the heart of Andean aesthetics. In the third column, the second figure from the top has blue-hued lower teeth, produced by a strong bath of indigo dye.

Wool (camelid) slit tapestry
H. 175.9 cm (69¼ in.), w. 159.4 cm (62¾ in.)
Charles Potter Kling Fund   1981.284

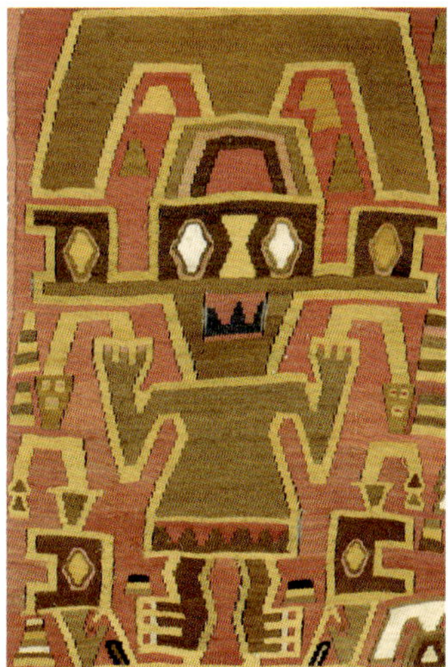

Incense burner

Maya, Early Classic Period, 350–650 CE
Department of Tiquisate, Pacific Coast, Guatemala

Throughout the ancient Americas, ceremonial and administrative buildings
were adorned with extravagant regalia, setting the stage for the formal activities that took place in them and along their staircases and platforms. Buildings
were decorated with carved stucco and painted images, woven or painted cloth,
and carved wooden elements displaying royal and sacred insignia. Magnificent
incense burners, such as this Maya version, ornamented the wide staircases,
the smoldering incense and modeled imagery activating sacred forces to sanctify the structures and the myriad rites of state and religion held inside the
buildings.

This incense burner replicates a Maya shrine adorned with divination mirrors, a flamboyant feather headdress, and emblems of the warrior's sacred obligations of war and sacrifice. Motifs flanking the building identify the censer
as a representation of the mythical Flower Mountain, a place of cosmic origin
and the after-death paradise for warriors. The bust of a figure, believed to
portray the mummy bundle of a deified ancestor-warrior, sits inside the shrine.
This style of censer was developed at Teotihuacan in highland Mexico, which
extended its imperial and economic influence to Guatemala's Pacific Coast during the third century and introduced the cult of sacred warfare and the veneration of warrior sacrifice.

Earthenware with traces of red and yellow post-fire paint
H. 43.5 cm (17⅛ in.), w. 43.3 cm (17 in.), d. 28 cm (11 in.)
Gift of Landon T. Clay 1988.1229a-b

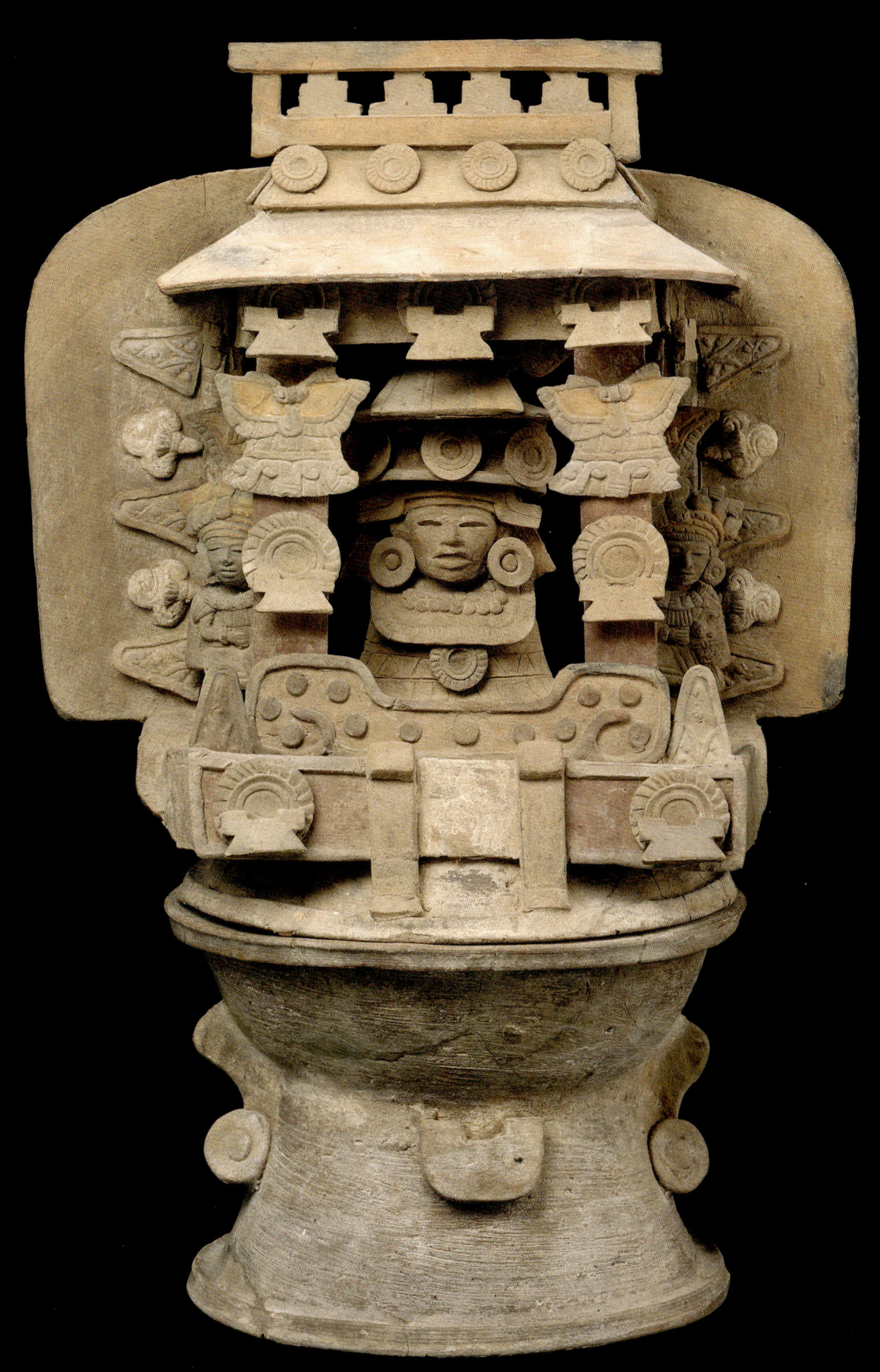

Incense burner stand

Maya, Late Classic Period, 700–800 CE

Tabasco or Chiapas, Mexico

The tall cylinder at the back of this censer elevated a dish filled with burning coals and smoldering incense to perfume the atmosphere and, according to Classic Maya belief, connect the human and divine realms. Lacandon Maya, who today live in the same region where the censer was made 1,200 years ago, equate copal incense smoke with rain clouds, and they collect the soot for use during rain ceremonies. The censer's imagery suggests its use during similar rain and storm-related rituals, its main figure being "God L" in his aspect as a rain and lightning deity whose loincloth ties terminate in serpent heads—a common lightning symbol. The vertical elements in the now-fragmentary headdress likely render God L's distinctive screech-owl hat with long feathers jutting upwards. Usually this deity is pictured as an old man. However, a youthful version, like this, is seen on stone monuments at sites in Tabasco, Mexico, a verdant and rainy land where ancient Maya artists made similar large, figural incense burners from a distinctive reddish clay as seen here.

God L is flanked by two Chahk deities (God B), recognized by their long, toothy snouts. Chahk is a four-part rain and lightning god, frequently oriented to the four cardinal directions and often represented holding a serpent or axe symbolizing lightning. Here they grasp long standards topped by axe-like blades adorned with mist/lightning curls. God L stands on a turtle shell signifying the earth, with an aged earth deity emerging from the earth/carapace.

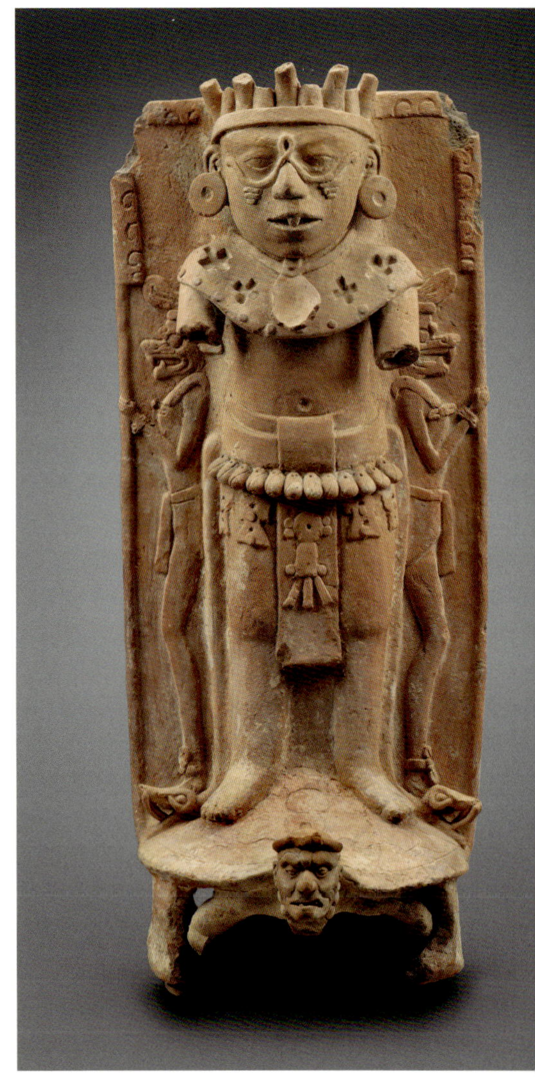

Earthenware with traces of stucco with a dark red
and post-fire blue paint
H. 40.6 cm (16 in.), w. 87.6 cm (34½ in.), d. 30.5 cm (12 in.)
Gift by Timothy Phillips in memory of Katherine Sullivan
2007.840

Incense burner

Nicoya, Potosí style, 500–1350
Greater Nicoya region, Costa Rica or Nicaragua

Two-part incense burners topped by fantastical crocodilian beings are unique to southern Nicaragua and northwestern Costa Rica. These ornate burners have been found on the slopes of an imposing volcano on Ometepe Island in the middle of Lake Nicaragua. The island has been inhabited for millennia, and the many intentionally broken incense burners strewn on the volcano's slopes affirm the island's long-standing importance as a ritual center.

The modeled imagery on Potosí-style censers pertains to universal concepts of the potency of fire and new life emerging from the widespread death caused by volcanic eruptions, a frequent experience for Central American societies living in an active volcanic zone. The smoke and ash from an erupting volcano were directly connected to its magical fertilizing powers. Further, smoke's simultaneous ability to reveal and conceal echoes the shadowy, fleeting nature of life force and the spirit world from which it originates.

Potosí incense burners mimic the geography of Central America and simultaneously represent the universe. The conical lid mirrors a volcano's shape, and the crocodile on top epitomizes the smoke and ash spewing from its summit. The base and lid depict the universe whose underworld was a mirror image of the heavens. The point of juncture in the middle is the disk of the earth, marked by hand-formed ridges like those on a crocodile's body. Among many cultures in Mesoamerica and Central America, the earth was likened to a crocodile floating in the cosmic ocean. Here the version atop the lid completes the model by simulating the continent's mountainous spine.

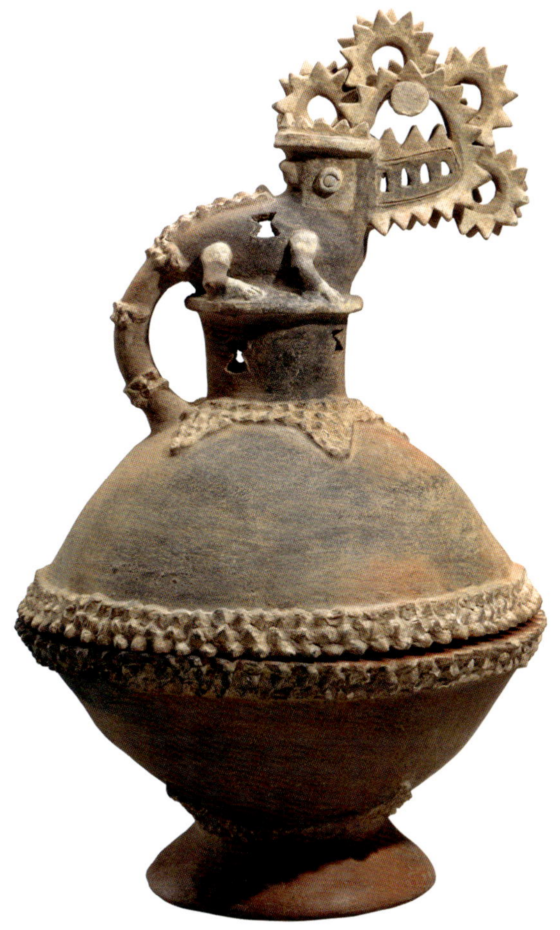

Earthenware with slip paint
H. 52.2 cm (20½ in.), w. 31.8 cm (12½ in.), d. 31.4 cm (12⅜ in.)
Promised gift of Timothy Phillips

Metate

Atlantic Watershed, 800–1400

Eastern Cordillera, Atlantic Watershed region, Costa Rica

Basalt

H. 10.8 cm (4¼ in.), w. 28.6 cm (11¼ in.), d. 14.9 cm (5⅞ in.)

Gift of J. Denis Glover and Sydney L. Glover   2011.2093

Metate

Guanacaste-Nicoya, 300–700 CE

Northwestern Costa Rica or southwestern Nicaragua

Basalt

H. 36.8 cm (14½ in.), w. 86.4 cm (34 in.), d. 35.6 cm (14 in.)

Museum purchase with funds donated by Jeremy and Hanne Grantham and Timothy Phillips   2008.169

The large, three-footed metate is an excellent example of the highly decorated ceremonial metates from northwestern Costa Rica and southern Nicaragua, which are renowned for delicate openwork carving and finely incised details. Although the word *metate* (from the Nahuatl word *metatl*, grinding stone) implies a common kitchen tool for grinding maize, seeds, or other plants, this elegant variety had different uses throughout the ancient Americas. Contemporaneous pottery sculptures in the Guanacaste-Nicoya region depict leaders and shamans sitting on decorated metates, indicating that some were ceremonial seats. In the sixteenth century, the Spanish observed metates serving as funerary biers. Some have been found deliberately broken and buried beneath house structures. The Spanish also described small versions, like the four-legged example here, being used to grind tobacco and other hallucinogenic substances ingested during shamanic rites.

Central American metates typically feature powerful animals, including jaguars, crocodiles, bats, and raptors. Such animals were esteemed clan symbols according to sixteenth-century Spanish writings, and they also were favored shamanic forms. The three-legged metate/seat may depict a shaman's animal spirit form given its composite zoomorphic features, which is a standard artistic format for picturing transformed shamans. It represents a ferocious feline—the jaguar's spotted pelt is represented by the latticework carving. Yet the ears are tiny crocodiles, and avian-like forms serve as the three legs. Completing the shamanic portrait is a nose-bar jewel—a common adornment worn by Costa Rican leaders. The carving on the top of the curved slab, patterned to represent textiles, also served to indicate an elite use.

The small, four-legged metate also portrays a jaguar, its spotted pelt rendered as a geometric design recalling the pulsating patterns experienced by shamans during visionary trance. This metate was found in a burial with more than a dozen other domestic and ritual objects, discovered in 1905 on land belonging to the Lindo family in Costa Rica.

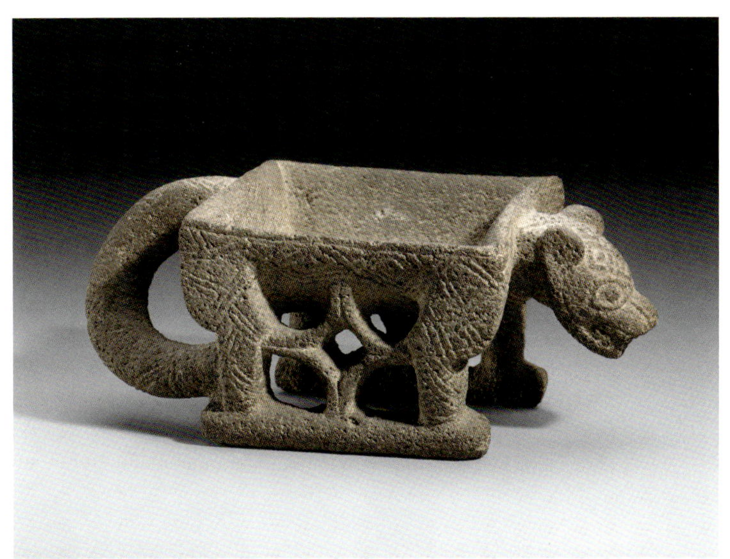

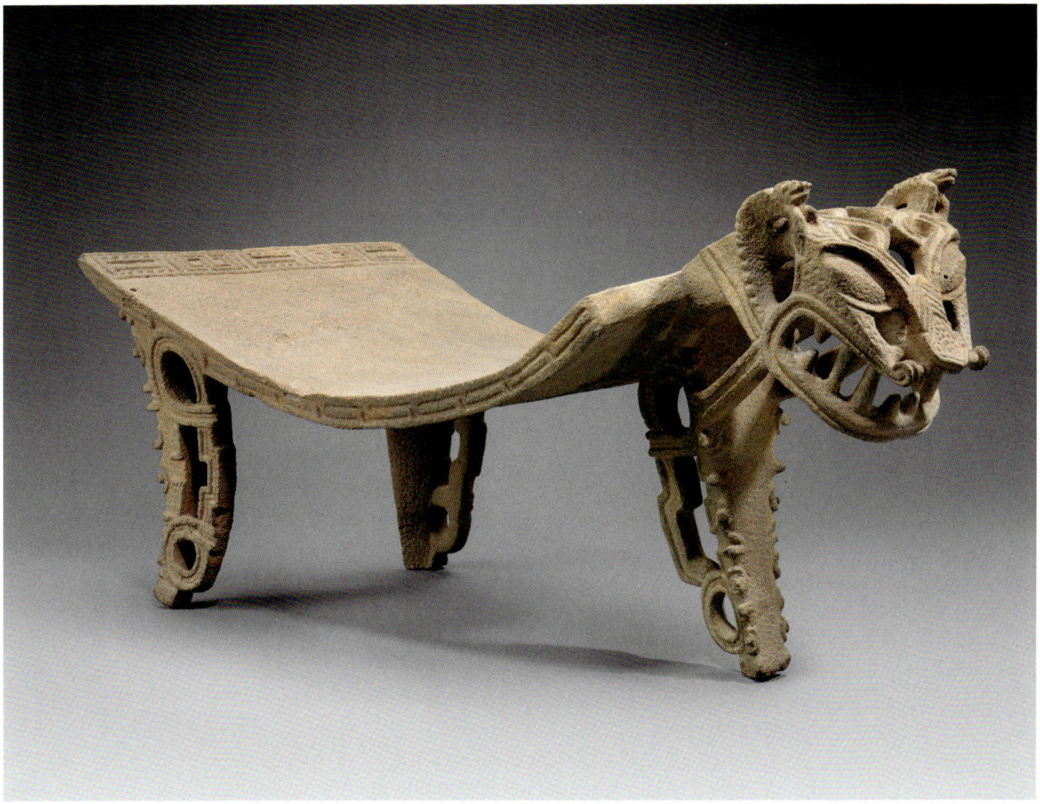

Ballgame yoke

Veracruz, Early Classic Period, 450–700 CE
Veracruz, Mexico

In Mesoamerica, the ballgame was both sport and solemn public ritual. Enclosed stone ball courts, which are today found in many archaeological sites in Mesoamerica, hosted games played by two teams (or individuals). The goal was to keep a solid-rubber ball from hitting the ground while batting it between opposing sides. The friar Diego Durán, who lived in Mexico City during the sixteenth century, described how, with "skill and cunning . . . in one hour the ball did not stop bouncing from one end to the other, without a miss, [the players] using only their buttocks [and knees], never touching it with the hand, foot, calf, or arm." Representations of Maya players illustrate them volleying the ball with forearms, hips, and thighs, all protected by special gear. Thick cotton-and-leather pads covered arms and legs, and a wide belt, called a yoke, was particularly effective for striking the ball.

This yoke made of stone—too heavy to be worn during an actual game, which demanded speed and agility of its players—was likely a trophy, ceremonial offering, or funerary article. Many surviving Veracruz stone yokes were expertly carved with imagery referring to sacred forces ritually activated during the game. This exquisite example features an anthropomorphic toad, its midsection ornamented with scroll motifs denoting water or mist. Mesoamericans associated the toad with rain, fertility, and spiritual transformation because of its curious life cycle. The toad begins life as a fish swimming in the water and then emerges to walk on land. In addition, toads become active when the rains arrive. The bearded human emerging from the toad's body may be the mythic hero Quetzalcóatl ("feathered serpent").

Stone
H. 13 cm (5⅛ in.), w. 37.5 cm (14¾ in.), d. 41.6 cm (16⅜ in.)
Gift of Lavinia and Landon T. Clay   2003.855

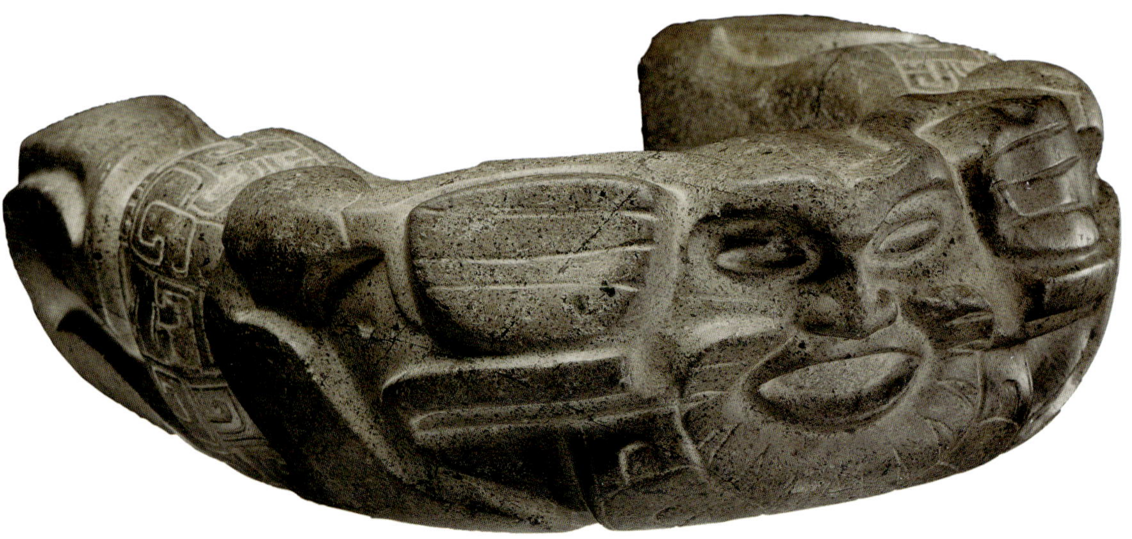

Hacha

Veracruz, Classic Period, 500–800 CE
Gulf Coast region, Mexico

This enigmatic type of object is known by the misleading name of *hacha*, meaning "axe" in Spanish, because its front edge narrows like that of an axe head. Classic period illustrations of ballplayers show hachas set atop yokes—the specialized wide belts worn by the players. Hachas functioned in tandem with palm-leaf-like attachments (called *palmas*) on the yokes' front, which were used to bat the ball. Stone hachas, found from Veracruz to Honduras, frequently are discovered in caches and burials, often grouped in numerically symbolic sets of three, nine, or fifty-two. Interestingly, only occasionally are they paired with yokes.

Ceremonial hachas display a wide range of imagery, including humans, animals, composite beings, animal or human body parts, and occasionally architecture. This skillfully carved version portrays an elderly male adorned with a large earflare. The wide band encircling his eye suggests a deity, perhaps Xiuhtecuhtli, the preeminent elderly god in the Central Mexican pantheon. He is the god of terrestrial fire and typically carries a fire brazier on his head. But here he supports a fangless serpent-like zoomorph, perhaps referring to the *xiuhcoatls*—fire serpents— associated with the sun.

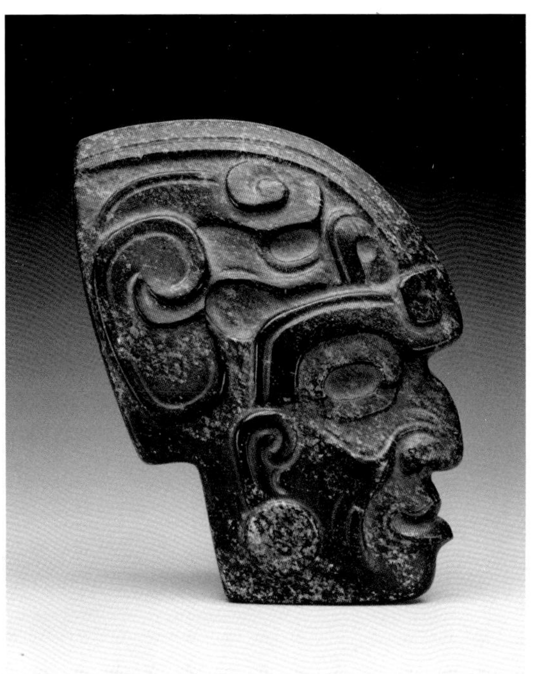

Black diorite with feldspar inclusions and cinnabar pigment
H. 17.8 cm (7 in.), w. 13.3 cm (5¼ in.), d. 5.1 cm (2 in.)
Gift of Mr. and Mrs. John Dolliver MacDonald   1972.1085

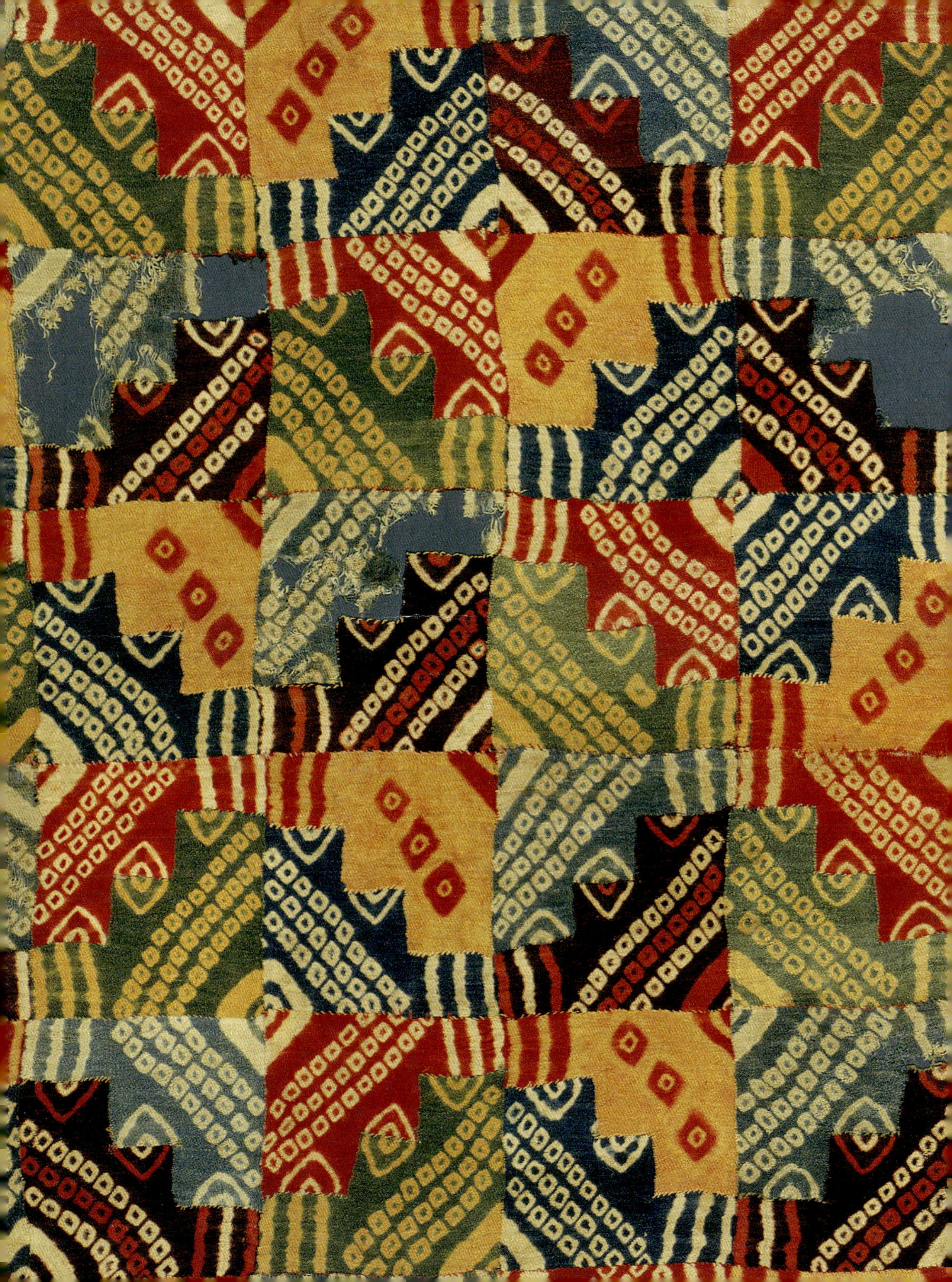

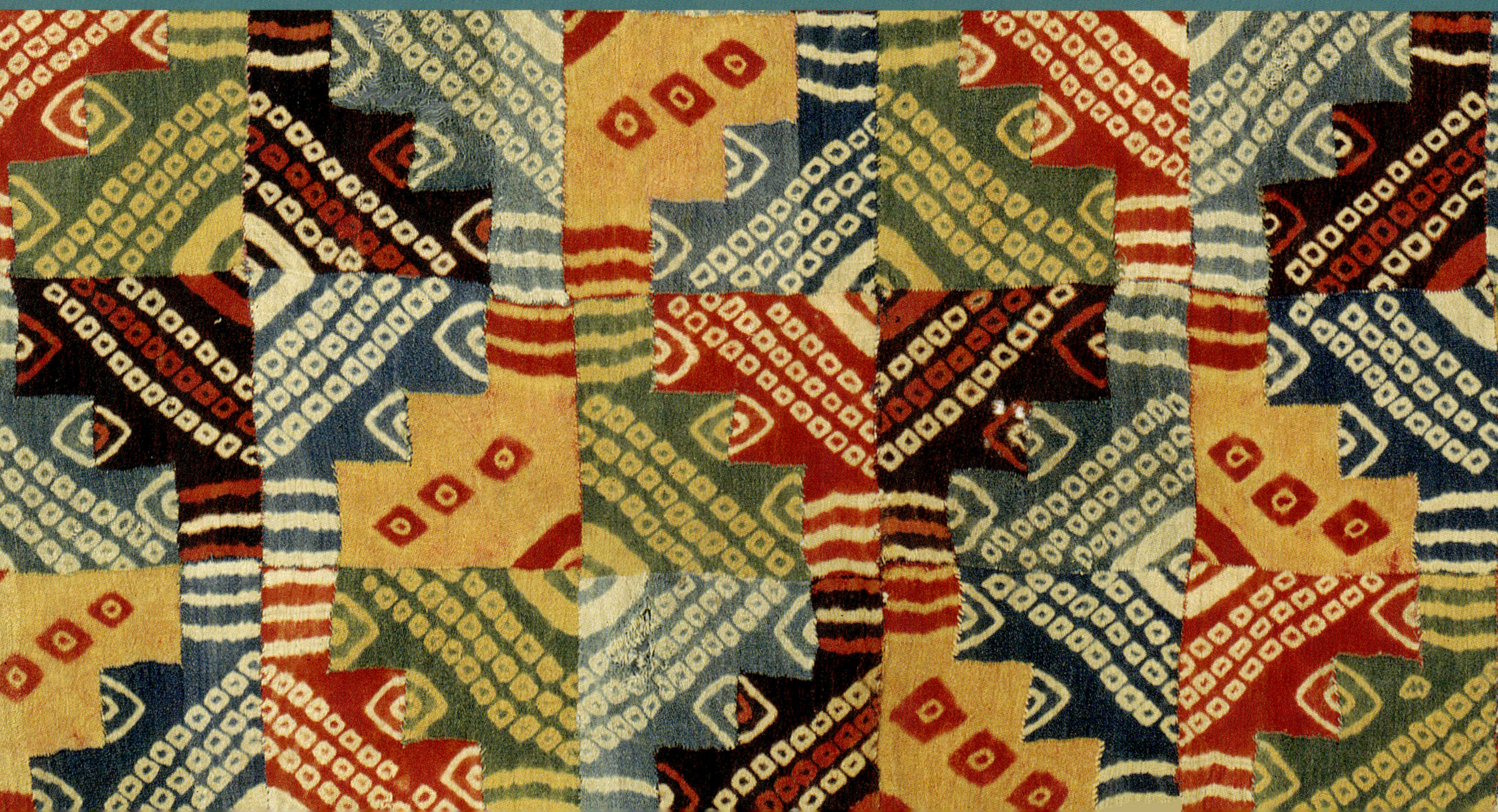

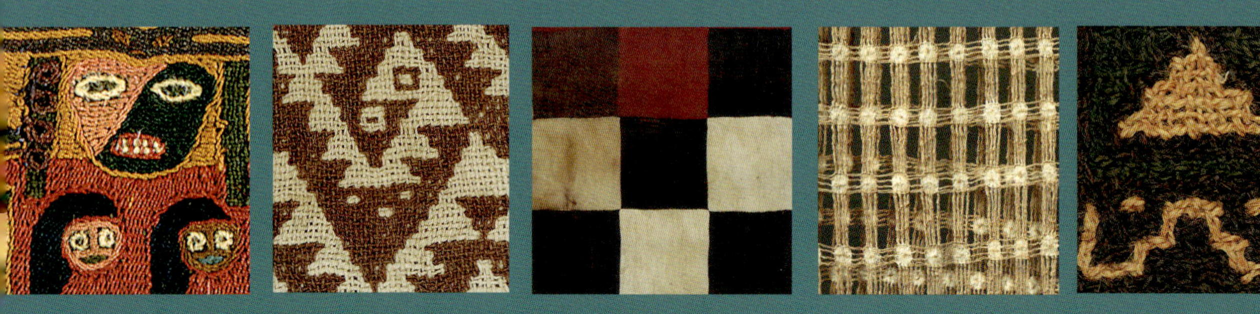

The ancient Americas enrich the world's textile heritage with stupendous fiber works—from utilitarian bridges spanning deep mountain gorges, to monumental hangings adorning buildings, to opulent clothing glorifying rulers and the honored dead. Yet cloth in the ancient Americas was far more than a simple product and covering to shield the body from discomfort. Cloth, and clothing made from it, was fundamental to economics, politics, and social interaction, and also played crucial roles in religious rites and beliefs. In ancient Peru and Bolivia, fiber artists developed many of the world's most sophisticated traditions, devising complex spinning, dyeing, weaving, and decorative methods. Cloth was so central to Andean civilization that it underlay the aesthetic system, shaping Andean pictorial formats in all media, including architecture and city planning. For example, the design layout of the famous "Gate of the Sun" in the Kalasasaya district at Tiwanaku, Bolivia, is based on the rectilinear geometry inherent to a warp-and-weft fabric.

In Mexico as in Peru, wealth and status were revealed by the amount of cloth controlled by a person. According to sixteenth-century Spanish writers, cloth was the leading item for paying tribute and tax obligations because it was the main exchange commodity for other goods, service labor, and political support. Across the Aztec empire cloth functioned as currency with fixed exchange rates. Value was based on fiber quality and finesse of weaving and decoration. The importance of cloth to the financial stability of the Aztec empire is revealed by the mass quantities yielded to the state, such as that recorded in the colonial manuscript *Matrícula de Tributos* (1522–30). Every eighty days, 51,600 mantles (long cape-like garments) were owed to the Aztec state from its subject polities, totaling roughly 235,296 full-length garments each year. Similarly among the Maya of Yucatan, cloth was a leading tax obligation and essential to market exchanges. Bishop Diego de Landa, the first bishop of Yucatan, remarks on the tax payment to the Spanish Crown of 13,480 cotton mantles by the town of Maní in 1549.

In Peru, cloth comprised the main tax payment to the Inka state, equal in value to all agricultural products. Peasant women produced plain cloth (*awasqa*) by spinning, dyeing, and weaving fibers from camelid (llama, alpaca, and vicuña) herds and plant fiber reserves. Cloth was awarded for service to the state, to encourage political alliances, and to integrate conquered peoples into the empire. Full-time specialists, mostly women but occasionally men, worked exclusively for the state to weave the highly coveted, opulent textiles. The Inka armies also required myriad items made of cloth—from shelter (tents and blankets) to clothing (tunics and headgear) to military equipment (slings and padded armor). Because Inka armies traveled light, warehouses were positioned strategically, from Chile to Ecuador, to supply the advancing militias. In essence, cloth bound together the Inka empire as a fabric-centered system of finance and social politics.

Textiles were so important to the Mixtec economy in southern Mexico that its rulers often had as many as fifteen wives who spent their time creating cloth. Textiles provided an economic and social advantage for the family's patriarch in three ways. First, he could exchange textiles for other commodities and service labor. Second, the family head could host feasts during which he distributed fabrics and other gifts to strengthen social ties and forge political connections. Third, large holdings of cloth ensured higher-status marriage partners for the patriarch's daughters. Among the Mixtecs, then, the ability to produce and give away cloth was key to one's economic, social, and political status.

As a political tool, the type of garment and its decorative pattern communicated important social information such as ethnic affiliation, economic status, ritual responsibilities, political association, and official accomplishments. In the Andes, clothing, headgear, and body adornments were cleverly controlled to accentuate sociopolitical bonds. For example, the Inka ruler Huayna Capac (about 1493–1527) would send gifts of fine, Inka-style clothing to conquered leaders while he donned their native garments during official visits. This clothing reciprocity acknowledged local traditions while non-aggressively introducing the textile customs of the conqueror to nurture acceptance of the new political hierarchy.

In Mexico, social status was communicated by the type of fiber—such as soft cotton versus coarse maguey threads—and the specific items of clothing an individual was authorized to wear. In the fifteenth century, members of the Mexica (Aztec) lower classes were restricted to clothing made from low-quality fibers and lacking the elaborate embellishments of upper-class attire. Commoner-class men could wear only knee-length mantles, whereas the elite were granted long, elegant tunics reaching to the ankles. Political relationships were communicated via specific types of clothing conferred by Mexica rulers on those who had given good service to the state. Decorative designs specified the type of service, such as the wind god Ehecatl's symbol and the "eyes on the edge" border motif that could be worn only by warriors who had taken at least three prisoners in battle.

Favorable climatic conditions in Andean South America have preserved woven fabrics from as early as 3200 BCE and twined fibers from before 13,000 BCE. The fiber-rich Andean archaeological record demonstrates the long-standing social, economic, and political importance of textiles, which continues today. Less favorable conditions in Mesoamerica have meant few survivals of the fiber works themselves. Yet myriad renderings of textiles and the many observations by sixteenth-century Spanish writers point to an equally long history and pivotal role for cloth in ancient Mesoamerica (see, for example, p. 121). Today indigenous peoples in Mexico and Guatemala wear traditional clothing as an apparatus of identity and ideology, intimating the seminal role of the fiber arts in ancient Mesoamerica as among their counterparts in the Andes.

Tunic

Inka, Late Horizon Period, 1476–1534
Peru

The Inka strictly regulated what types of
cloth and clothing were worn, each catego-
rized by the design and quality of fiber and
weaving. The finest cloth, *cumbi*, woven by
men called *cumbicamayos* ("ones in charge
of fine cloth"), was reserved for esteemed
warriors, military leaders, and the ruling
elite. Throughout the empire, every town
and social group was limited to exclusive
patterns and colors to publicize the wearers' affiliation and status. Spanish chronicler Francisco de Xérez described in 1534
the marvelous sight of the arrival at Caja-
marca of "a squadron of Indians [in the Inka
emperor Atahualpa's army] dressed in livery
of colors in the manner of chessboards . . .
all singing and dancing." This military uni-
form was worn into the seventeenth century
as illustrated by the Inka artist Guaman
Poma de Ayala. The Spanish banned its use
because, as a symbol of indigenous power,
it undermined colonial control.

This warrior's tunic features a red stepped neck
yoke and alternating white and deep purple squares.
Its edges and vertical neck slit are finished with fine
embroidery to amplify its value. The design, repeated
on both sides in keeping with Andean aesthetics, may
pertain to the *collca*, the checkerboard-like architectural compound of administrative storehouses where
tunics, food, regalia, raw materials, and other tribute
items were kept. Keeping the state storehouses full to
maintain the empire's taxation system and complex
social and political networks (via royal gift-giving)
was a prime factor driving conquest.

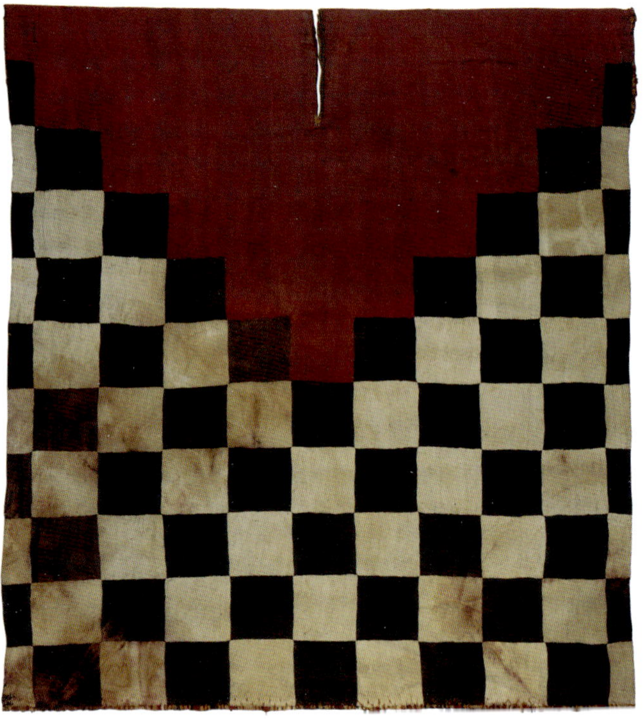

Wool (camelid) interlocked tapestry
H. 84.5 cm (33¼ in.), w. 78 cm (30¾ in.)
William Francis Warden Fund   47.1097

Hunter effigy vessel

Chancay, Late Intermediate Period, 800–1450
Central Coast, Peru

Modeled in the form of a mummy bundle, this jar renders a hunter carrying a trussed deer on his shoulder. The deer was a prized animal throughout Peru, hunted for food and also captured alive to be sacrificed during religious rites pertaining to agricultural fertility. Andean artworks often portray ritual deer hunts and hunters wearing the finery of the elite—not the "field clothing" of a common huntsman.

The high-status attire depicted here includes a richly woven head wrap with a large diadem at the forehead and matching ear pendants. The dark-hued tunic features a decorated neck opening and intricately woven motifs on the armholes' border. The bottom edge is adorned with a step-fret design, a pan-Andean symbol for architecture perhaps referring to a sacrificial platform. The man's legs are subtly suggested by the modeled tips of the hunter's feet below the tunic's hem. The three vertical bands on each cheek are a recurring Andean symbol whose meaning is unclear.

Earthenware with slip paint
H. 41.9 cm (16½ in.), w. 25.4 cm (10 in.), d. 26.7 cm (10½ in.)
Helen and Alice Colburn Fund   2015.2221

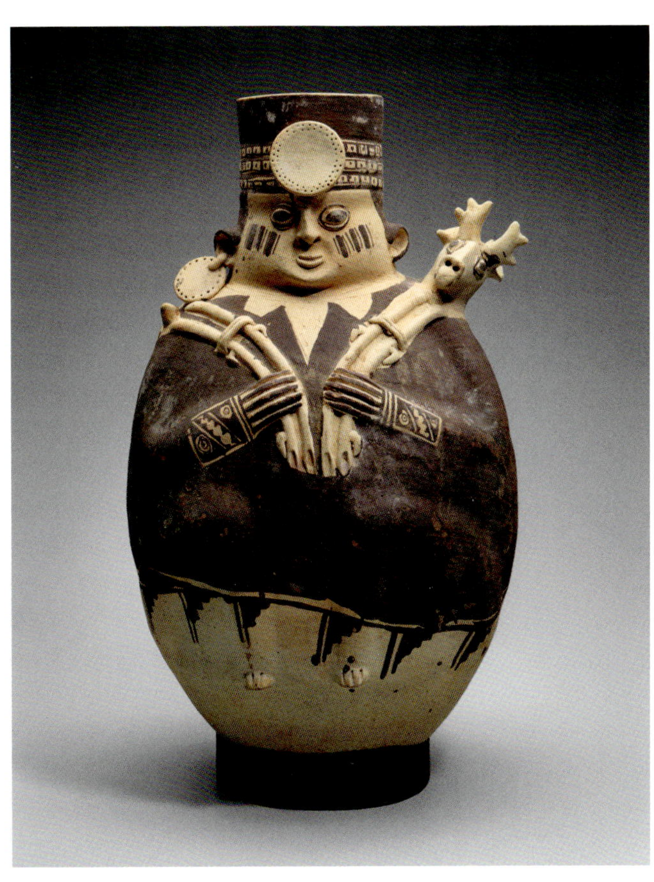

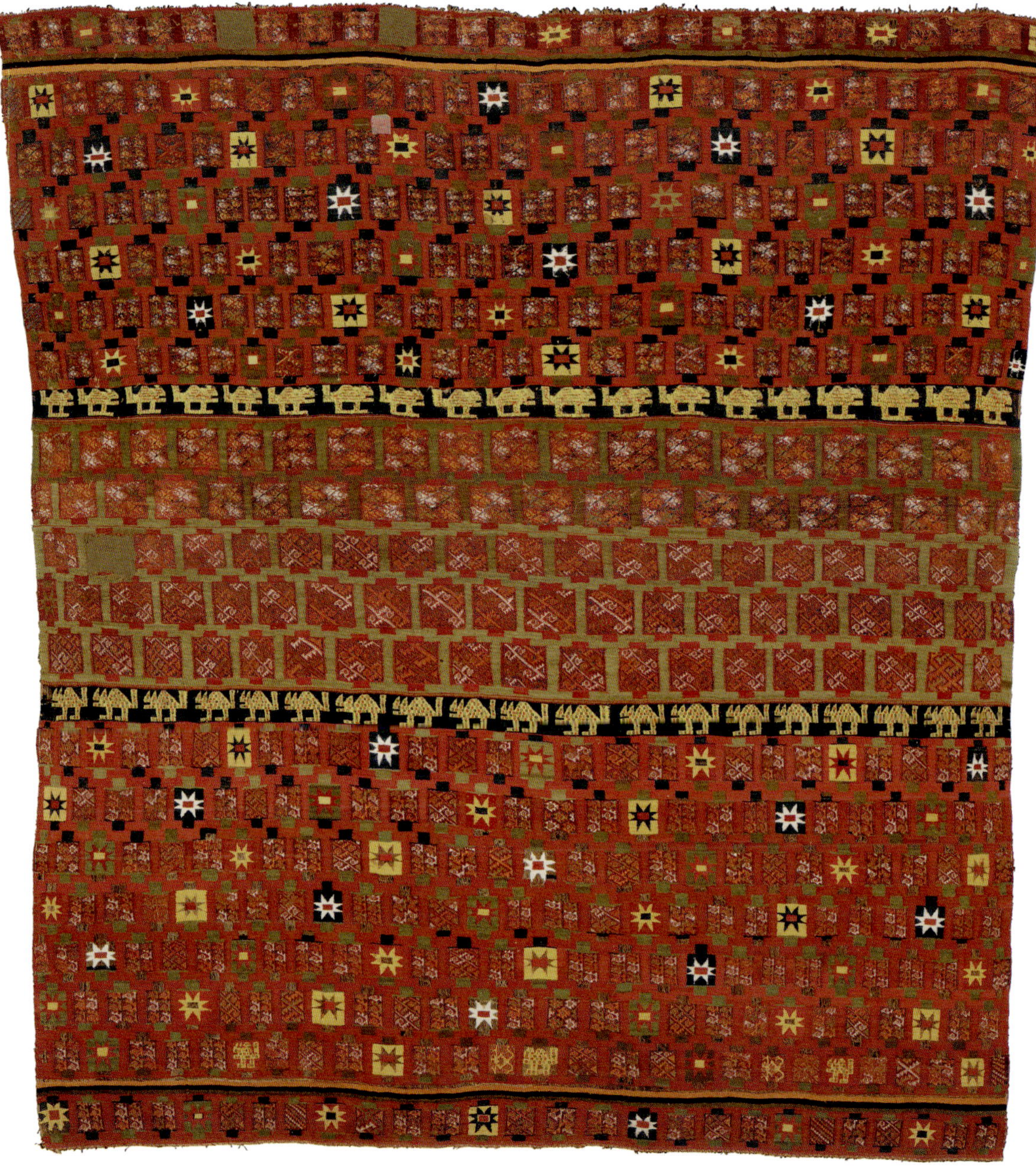

Large folding mantle (*lliklla*)
Provincial Inka, probably Late Horizon Period, 1400–1550
South Coast, Peru

This type of textile, called a *lliklla*, is a rectangular shoulder cloth worn by Andean women and fastened at the front with a large, decorated silver pin or *tupu*. This uncommonly large *lliklla* was made to be folded horizontally along a very thin red line woven across the central section, the line indicating where to double the mantle before draping it over the shoulders. When folded, a typical fabric would expose both the back and the front of the cloth, which was not acceptable to Andean custom because the folded-over half exposes its unfinished side to public view. To avoid this, the fiber artist reversed the weaving at the thin red line so that the back side of the upper half faces inward when the cloth is folded. According to Andean beliefs, the inherent qualities of technical and aesthetic perfection in this textile were transferred to its wearer.

The imagery comprises three rectangular sections, oriented horizontally and separated by a row of spotted felines. The sections contain—from top to bottom— six, five, and seven bands of squared motifs. The bands in the upper and lower sections are composed of three rectilinear forms separated by an eight-pointed star, a common motif on contemporaneous pottery of the South Coast. The design regularity is interrupted by such anomalies as the three felines and two frogs incorporated in the band at the bottom of the third section, refreshing the otherwise static pattern.

Wool (camelid or sheep) interlocked tapestry with complementary weft weave
H. 219 cm (86¼ in.), w. 207.5 cm (81¾ in.)
Museum purchase with funds donated by the Class of the Museum 62.1180

Female effigy bottle

**Nasca, Early Intermediate Period,
Phase 7, 550–650 CE
South Coast, Peru**

This finely dressed woman wears the wrap skirt
(*aksu*) and mantle (*lliklla*) typical of women's clothing
throughout ancient Peru. Her *aksu* is embellished
with lobsters and pollywogs. The profusely decorated *lliklla*, which falls from her head to her lower
back, features an archetypal Nasca supernatural
nicknamed the "Fan-Headed Anthropomorphic Mythical Being" (AMB-7-A). This mythic being is the most
frequently encountered sacred theme in Nasca art
with ancient origins in the region. The AMB is thought
to be a symbolic representation of nature's powerful
forces, each force represented by a different manifestation distinguished by specific motifs.

The Fan-Headed AMB typically is represented only
by his head topped by a fan-like element. Here plants
emerge from his mouth and radiate around the vessel
tracing the *lliklla*'s hemline; the foliage indicates that
this AMB may pertain to agricultural fertility. The pollywogs and lobsters decorating her *aksu* expand this
theme to life-giving bodies of water—both fresh and
marine. A tiny hole at the top of the woman's head
creates a whistling sound when liquid exits or air is
blown into the bottle.

Earthenware with slip paint
H. 17.1 cm (6¾ in.), w. 13.3 cm (5¼ in.), d. 13.3 cm (5¼ in.)
Gift from the Collection of Shirley and Hy Zaret
2008.192

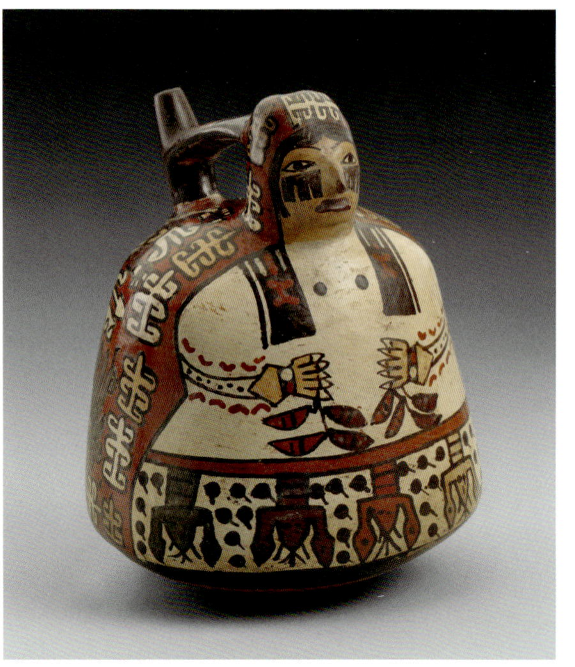

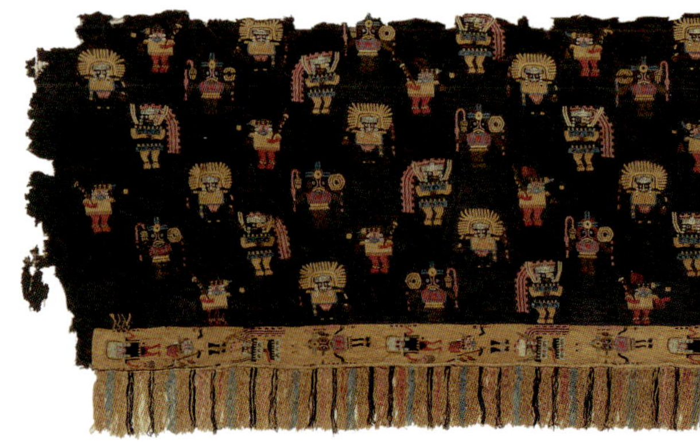

Wrap skirt (*aksu*)

**Paracas, Early Intermediate Period,
Phase 1, 1–100 CE
South Coast, Peru**

This wrap skirt (*aksu*) belongs to a singular category of ancient Paracas textiles in which groups of four different figures recur across the fabric rather than the more common single image. This repeated grouping suggests a specific narrative although its significance is unknown. Each figure is distinguished by a headdress and the items held in the hands. Two figures wear gold headbands. One of them sports an impressive rayed headdress and carries a large baton and trophy head. The other figure's headdress features long streamers, and he holds two double batons and a tiny trophy head. The topmost figure's headband is festooned with a large circular gold-colored diadem, and he clutches a curved staff and baton. The fourth figure—on the grouping's right side—wears a headband with four tall feathers, and he carries a spear-thrower (*atlatl*) and a short baton.

This textile came from a funerary bundle; its multiple cloth layers protected the innermost garments, including this *aksu*. Paracas bundles were placed in stone-walled chambers buried in Peru's South Coast desert, one of the world's driest areas. These burial fabrics are decorated with embroidered imagery that often covers more than 75 percent of the garment's surface with tiny stitches. The excessive amount of skilled labor needed to create the fabric would have lent greater prestige to its wearer. This aspect was especially important for fabrics used in sacred settings, where the textile amplified the sanctity of the rite, its participants, and the ceremonial setting—in this instance the burial of a revered family member.

Cotton plain weave embroidered with wool (camelid)
H. 60.8 cm (23⅞ in.), w. 286.7 cm (112⅞ in.)
Denman Waldo Ross Collection   21.2563

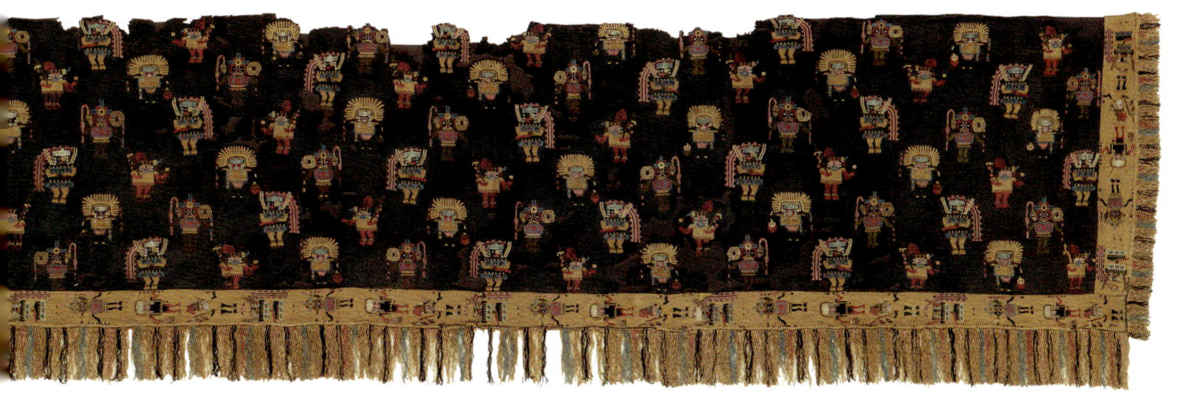

Mantle (*lliklla*)

Paracas, Early Intermediate Period, Phase 1, 1–100 CE
South Coast, Peru

Paracas textiles focus on three themes—blood sacrifice, fertility, and transformation into revered ancestors and spirit beings. Blood sacrifice is referenced
by figures carrying sacrificial knives and severed
human heads. Fertility is symbolized by seeds or
plants sprouting from the figures, and transformation is expressed by humans shifting into composite
human-animal beings.

Transformation and sacrifice are the principal
themes of this complex *lliklla*. The repeating image
depicts a male figure becoming a condor-like spirit
being, his outspread arms sprouting wings decorated
with severed human heads like those adorning his
short tunic. The bent arms, legs, and feet are a Paracas artistic convention for rendering the unseeable
mystical transformation. Blood sacrifice is implied
by the tunic's red color, the knife-like implement
in the figures' raised hands, and the trophy heads.
Those in the figures' left hands sprout a flower to
signify the causative link between blood sacrifice
and fertility/regeneration.

This mantle, exhibiting the highest levels of Paracas fiber artistry, was found with other fragmentary
textiles in 1916 in an ancient burial site located near
Pisco on the South Coast.

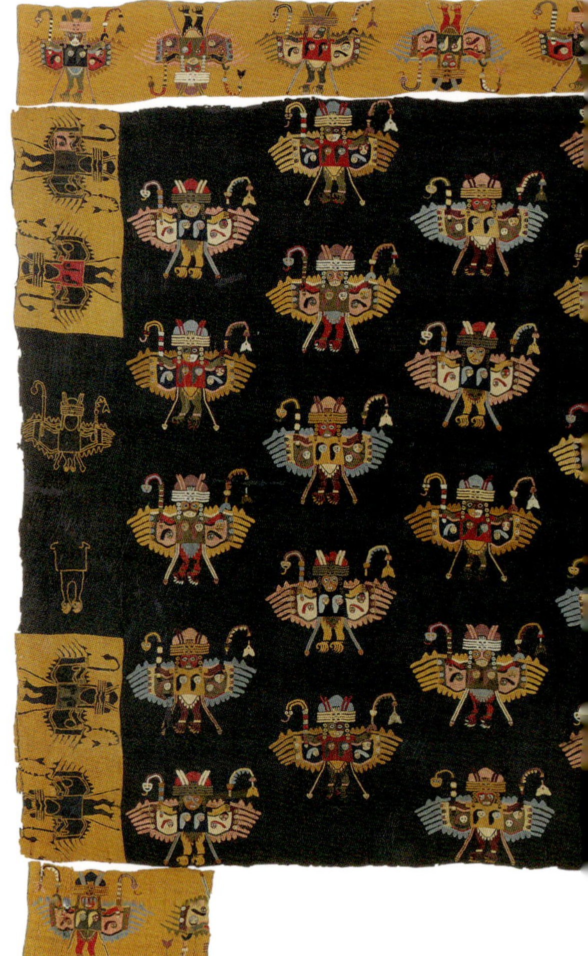

Wool plain weave, embroidered with wool (camelid)
H. 14 cm (5 ½ in.), w. 25.2 cm (9 ⅞ in.)
Denman Waldo Ross Collection   16.34a–c

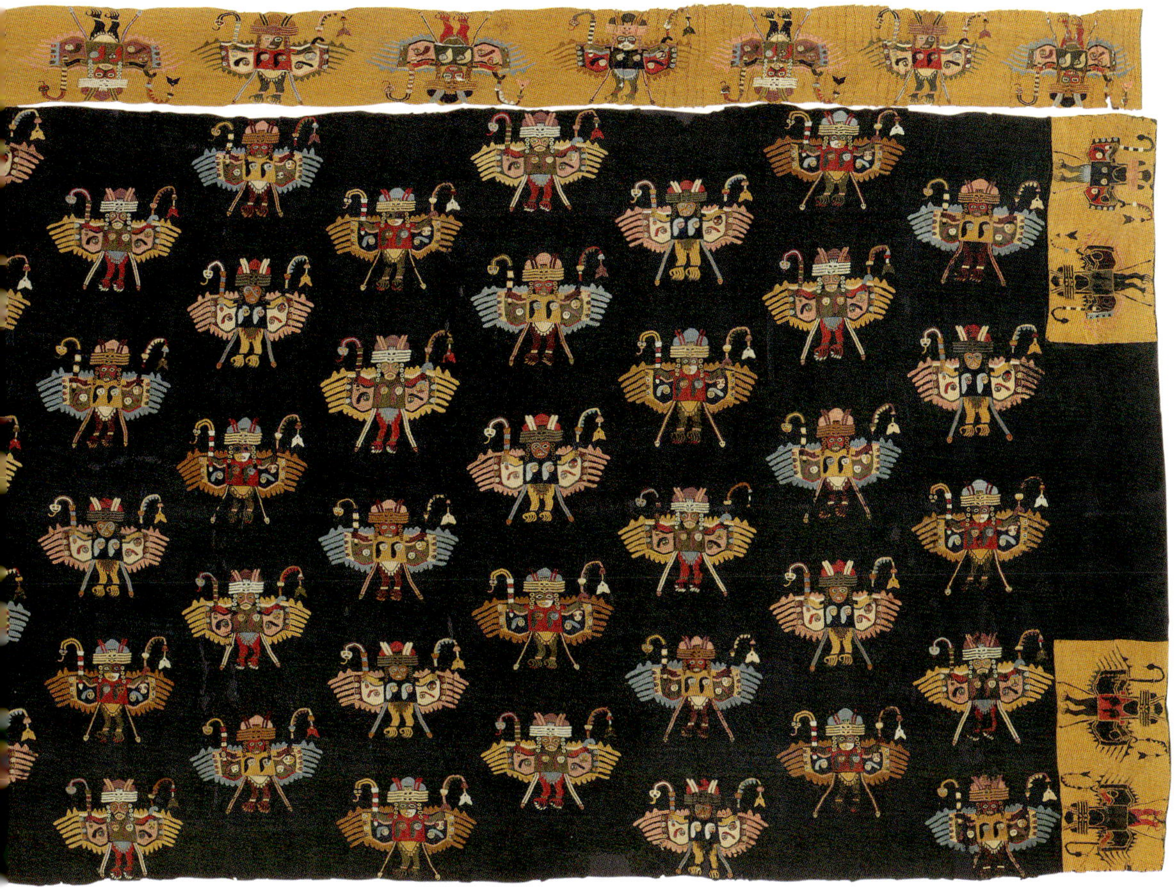

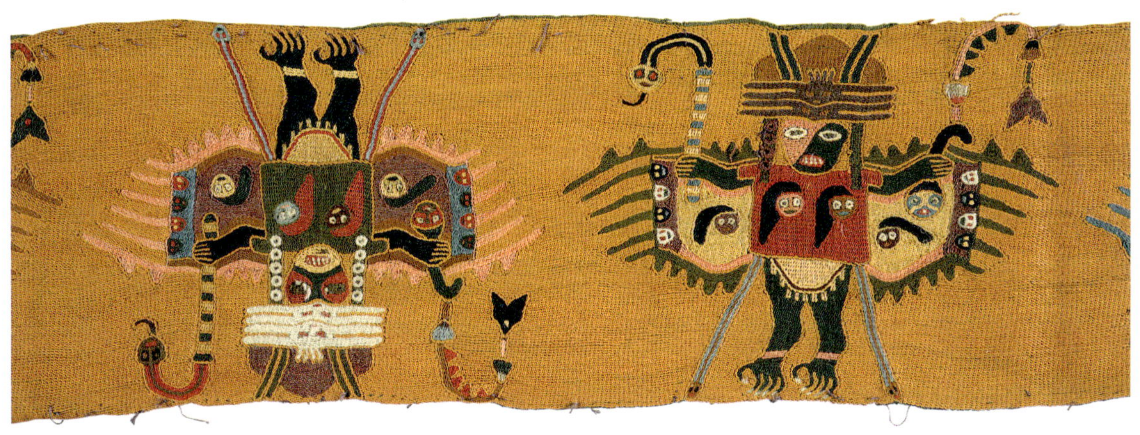

Pair of miniature shoes

Late Intermediate Period, 1000–1476

North Coast, Peru

These diminutive shoes are symbolic versions of actual high-status footwear worn by the elite. Miniature clothing and accessories of the finest craftsmanship often are found in ritual caches and burials on Peru's North Coast, and are thought to be offerings made by people lacking the economic means to acquire the full-size versions. Tiny clothing is the most common, although minute versions of musical instruments, tools, and even fiber-woven plant effigies also are known.

Although small in size, these petite shoes demanded considerable effort to produce. The exterior tapestry wool fabric is richly dyed in cochineal to produce the deep red color. Cochineal is a natural carmine dye made from the dried carcass of an insect (*Dactylopius coccus*) mixed with aluminum or calcium salts. A plain-weave cotton textile lines the shoes, and the soles are thin sheets of cold-hammered silver alloy. More than fifty small squares of this precious metal cover the shoes, each hammered to an exceptional thinness of less than half a millimeter and ornamented with a circle-and-dot motif produced by the repoussé technique. The now-tarnished alloy masks the shiny metal's once impressive silver flash against the fabric's rich red color.

Wool (camelid) and cotton tapestry, cotton plain weave (lining), appliquéd silver alloy plaques, and silver alloy soles
H. 10 cm (3 7/8 in.), w. 9.2 cm (3 5/8 in.), d. 6.5 cm (2 1/2 in.)
Gift of Landon T. Clay   1975.662a-b

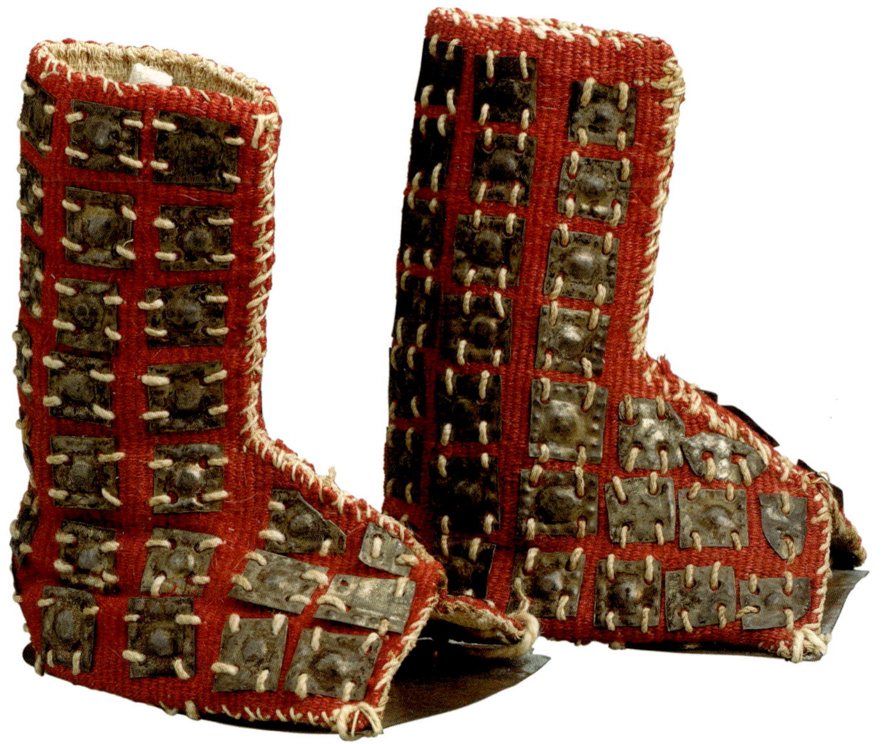

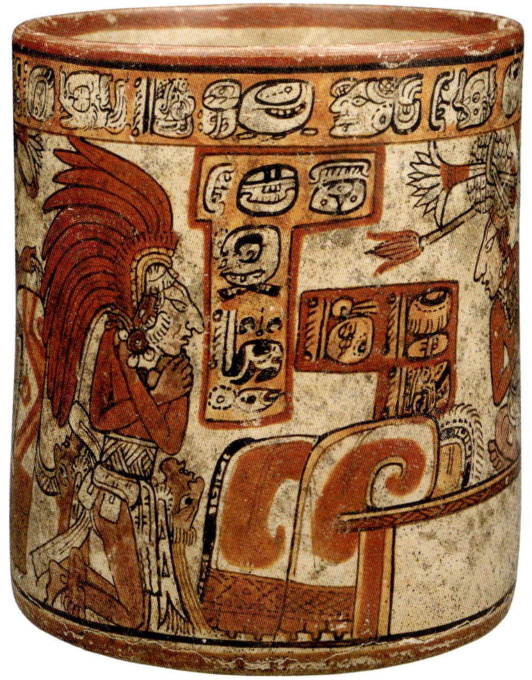

Drinking vessel
Maya, Late Classic Period, 650–800 CE
Nebaj area, Southern Highlands, Guatemala

Cloth was a valuable commodity among the Maya, yet only small fragments and impressions on tomb floors and the bottoms of pottery vessels have survived the wet environmental conditions. Representations on the pictorial pottery, however, provide a glimpse of the sumptuous clothing worn by the elite. From these images we can infer the marvelous skill of Classic Maya weavers and the social and economic importance of cloth.

This vase commemorates the capture of a high-status lord identified in the hieroglyphic text separating the kneeling captive and enthroned victor, who is named in the rim text as the vase's owner. The imagery records the public presentation of the spoils of war—here the captured warriors and fine cloth they present to the victorious lord. The fabrics' tabbed ends may denote use of the discontinuous warp-and-weft technique. The diagonal decoration could be a supplementary weft design. The cloth draped on the throne has a fringed edge or feathers interwoven into the selvedge. Its curvilinear motifs likely are a painterly device to denote a lively fabric-wide patterning.

Writings by sixteenth-century Spanish observers of Maya society describe cloth as a principal commodity and tribute item as well as the most important gift distributed during elite-sponsored feasts. The goal of these ceremonious gatherings was to advance the host's social and political position by gaining the guests' allegiance. The feast's success relied heavily on copious amounts of gifts provided for the guests, with cloth being among the most favored and valued item bestowing esteem upon both host and guest.

Earthenware with red, orange, pink, and black on cream slip
H. 16.3 cm (6⅜ in.), diam. 14.8 cm (5⅞ in.)
Gift of Landon T. Clay   1988.1170

Mantle or shroud

Neo-Inka, Late Inka to Early Colonial Period, about 1500–1550
Peru

This is one of the finest surviving examples of Inka tapestry in both its technique and narrative content. Technical mastery is evidenced by the astounding 195–200 weft threads per square inch, which reaches the upper limits for hand spinning and weaving. It is the only known mantle of this size completely covered by *tukapu* (or *tocapu*) motifs, which make up a graphic system of communication. *Tukapu* designs were reserved for textiles worn by the highest social ranks in Inka society. They are prevalent on royal tunics of the type called *capac unku*, "rich and powerful shirt," by the Basque friar Martín de Murúa in his 1580–1616 chronicle of Peru. This mantle's relatively small size and the location of burial stains suggest its final usage as the funerary shroud for an adolescent boy, although its *tukapu* narrative intimates earlier use among the living.

Recent scholarship has proposed that the mantle can be read as a historical document placed within a commemorative five-year calendar. Its 1,824 *tukapus* represent the number of days in five solar years (5 x 365 = 1,825). Five-year periods hold special mythological, social, and administrative significance among ancient and contemporary Andean societies. Here the individual *tukapu* types are positioned in a complex arrangement within the five solar divisions. The narrative scheme comprises three main sections defined by format and color, with the motifs arranged in 38 rows of 48 columns and assembled into two unequal sets. These idiosyncratic positions may recount place names or social identities, such as personal titles or the name of a sociopolitical group (*allyu*), allowing the mantle thereby to serve as a historical record.

Wool (camelid) and cotton interlocked tapestry
H. 119 cm (46⅞ in.), w. 171 cm (67⅜ in.)
Charles Potter Kling Fund   1988.325

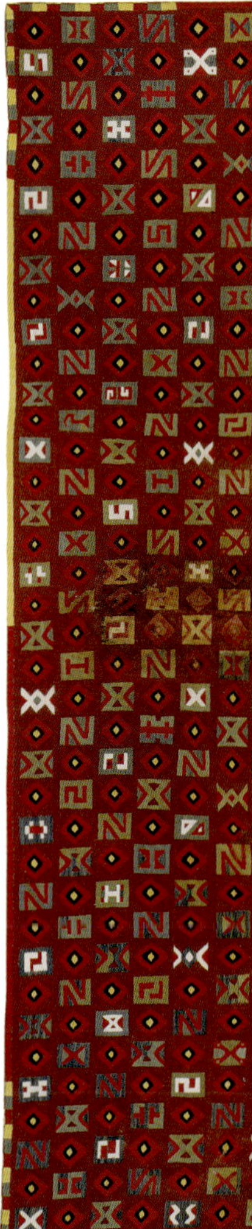

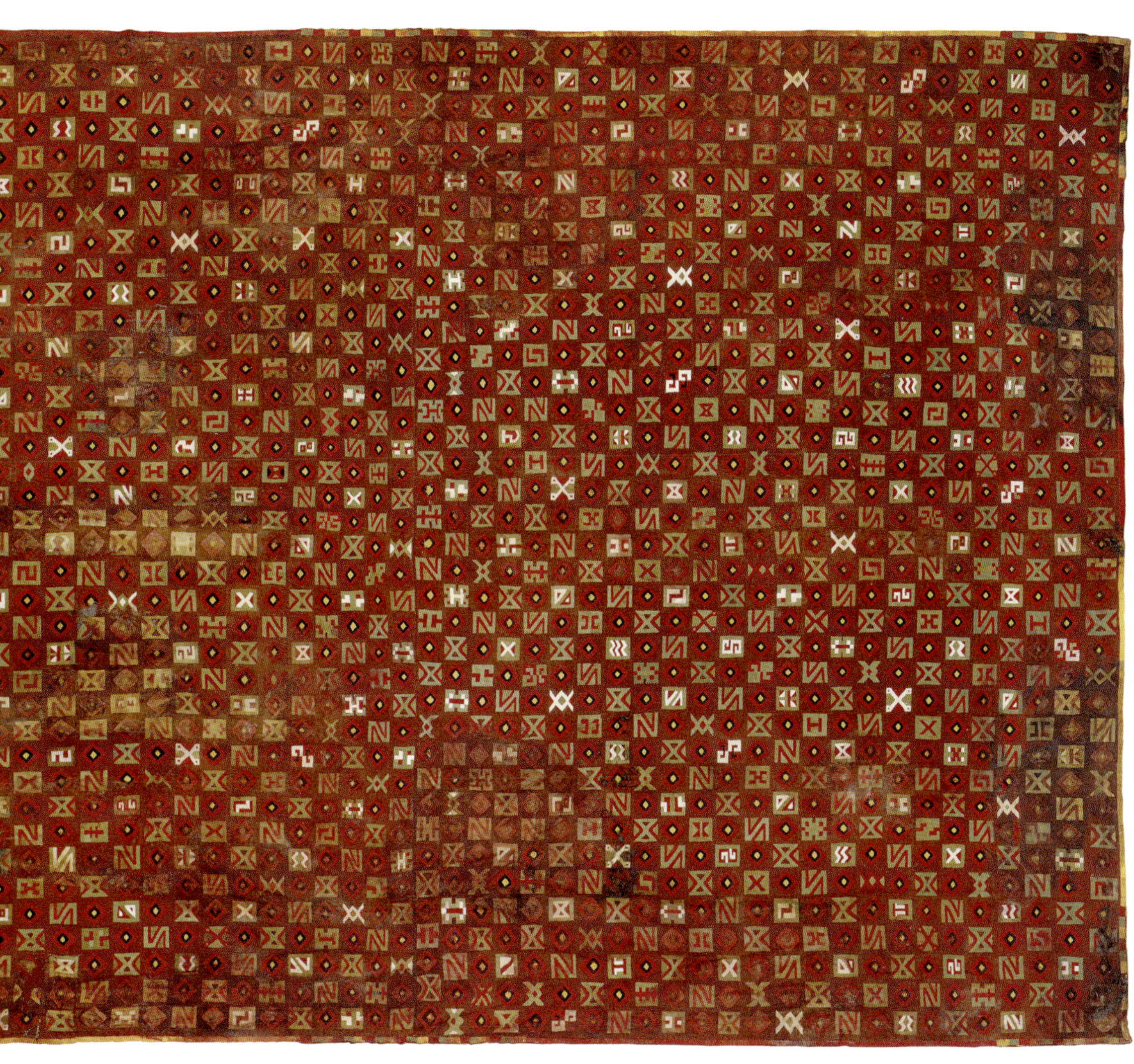

Fragments of a hanging

Paracas-Nasca transition,
Early Intermediate Period, about 200 CE
South Coast, Peru

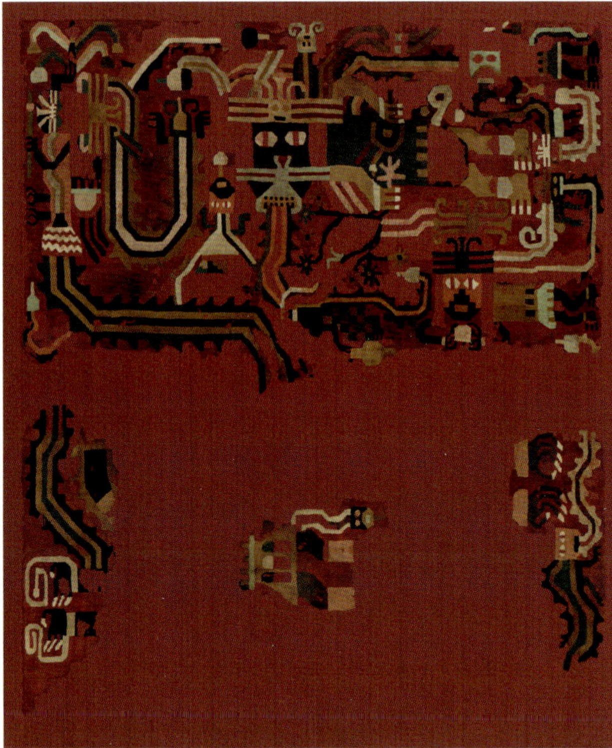

The large textile represented by these fragments is
one of the most elaborate examples of discontinuous
warp and weft technique from any Andean culture.
This method requires temporary scaffold yarns to
support non-contiguous warp and weft yarns during the weaving process of each of the sections. The
scaffold yarns were later removed after interlocking each motif segment onto its neighboring shape.
The specialized skill needed to create such a fabric
likely was attained by only a few individuals, and its
original size—more than 2,500 square inches (6,350
square centimeters)—suggests the work of experts.

The textile probably festooned a ceremonial building
or served a ritual function, its technical virtuosity
and mythic imagery imbuing the rite or architectural
space with sacredness.

The discontinuous warp and weft
technique uses threads that are not con-
tinuous along the length and across the
width of the fabric. This method allows
the weaver to create separately woven
sections, distinguished by color, which
she interlocks to create the finished textile. Temporary scaffold yarns support
the non-contiguous warp and weft yarns
during the weaving process. Thread and
fabric tension had to be carefully controlled so as not to pull out of alignment
any of the imagery when the scaffold
yarns were removed.

This labor-intensive method allowed
the fiber artist to create a sheer but colorful cloth, here refined to the highest
aesthetic level by a plethora of diagonal lines and curved forms within an
irregular design. Exceptional expertise is
also evidenced by at least fourteen yarn
colors enlivening the complex images,
spanning the visual color spectrum and
including blue, lavender, red, pale orange, black, and
cream-white (the natural color of wool). Shades of
yellow, green, gray, brown, and pink were produced
by spinning together white and yellow, black, or red
fibers, depending on the desired hue and value.

Wool plain-weave with discontinuous warps and wefts
H. 69.9 cm (27½ in.), w. 113.6 cm (44¾ in.)
Edwin E. Jack Fund   67.313a-d

Double-cloth bag

Chancay, Late Intermediate Period, 1000–1476
Central Coast, Peru

At first glance, the lively design panels on this carrying bag appear to have been made separately and sewn together to create a patchwork fabric. In reality, the bag was created as a single fabric and woven to shape with curved top and bottom edges. The fabric then was folded and stitched together to form the bag. Andean ideology favored fabrics with four finished selvages, and clothing was fabricated without cutting or piecing together its sections. This fundamental tenet is expressed in this practical carrying bag as a key accessory for both women and men.

Even more complicated, this bag is made of double-cloth (a cloth with two layers). To produce double-cloth, the weaver pulls alternate warp threads to the front and back, each set of warps using its own group of wefts to create separate planes of cloth. The planes trade faces to form the same pattern on each side but in reverse colors. The twenty-one panels on this bag may comprise an inventory of the weaver's design repertoire, including frontal human faces, birds, monkeys, deer, interlocking serpent patterns, and step-fret motifs. They are arranged in broad horizontal bands filled with the motifs, each one following the same diagonal format. The horizontal bands are delimited asymmetrically by thin vertical stripes. The overall effect of the interplay of horizontal and diagonal patterning creates a visually dynamic artwork.

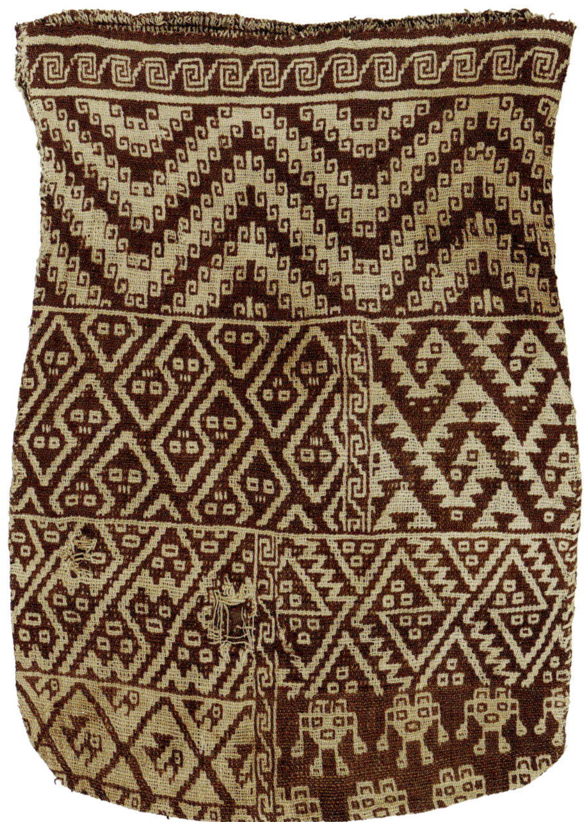

Cotton plain weave double-cloth
H. 35.5 cm (14 in.), w. 26 cm (10¼ in.)
Samuel Putnam Avery Fund 52.482

Triple-cloth border fragment
Early Horizon, Phase 9, about 500 BCE
Ocucaje, Ica Valley, South Coast, Peru

Textiles are the oldest and most esteemed medium
for artistic expression and cultural value among
Andean cultures. The earliest surviving fabrics (from
about 3200 BCE) are expertly woven using complex
techniques, indicating an even earlier origin for
the medium. As shown by these ancient examples,
Andean textile tradition afforded equal importance
to construction technique, aesthetics, and style.

The complex, esoteric imagery of Peru's Early
Horizon (900–200 BCE) artworks, including this fabric fragment, is thematically multilayered and rich
in modes of representation. Artists explored such
narrative devices as metaphorical substitution and
visually shifting designs. These features were devised
intentionally to confuse and surprise the viewer.
They also reflect key Andean principles of complementarity, duality, and transformation. Of equal
importance in Andean aesthetics is the doctrine of
essence over appearance: the goal of the artwork is
to convey a fundamental principle or meaning rather
than a simple representation. As seen on this tiny
fragment of triple-cloth, the weaver repeated the
feline design pattern among its three layers, which
were created simultaneously using black, dark green,
and ocher yarns. The viewer knows the inner layer's
feline image exists—yet it cannot be seen. Even the
two visible images (on the front and back of the fabric) are purposely obscure, emphasizing the feline's
essence rather than its simple representation.

Wool plain weave triple-cloth
H. 11.4 cm (4½ in.), w. 6 cm (2⅜ in.)
Mrs. Samuel Cabot's Special Fund
47.1084

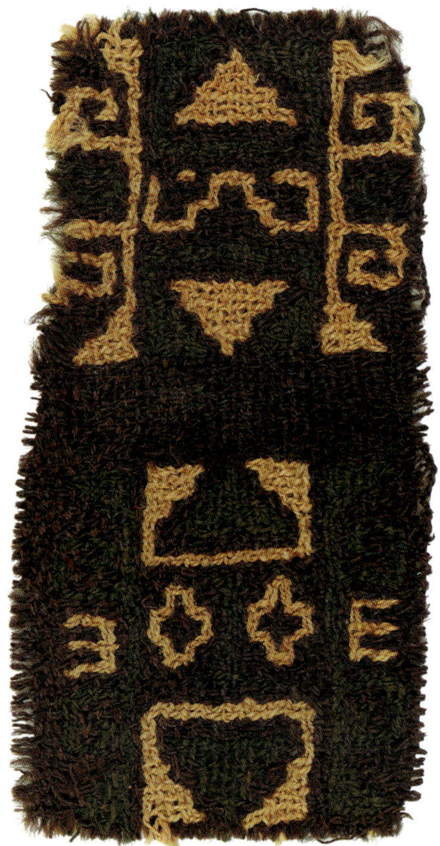

Head cloth (*ñañaqa*)
Chancay, Late Intermediate Period, 1000–1476
Central Coast, Peru

Locally grown cotton yarns were the dominant fiber
used by Chancay weavers because camelid yarns,
imported from the distant highlands, were more
costly. Women's head cloths (*ñañaqas*) are usually
sheer fabrics with subtle designs in contrasting
densities of the yarns and the embroidered square-
mesh openwork. Decoration was also produced by
pigmentation (painting), although it is relatively rare
because the Chancay weaving aesthetic embraced
texture rather than the color fields typical of most
other Peruvian cultures.

The ephemeral yet strong patterning of this *ñañaqa* was created by laying out a loose grid of warps and wefts, then embroidering the four-band pattern on the diagonal. The design alternates between interlocking serpents and felines, the serpents' eyes and feline body contours accentuated by extra groups of threads. The pattern, which runs 45 degrees from the direction of the weaving grid, is emphasized by thin pigmented bands in ocher and brown. The flexible fabric collapses when placed on the head and the motifs disappear, leaving only a hint of design from the pigmented bands. When blown by the wind or responding to the wearer's motions, the head wrap shifts form and patterns, reflecting the Andean aesthetic preference for shifting imagery and for knowing that certain motifs exist without always being visible.

Cotton gauze weave with embroidery and pigment
H. 84 cm (33⅛ in.), w. 80.8 cm (31¾ in.)
Gift of Mrs. Samuel Cabot   60.1135

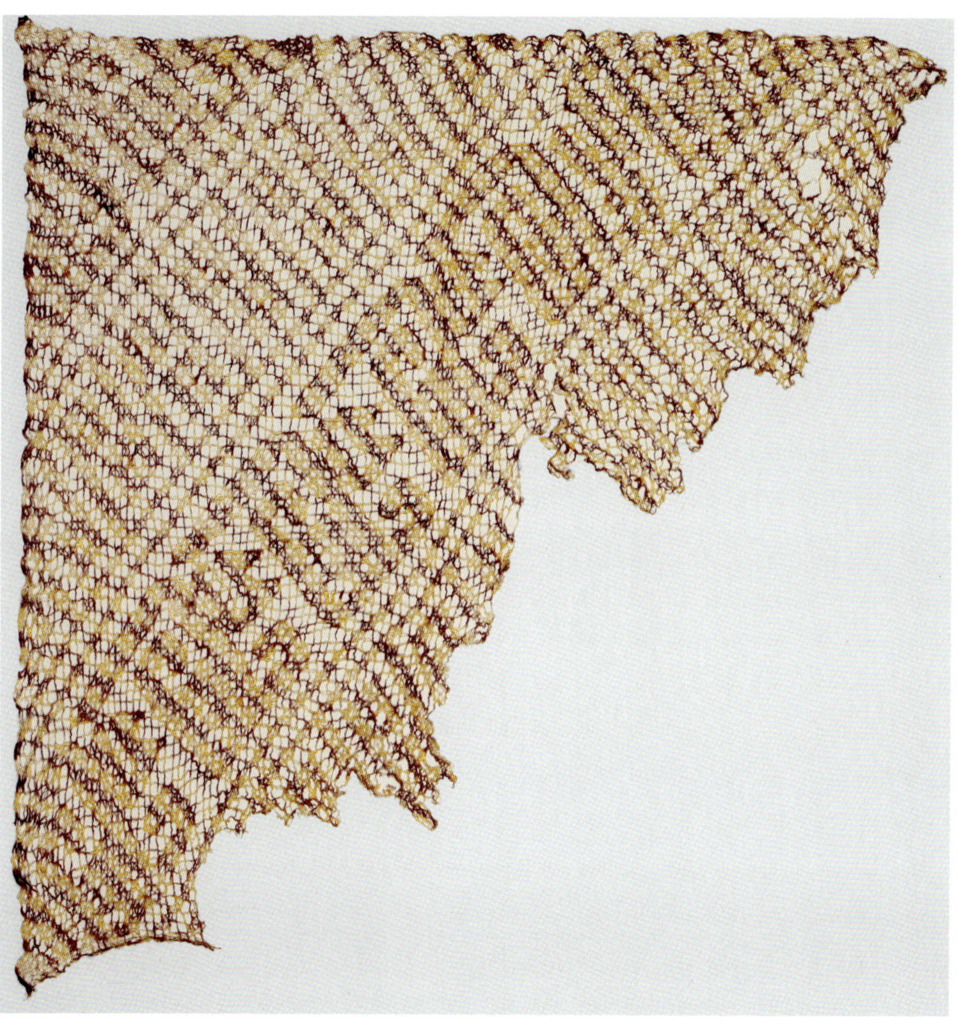

Openwork tunic

Late Intermediate Period, 1000–1476

North or North-Central Coast, Peru

The muted colors and repetitive designs of this sheer tunic belie its effect when worn, especially if donned over a brightly colored fabric to create a dynamic field of contrasting color and pattern that shifts with the wearer's movements. A variety of weaving techniques accentuates the fabric's subtle designs while the strong borders define the garment's contours. The borders are executed in two types of weft patterning (interlocked and slit tapestry) and warp patterning (warp substitution and complementary warp), expressing the Andean ideology of duality and complementarity. The sleeves, an unusual feature for Andean tunics, comprise a slit tapestry band of stepped motifs terminating in thick fringe.

The tunic's plain weave structure is invigorated by the open rectangular spaces evenly distributed among the densely woven areas. The countless points of intersection of warps and wefts were individually stitched around their edges to hold their shape. The fabric was then tie-dyed to produce the brown and cream-white design. The bound intersections preserved the original light color of the cotton yarn, creating a contrasting pattern of tiny cream-colored circles within a dark brown pattern of slightly larger rectangles. Less laborious approaches could produce a similar effect, but in accordance with Andean practice, the finesse of the final visual effect took precedence.

Cotton plain weave with spaced warps and wefts, tie-dyed; interlocked tapestry with weft loop fringe (sleeves); slit tapestry, plain weave with warp substitution, and complementary warp weave (lower borders)

H. 70 cm (27½ in.), w. 99.5 cm (39⅛ in.)

Gift of Edward W. Hooper   78.64

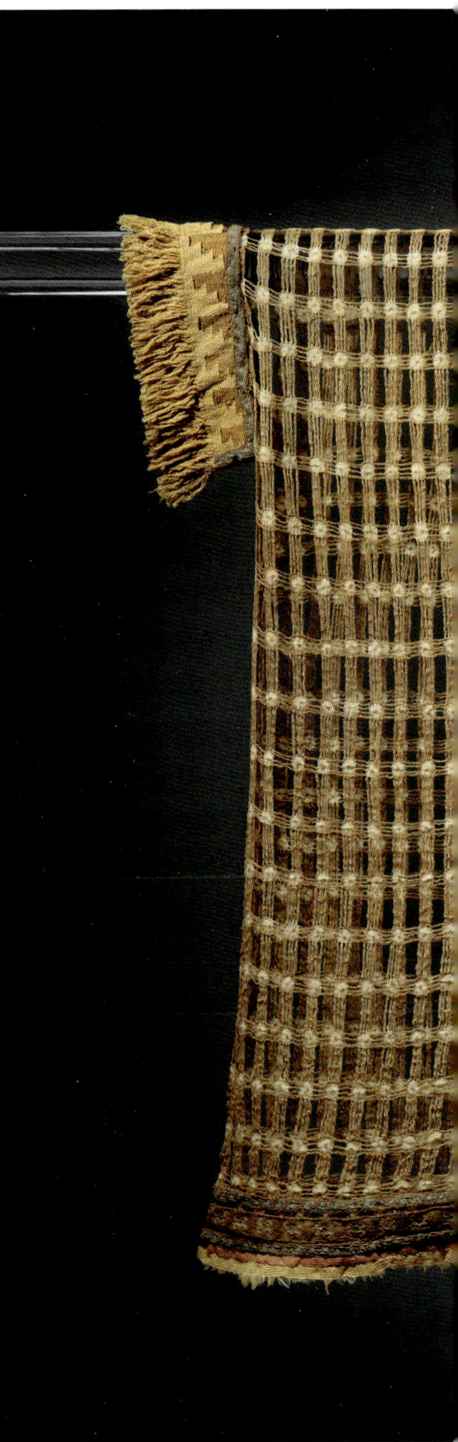

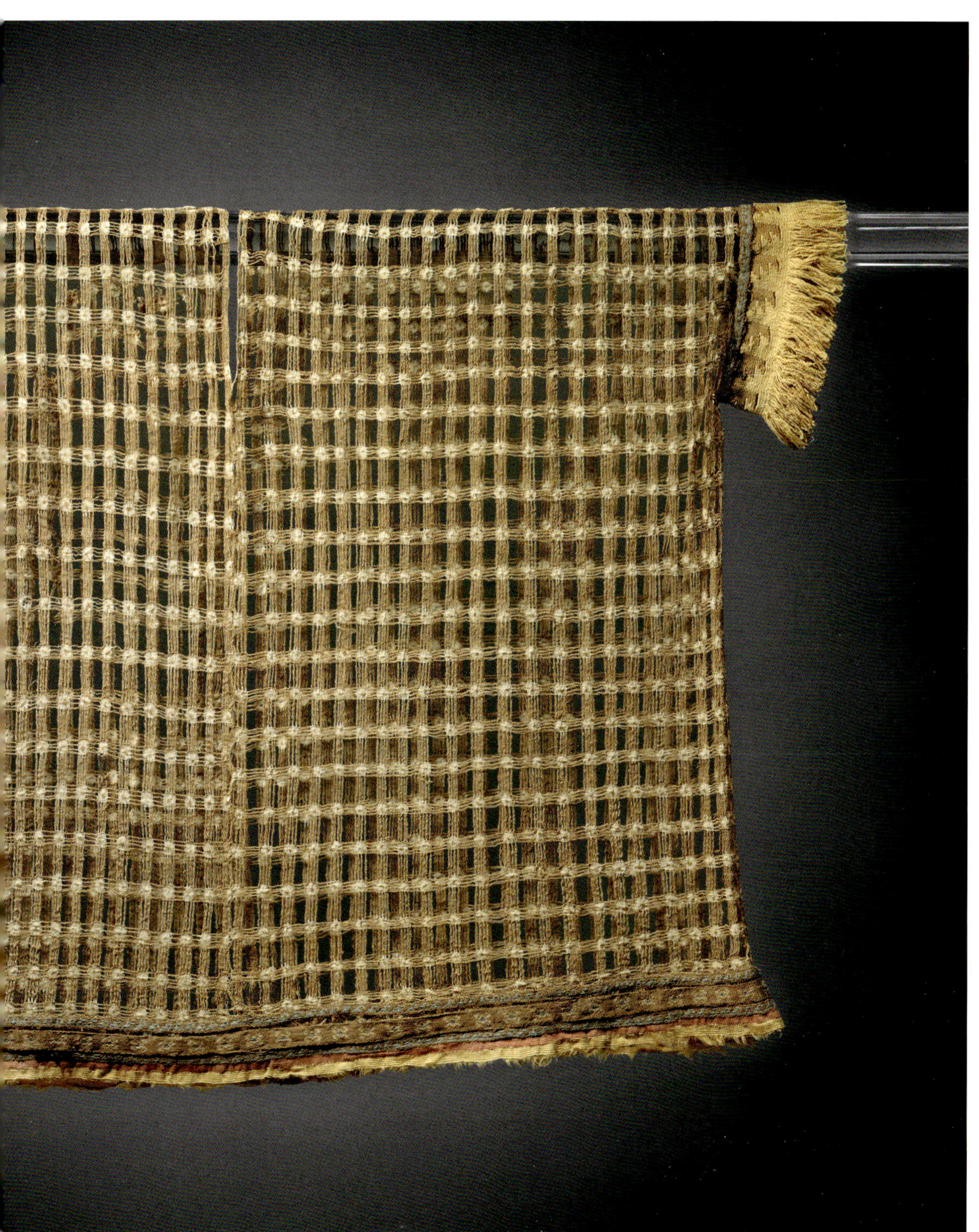

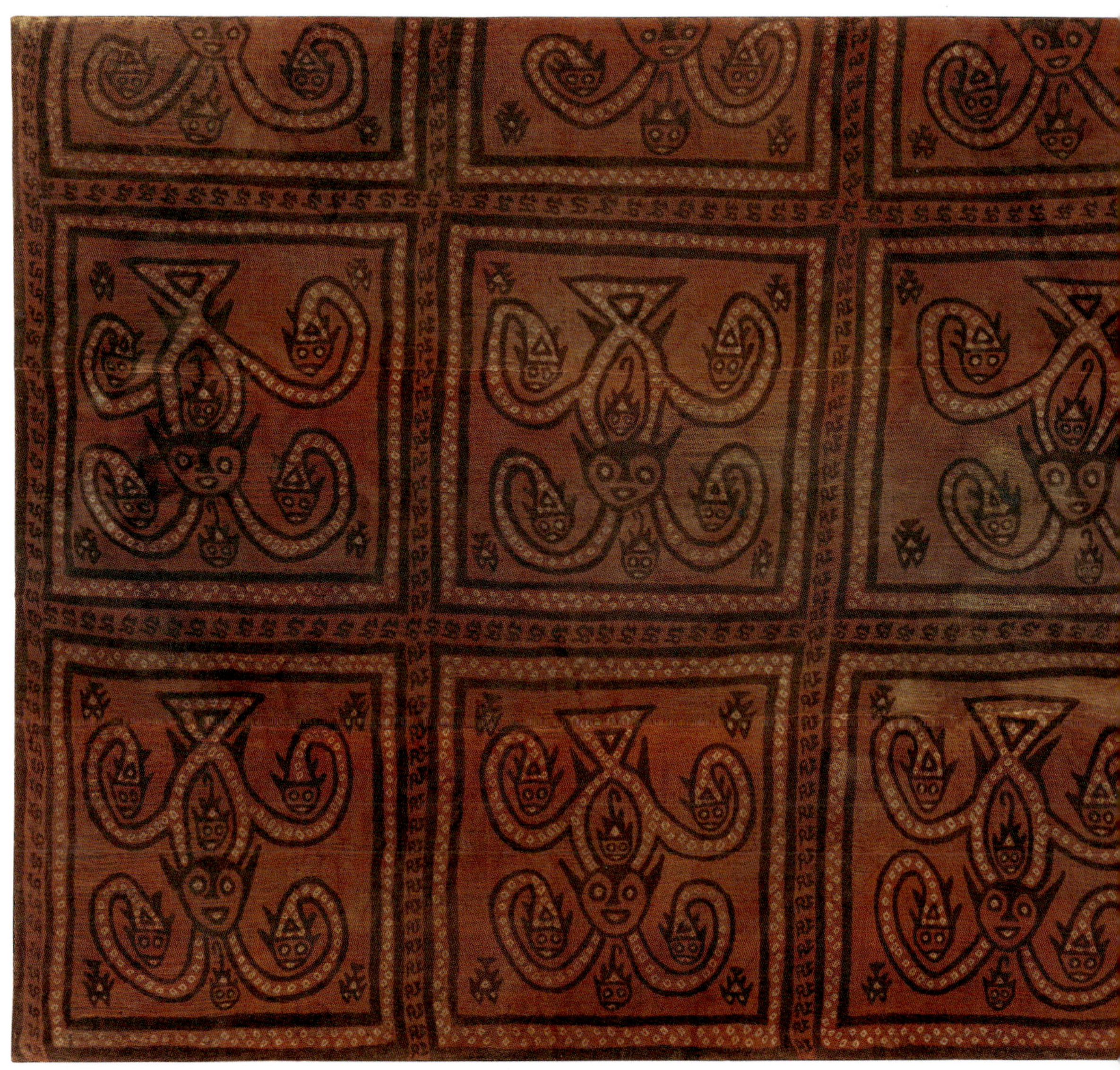

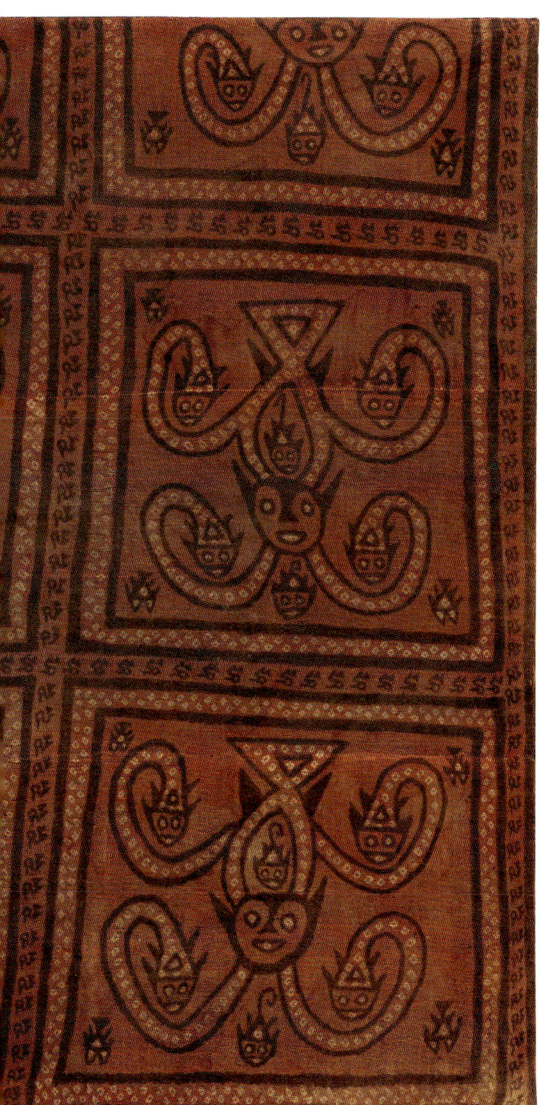

Hanging

Chancay (?), Late Intermediate Period, 1000–1476
Central Coast, Peru

Very fine gauze weaves typify textiles from Peru's Central and South Coasts. Many are extremely sheer, like this sizable hanging, which was woven using single unplied threads. Sheer fabrics take on the coloration of their immediate environment; this fine cloth appears very dark when mounted on a black fabric (as here), whereas a light-colored background reveals a translucent, pastel cloth. Half-images at the hanging's top indicate it was originally a larger piece of fabric. Although its original use remains speculative, large textiles often adorned buildings. The quadrilinear format mirrors that of textile-like, stucco-and-painted murals found on the interiors and exteriors of important buildings at many coastal sites. The organic stain patterns across the hanging's surface reveal its final function as a funerary wrapping.

The fabric's production is complex. Each panel was woven separately and the panels were then assembled into a single textile, with black paint delimiting each square and its decorative motifs. Next, the fabric was tie-dyed with reddish-brown color to produce the dark ground and the rows of cream-white dotted circles. The motifs—including a large fish surrounded by four smaller ones and a stingray below each fish's head—reflect Chancay reliance on the sea for sustenance. Four serpent-like stingray-headed appendages emerge from each fish, and the fishes' bodies include another stingray image. Single rows of tiny waterbirds outline each panel.

Cotton plain weave, tie-dyed and painted
H. 142 cm (55⅞ in.), w. 239 cm (94⅛ in.)
Textile Income Purchase Fund   1970.30

Sleeveless tunic

Wari, Middle Horizon Period, 700–900 CE

South Coast, Peru

The recurring configurations of color and shape on this vibrant tie-dyed textile are sporadically interrupted by subtle breaks in the pattern, in keeping with the Wari emphasis on predictably varied designs enriched by random anomalies. Such virtuosity reveals the creativity of a master fiber artist, whose composition can be read simultaneously as diagonal bands of uniformly decorated rectangles (from upper left to lower right) and as horizontal groupings of four squares forming a large quadrant with a diamond-shaped center. Each square contains the same geometric shapes, but different colors enliven the repetitive design. The configurations of pattern and color impart a dynamic three-dimensionality to the fabric in keeping with Andean principles of duality—here stasis/dynamism and flatness/volume.

Skillful deployment of the resist dyeing process and the discontinuous warp and weft technique helped achieve the sophisticated pattern. After weaving strips with stepped sections joined by temporary scaffold yarns, the artist selectively tie-dyed each strip a different color or colors. Then the scaffold threads were removed to allow the disassembly of the individual stepped triangles. Next, the sections were reassembled to create the finished textile. The weaver worked off-loom, inserting a yarn through each of the stepped triangles' looped-edge warp threads to dovetail with those of its neighbors. And last, the weft slits were sewn together.

It would have been far easier to produce this textile by cutting the stepped triangles from finished fabrics and joining the fragments. However, cutting fabric violated every principle of Andean textile ideology, and thus the extensive amount of labor needed to create this tunic was of little concern to the fiber artist and the wearer of this dazzling garment.

Wool (camelid) plain weave with discontinuous warps and wefts, disassembled, tie-dyed, and reassembled
H. 114 cm (44⅞ in.), w. 187 cm (73⅝ in.)
Textile Fund and Helen and Alice Colburn Fund   1983.252

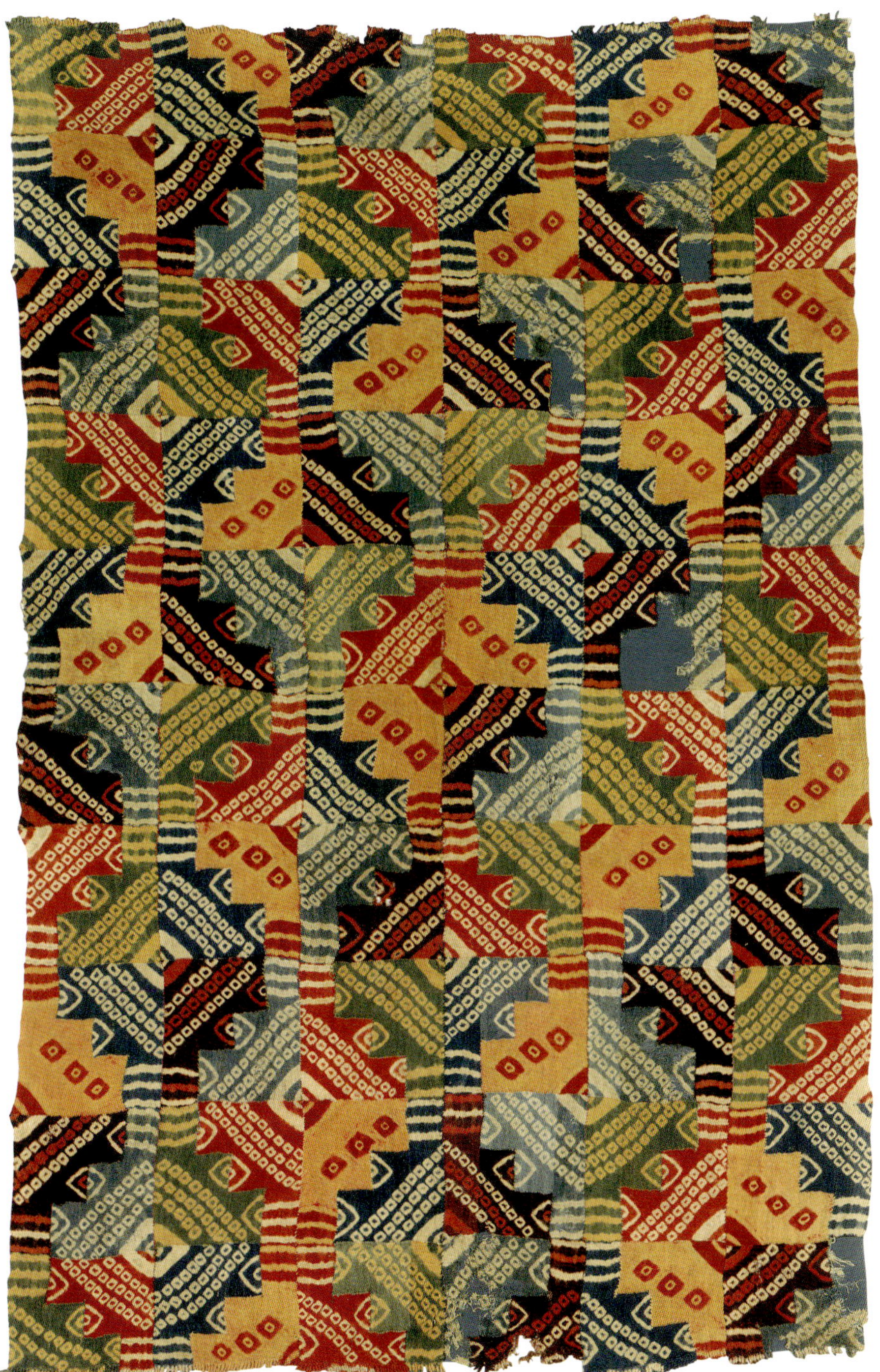

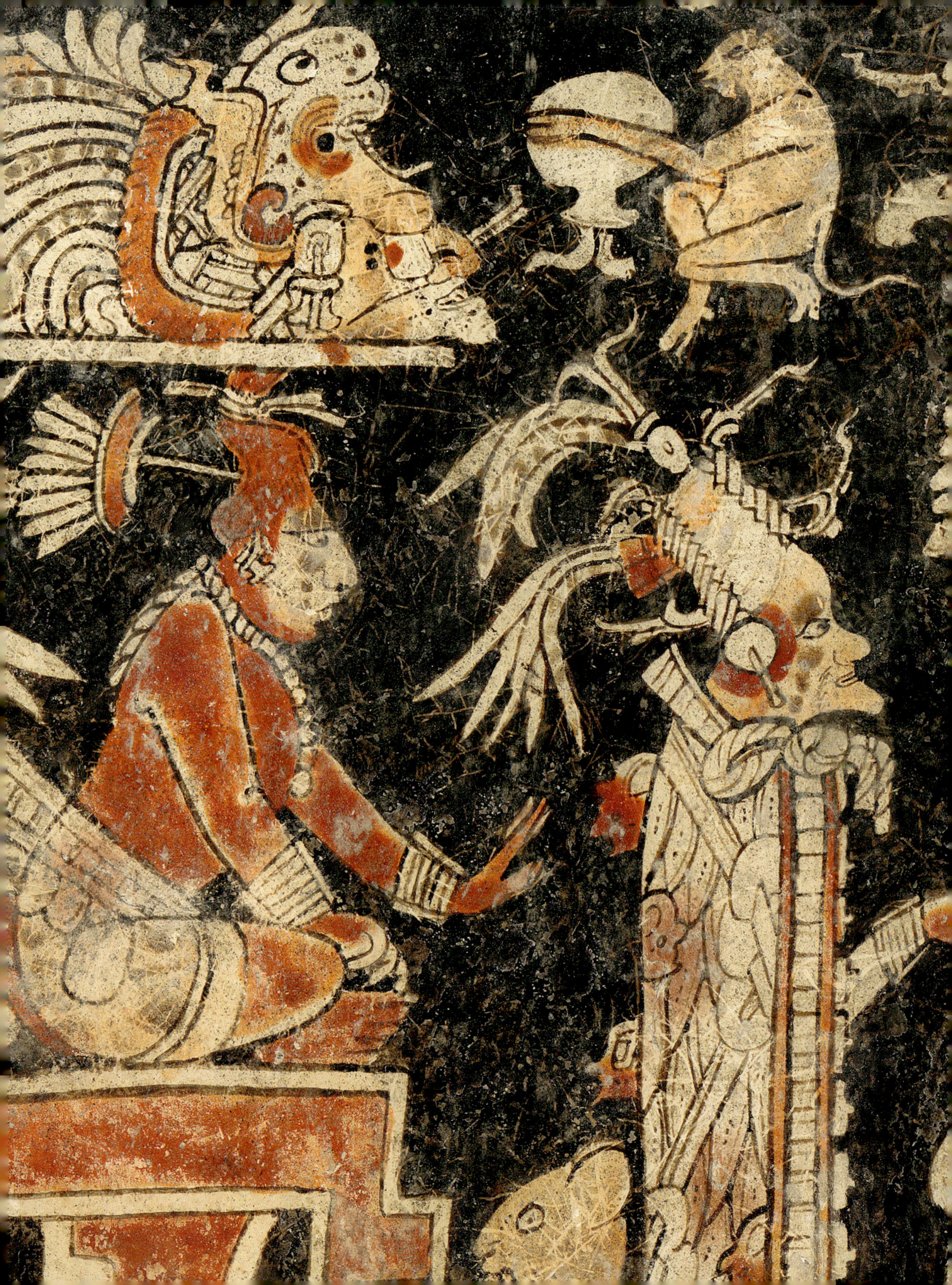

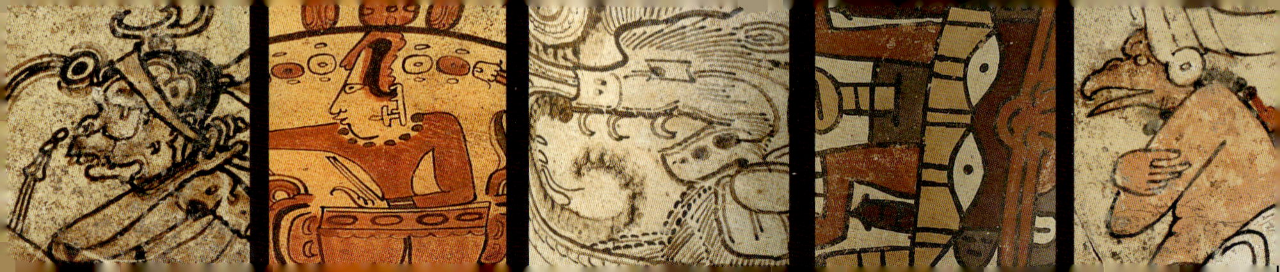

Feasting

Feasting has been at the center of human gatherings throughout history. The consumption of food in the company of others satisfies not only the body's demand for nutrition, but also the soul's thirst for companionship and society's need for community. In the ancient Americas, feasts were held at every level of society, from humble households to opulent palaces of the ruling elite. Refuse from feasting events is found at many archaeological sites, often including the bones of deer, turkeys, and fish, ash from cooking fires, and broken food containers. Intact examples of food service vessels survive because they were placed in tombs, and many are depicted in use on artworks from pottery to screen-fold books.

Ancient American feasting wares originate in the humble gourd, the food service vessel for millennia. Even after the development of basketry and pottery, gourds continued to dominate the table. Mesoamerican potters often made ceramic replicas of gourds, decorating these imitations with painted or incised images. And still today in Latin America, inexpensive plastic ware has not completely supplanted the gourd. In ancient times, pottery became a prime medium for artists to paint or carve complex pictorial narratives that provide specifics of their social context of use as well as details of history, religion, and cosmology. What were the factors that prompted such dramatic artistic developments for eating and drinking utensils?

Sixteenth-century writings by Spanish and Native chroniclers provide the answer. In Peru, Felipe Guaman Poma de Ayala, an Inka of noble descent who penned a history of Peru sometime between 1567 and 1615, describes feasts held to honor the dead and at the conclusion of communal labor projects. Vast amounts of food and drink (especially *chicha*, maize beer) were served to guests who sometimes numbered in the hundreds. Guaman Poma also notes the use of specially decorated service vessels, some made of silver and gold. Antonio de Herrera de Tordesillas, the official chronicler of the Americas under Spanish king Philip II, noted the importance of formal feasts, which frequently included musicians and performers to entertain the guests. Feasts also accompanied religious observances, especially those pertaining to important days in the solar and lunar calendars that commemorated mythic events. Today, they have been supplanted by dates in the Christian calendar such as saints' days, yet feasts continue to commemorate these ritual observances.

A second goal of the feast was the social and political advancement of both the host and guests. Bernardino de Sahagún, a Franciscan friar who arrived in Mexico in 1529, recounts how the Aztec (Mexica) ruler Motecuhzoma would invite leaders to a feast, welcoming supporters and adversaries alike. The gathering's overarching purpose was political—to honor the allegiance of confederates and prompt new alliances via the host's palpable power and generosity. Both were expressed by the presence of large amounts of fine food served in high-quality vessels and the presentation of impressive numbers of lavish gifts (including finely made vessels). Aztec banquets are reminiscent of nineteenth-century Zuni (Zuñi) feasting rites in New Mexico described by the anthropologist Frank Hamilton Cushing. The Zuni used feasts to forge ties via the physical bonding achieved by sharing food, the new ties perhaps averting future hostilities and prompting new support. The Aztec feasts described by Friar Sahagún elevated this opportunistic platform to the highest level of state politics.

Performances facilitated the feast's objectives by re-enacting local events and mythological parables, as described in early colonial documents from Oaxaca. These dramas chronicled the glorious deeds of Mixtec rulers, the illustrious history of local aristocratic families, and the sacred foundation of political power. Together, the sumptuous foods, fine serving vessels, and extravagant performances constructed an impressive arena in which to advance the host's social, political, and economic endeavors. Not surprisingly, sixteenth-century Spanish clergymen quickly adopted the feast with its requisite performances as an effective tool for establishing the new Catholic faith. They devised pageants recounting Biblical teachings and European history to pursue their apostolic goals and convey Iberian culture. Many early colonial observances survive throughout Latin America as magnificent public events celebrating the Christian story, particularly those of Carnival and Holy Week. Feasts, with their special food and drinks, remain a focal point of these celebrations.

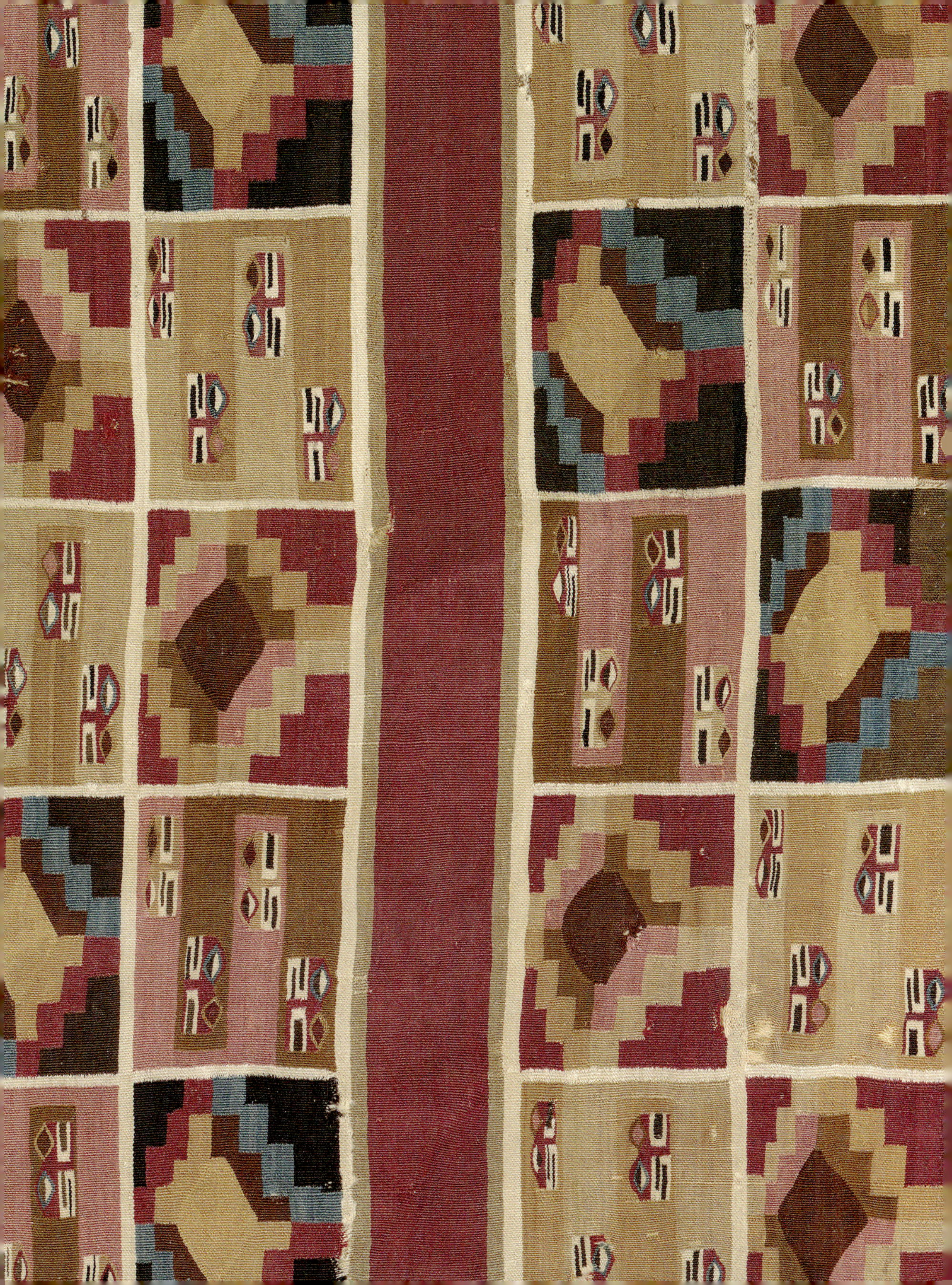

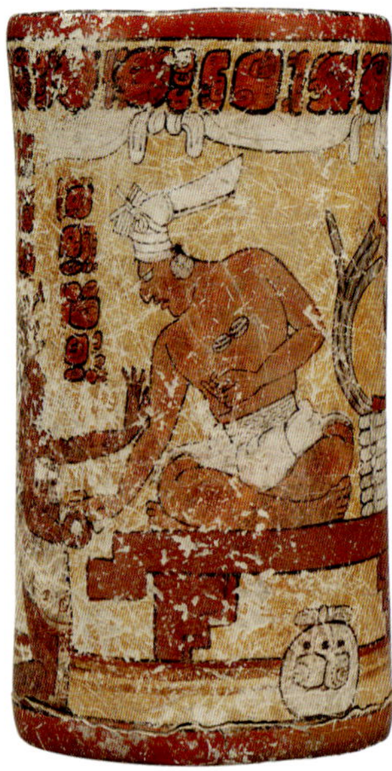

Drinking vessel

Maya, Late Classic Period, about 700 CE
Lake Yaxhá-Tikal region, Department of El Petén,
Guatemala

A crucial moment of détente between the two most powerful polities during the Classic Period—Tikal (in Guatemala) and Calakmul (in Mexico)—is recorded on this drinking vessel, its hieroglyphic text documenting the event's date of October 7, 691. A nobleman named K'ahk' Hix ("Fiery Jaguar"), an emissary of Calakmul's ruler Yuknoom Yich'aak K'ahk' ("Earth-Shaking Claw of Fire"), kneels before his overlord's archenemy Jasaw Chan K'awiil ("K'awiil that clears[?] the sky"), the holy lord of Tikal. The emissary offers him a bundle of gifts borne on the nobleman's back. The enthroned ruler's reciprocity is implied by the stack of cloth and sheath of quetzal feathers behind him and the sack of 24,000 cacao beans in front of the dais. These high-value commodities are the gifts and tribute payments most frequently depicted in Classic Maya art.

Maya feasting vessels often are decorated with a formulaic hieroglyphic text nicknamed the "dedicatory phrase." Its three parts are an opening dedication, a statement of the vessel's function and contents, and the name of the vase's owner or patron. Typically, the glyph recording the function of cylinder vases phonetically spells the phrase *y-uk'ib* ("his/her drink-thing," or drinking vessel). On this example the artist substituted a logograph of a profile human head with the glyph for "water" in its mouth to invoke "drink-thing." The following two glyphs specify the liquid contents as "cacao sustenance." This relatively rare version of the function-and-contents phrase leaves no doubt that cylindrical vessels were intended for drinking beverages, usually cacao-based, the most esteemed draft throughout Mesoamerica and the proper brew for a feast.

Earthenware with red, orange, brown, and black on cream slip
H. 21.3 cm (8⅜ in.), diam. 11.7 cm (4⅝ in.)
Gift of Landon T. Clay   2004.2204

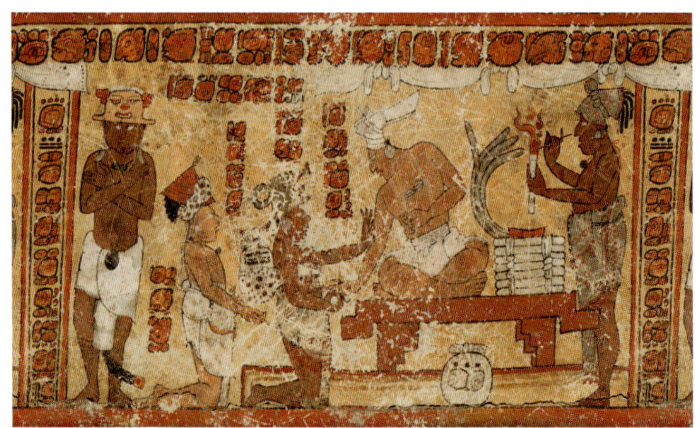

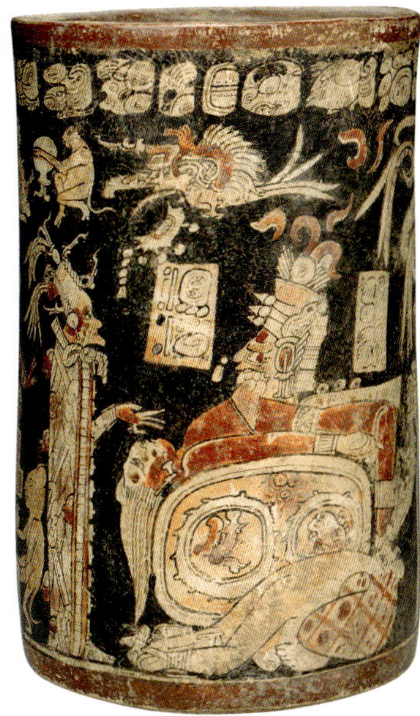

Drinking vessel

Maya, Late Classic Period, 650–800 CE
Tikal-Uaxactún area, Department of El Petén,
Guatemala

In ancient Mesoamerica, cacao was a mainstay beverage for feasts, as witnessed by sixteenth-century Spanish attendees at Aztec feasts that were renowned for their countless servings of chocolate drinks. Europeans also took note of the high cost of cacao beans and marveled at the wealth of Aztec merchants who controlled the long-distance trade networks supplying this valuable commodity to the Mexican highlands— mainly from Veracruz but also from Tabasco, Yucatan, Guatemala's Pacific Coast, and northern Honduras. Merchants were obligated to sponsor feasts in gratitude for financial success, providing plentiful food and drink and well-crafted items for the many guests. Afterward, the remaining food and gifts were distributed to the old, the infirm, and the poor. In essence, feasts redistributed wealth throughout the community, strengthened communal relationships, and reinforced the civic and sacred principles of hierarchy and authority.

This feasting vessel held a drink described in its hieroglyphic text as "tree-fresh cacao," followed by a series of titles naming its noble patron or owner. The large size indicates its use for presenting the prepared beverage, which then was served in smaller cups. The painted scene features a mythological saga from primordial time, signified by the black background. It may be a missing episode from the *Popol Wuuj*, describing how the Hero Twins resurrected their sacrificed father, the Maize god. The twins Juun Ajaw and Yax B'ahlam are shown pulling pages from a jaguar-pelt-covered book that may contain the secrets to reviving their sacrificed father. He lies supine over a sacrificial altar with a deity-incense burner embedded in his open chest, while a robed underworld lord oversees the rite.

Earthenware with red, orange, and black on cream slip paint
H. 25.4 cm (10 in.), diam. 15.3 cm (6 in.)
Gift of Landon T. Clay   1988.1179

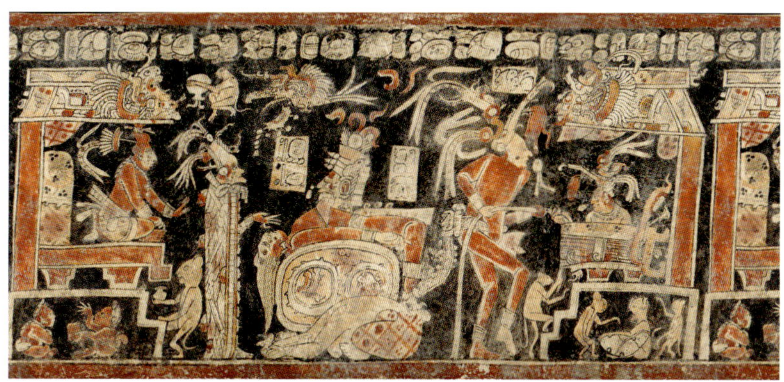

Incense burner

Maya, late Early Classic Period, 400–550 CE

Department of Tiquisate, Pacific Coast, Guatemala

An aromatic atmosphere was essential to a successful feast and indispensable to religious ceremonies.
The hourglass-shaped base of this effigy incense
burner held the smoldering coals and copal incense;
the scented smoke rose through a small cylindrical
tube behind the seated female figure representing a
cacao deity. She cradles a ripe cacao pod in her lap,
and cacao flowers adorn her head.

This style of incense burner is characteristic of
Guatemala's Pacific coastal zone where cacao imagery is prevalent in art and architecture. The region
is renowned for ideal cacao growing conditions, and
today some of the finest cacao and coffee is grown
there. Agricultural bounty nurtured robust societies
and attracted outsiders for millennia, beginning in
the sixth century BCE with the Olmecs, continuing
during the first millennium CE with Teotihuacan, and
culminating with the Aztecs in the sixteenth century,
each bringing new ideas and art forms from Mexico
to the Maya region. Such influences are reflected in
the deity's Maya-style jewelry and the Teotihuacan-
style divination mirror around her neck. Similarly,
her triangular-shaped face and elongated eyes are
typical of West Mexico and Teotihuacan sculptural
styles.

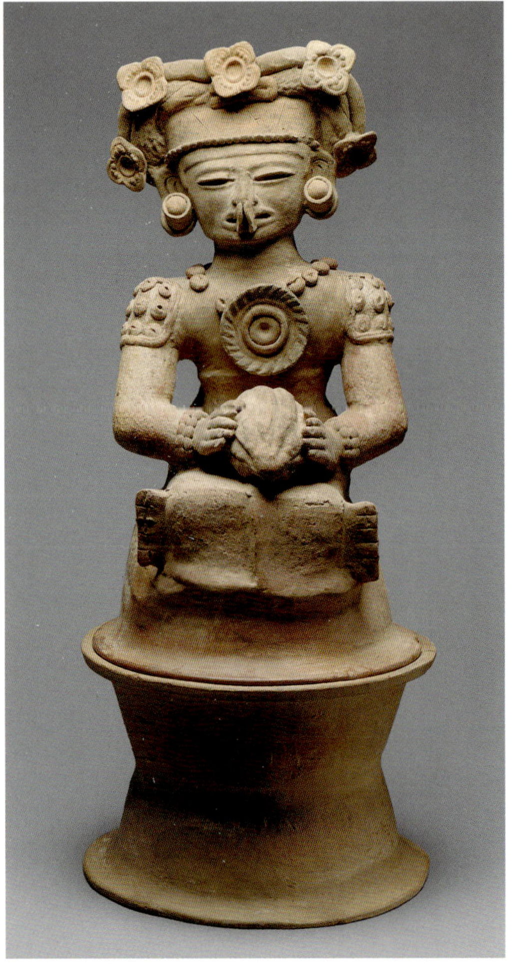

Earthenware with traces of specular hematite (red), white,
and black slip paint
Top: h. 43.2 cm (17 in.), diam. 24.7 cm (9¾ in.)
Base: h. 17.2 cm (6¾ in.), diam. 26.8 cm (10½ in.)
Gift of Landon T. Clay   1988.1227a–b

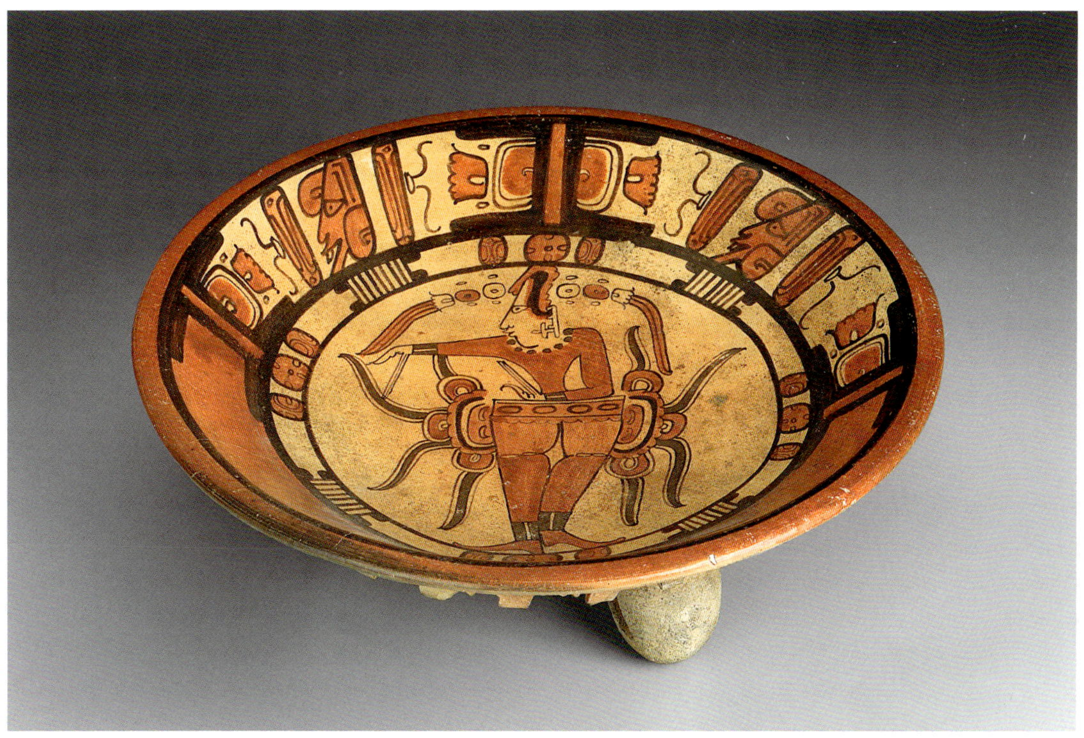

Tripod plate

Maya, Late Classic Period, 550–700 CE
Tikal area, Department of El Petén, Guatemala

Here, the Maize god strikes a standard dance pose in Maya art, raising his left heel and extending his right arm. Among the Classic Maya, formal political and religious observances often included performances such as re-enactments of mythological sagas. Two of the most frequent ones concern the Maize god's dance at cosmic creation and his resurrection from the underworld. In both sagas, the Maize god's formal dance position conveys the concept of performance rather than depicting a specific choreography. This plate's imagery portrays the Maize god's dance of resurrection at the center of the cosmos, a mythic location indicated by the four "great/red sun" motifs encircling the deity and marking the cardinal direc-

tions. Half of the plate's interior wall is painted red whereas the other half is marked by an emblematic hieroglyph naming the deity as the "great/red maize god."

This style of plate with its Maize god narrative was produced at Tikal and in nearby centers, and likely served as the polity's official sacred emblem. These plates also were traded to sites further afield in Guatemala and Belize, and thereby reveal Tikal's connections and relations. The large number of dancer plates also suggests that feasting and gift-giving were important political strategies for the polity's leaders.

Earthenware with red and black on cream slip paint
H. 10.1 cm (4 in.), diam. 30.9 cm (12⅛ in.)
Gift of John B. Fulling   1987.708

Fish effigy

Rimac (?), Late Intermediate Period, 1000–1476
Central Coast, Peru

Superb technique was highly prized among Andean textile artists and their patrons. This extraordinary portrayal of a large fish is noteworthy for all aspects of its creation, from skillful dyeing of the richly colored cotton threads, which characteristically are resistent to pigmentation, to the inimitable manipulation of the slit tapestry technique to accentuate the living creature's gills, teeth, and vertebrae. This fiber portrayal, finished on all of its twenty-five edges (including those of the interior tapestry slits), features warp threads running the length of the piece. During the weaving process, the warp threads were necessarily interlocked to scaffolds in order to maintain even tension throughout the loom; yet only a few scaffold threads remain visible along the contour edges.

The Rimac style was developed on Peru's Central Coast north of present-day Lima. Rimac art is not well represented in museum collections nor is the culture well-known archaeologically. However, the pictorial artistry and technical virtuosity of Rimac textiles are among the finest in the Andean world. This representation of a single fish is unusual for Peruvian textiles, which typically use fish as a repetitive decorative motif within a larger composition. Equally remarkable is the "X-ray" rendering of the fish's body, revealing five tiny fish inside its belly. Perhaps this atypical composition conveyed a message of fertility and sustenance, reflecting the animal's central place at the Andean table.

Cotton single interlocked, dovetailed, and slit tapestry
H. 17.7 cm (7 in.), w. 49 cm (19¼ in.)
Harriet Otis Cruft Fund   31.710

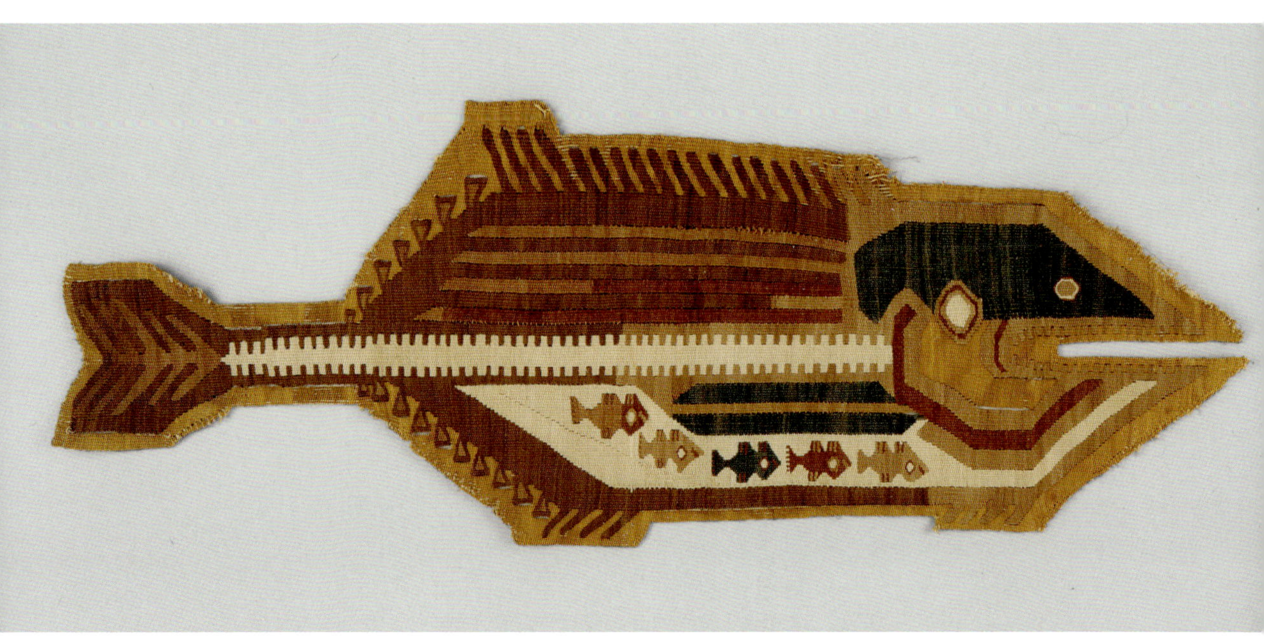

Ceremonial drinking vessel (*qero*)

Nasca, Phase 5, Early Intermediate Period,
about 450 CE
South Coast, Peru

This specialized beaker-shaped cup is called a *qero* (also spelled *kero* or *quero*) in K'echwa (Quechua), the primary indigenous language in Peru. The qero was the archetypal ritual libation vessel in the Andes; its distinctive shape became prominent during the Early Intermediate Period (200 BCE–500 CE) and survives today in Peru and Bolivia. Maize beer, called *chicha*, was—and remains—the primary draft consumed from this specialized vessel especially during feasts and other ceremonial gatherings.

The Early Intermediate Period witnessed a dramatic increase in the number of elites and the pageantry associated with social hierarchy and political authority. New palaces and ceremonial buildings were constructed, and many ritual objects such as finely made drinking vessels were produced for aristocratic feasts. As occasions for promoting social and political aspirations, the feast's success was based, in part, on serving large amounts of chicha in qeros whose artistic quality and decoration boosted the prestige of the event. This qero is decorated with the bird manifestation of the so-called Anthropomorphic Mythical Being, a Nasca icon pertaining to universal sacred forces. This version is based on a falcon or other raptor such as a condor, birds that were revered for their predatory skill and supremacy in the skies. These qualities make the raptors appropriate emblems for conveying a feasting host's power and prestige.

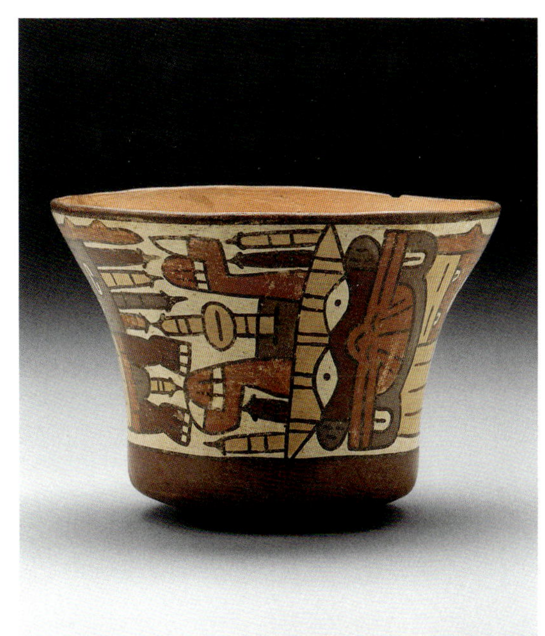

Earthenware with light orange, red, dark red, gray and black on cream slip paint
H. 11 cm (4⅜ in.), w. 15 cm (5⅞ in.)
Anonymous gift   2001.150

Ceremonial drinking vessel

Eastern Nahua, Postclassic Period, 1300–1521
Puebla or Tlaxcala, Mexico

Eastern Nahua–style painted bowls were among the finest ceramics in highland Mexico during the Postclassic period. They were used among the aristocracy for drinking prized beverages especially during feasts. The Aztec emperor Motecuhzoma Xocoyotzin (1466–1520) was said to eat only from such vessels adorned with images of his patron gods and other religious motifs. The style, known today as Puebla-Tlaxcala or Eastern Nahua polychrome, was made in workshops in the modern states of Puebla and Tlaxcala located east of the Valley of Mexico.

This bowl features symbols of the deity Mixcoatl Camaxtli, most notably the crossed-arrows motif and the decorative band of eagle-down balls adorning the rim. Mixcoatl, the patron god of the Eastern Nahua people, was the god of war and hunting, the first to make fire by striking flint, and the father of the Aztec deity–culture hero Quetzalcoatl ("Feathered Serpent"). The crossed-arrows motif alternates with an enigmatic icon composed of pointed bloodletting ritual implements configured as a mask of the deity Tlaloc, the god of rainstorms and lightning—perhaps alluding to the conceptual links among sacred warfare, blood sacrifice, and water/fertility. The vessel's tripod supports are painted to resemble eagle heads, which may refer to the famed eagle warrior order of the Aztecs, a fitting emblem for Mixcoatl Camaxtli. The god's main temple was located at Huexotzinco, Puebla, near the famous pilgrimage town of Cholula, which was one of the primary locations of Eastern Nahua pottery workshops.

Earthenware with yellow, orange, red, white, and black on cream slip paint
H. 14.6 cm (5¾ in.), diam. 17.1 cm (6¾ in.)
Museum purchase with funds donated by Timothy Phillips and Jeremy and Hanne Grantham 2015.2

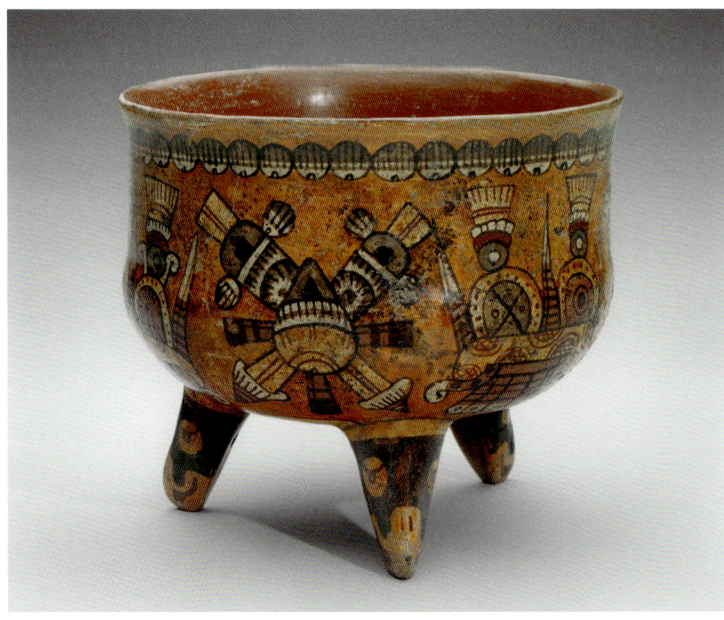

Drinking vessel

Maya, Late Classic Period, 740–780 CE
Motul de San José area, Lake Petén Itzá region,
Guatemala

The complex imagery of this Maya feasting vessel
features the birth of a deity nicknamed "Baby Jaguar," who lies in a dish with a "birth serpent" umbil-
icus rising from his body. His parents bracket the
scene and gaze at the newborn. Two open-mouthed
serpent heads below the parents indicate the place
of his birth, which is named "white mountain" in the
hieroglyphic text. The black background signifies
primordial time before the creation of humanity,
and the text records the birth's mythical date (1 Ix 2
Muwaan) and the Baby Jaguar's name Huk Yeh Tok'
("Seven Edges of Flint"). Large flint blades adorn his
and his mother's headdresses.

Feasting events required the presentation of
enormous quantities of special foods, such as cacao-
based beverages, meat tamales, and other fancy
dishes, as well as cigars. Sixteenth-century Spanish
witnesses of Maya feasts marveled at the sumptuous gifts provided for the guests, noting especially
the rich clothing and beautiful ceramic vessels.
These wares were often ornamented with imagery
featuring the gods, the nobility's special relationships with divinity, and the mythic histories that
validated elite privilege. Technical skill and artistic
creativity, exemplified by this vessel, amplified the
prestige of such gifts.

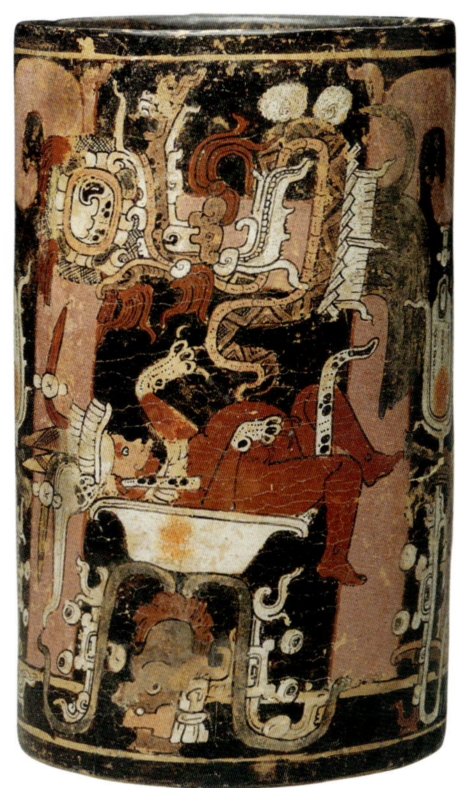

Earthenware with red, pink, white, gray,
and black on cream slip paint
H. 22.7 cm (8⅞ in.), diam. 13.7 cm (5¼ in.)
Gift of Landon T. Clay   1988.1184

Drinking vessel

Maya, Late Classic Period, 680–750 CE
Pacaya area, southern Mirador Basin,
Department of El Petén, Guatemala

Maya pottery artists developed distinctive painting styles that were exclusive to a site or royal patron, so that each would be recognized as coming from a specific place and person. One of the most conspicuous Maya pottery styles is the so-called codex-style, with its characteristic red-and-black-on-cream palette and fluid painted lines. The name derives from the style's similarity to ancient Maya books, called "codices" (singular "codex"), whose pages are delimited by red bands and whose imagery is painted in fine, calligraphic black lines on a cream-white background. Although only three Maya codices survive, hundreds of codex-style pottery vessels are known.

Maya writing—whether on pottery, paper, stone, or stucco-covered walls—was done with a brush and not a stylus (pencil or pen). In essence, all Maya writing is painting, and text and image are interconnected, much like the relationship between calligraphy and pictorial images in Chinese and Japanese scrolls. This vessel displays a harmonious integration of text and image; the artist used the same fluid outline for the peccary (a wild pig) and the hieroglyphic text, which surprisingly is painted in mirror image.

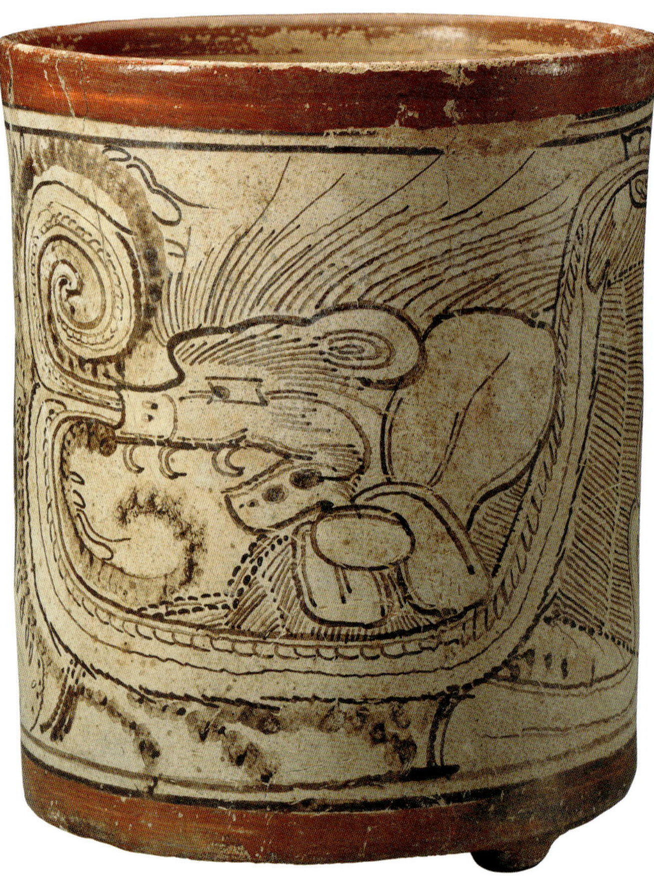

The masterful brushwork and unexpected pictorial format transform the simple drinking cup into a prized feasting vessel. The imagery likely pertains to a forgotten myth, although the peccaries and turkeys pictured also were favored banquet foods.

Earthenware with brown-black and red on cream slip paint
H. 12.8 cm (5 in.), diam. 11.1 cm (4⅜ in.)
Gift of Landon T. Clay   1988.1172

Drinking vessel

Maya, Late Classic Period, 680–750 CE
Nakbé area, Department of El Petén, Guatemala

The social position and political power of a vessel's patron were potent sources of its worth, especially when it was given to a banquet guest. For this reason, the dedicatory text typically ends with the patron's name or elite titles. Sometimes only titles were used to convey status appropriate to both the host and receiver, while also accentuating their mutual rapport embodied by the gift and the feast during which it was acquired.

The work of the painter of this drinking vessel, recognized as one of the best codex-style artists, is distinguished by strong brushwork and expressive glyphic forms. The patron's name is composed of five noble titles, beginning with the glyph for "artist/wise person." The three vertical texts in the scene make reference to lords from three different sites, each ending with an "emblem glyph" naming a site or its ruling dynasty—here Calakmul, Ceibal (Seibal), and an unassigned emblem. The text in front of the jaguar, who swims in a lake, identifies it as the spirit companion of a lord from Ceibal: "waterlily jaguar is the spirit form of the Ceibal lord." Some emblem glyphs come from the names of supernatural places, and ruling dynasties co-opted these mythic places to strengthen claims of divine origin for their political authority. For example, Ceibal's emblem glyph is the name of Three-Stone-Place—the mythic hearth of cosmic creation—which ties its rulers to the beginning of time.

Earthenware with black-brown and red on cream slip paint
H. 14.3 cm (5⅝ in.), diam. 11 cm (4⅜ in.)
Gift of Landon T. Clay   1988.1171

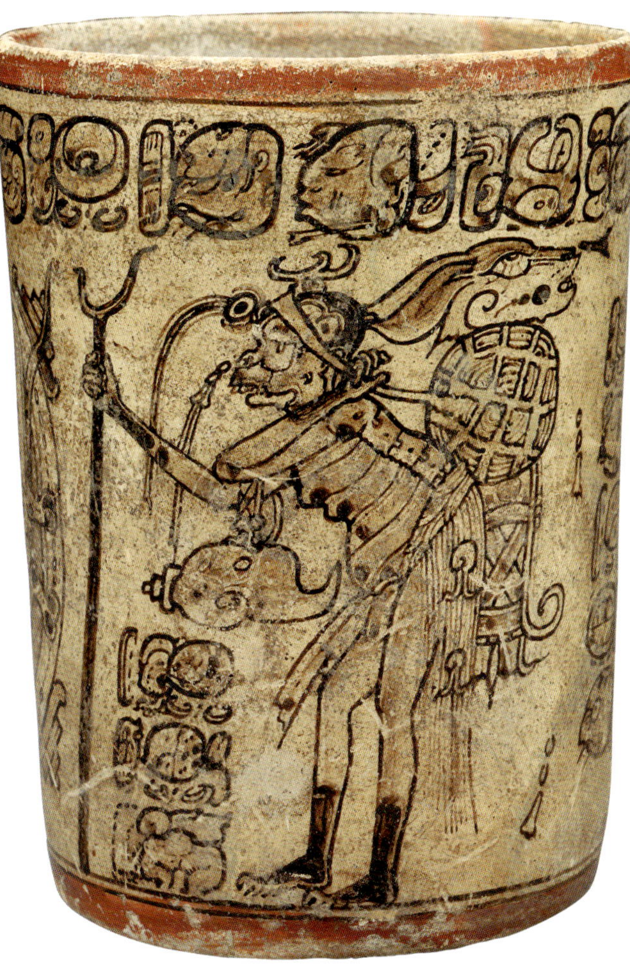

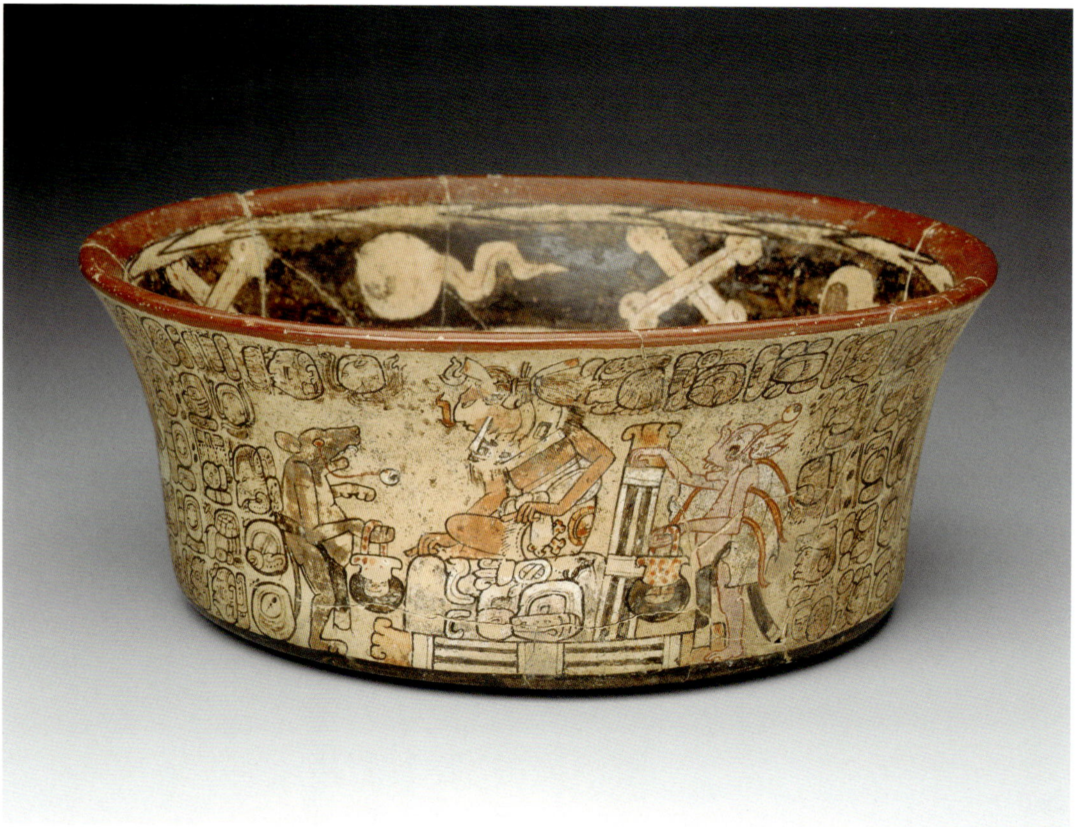

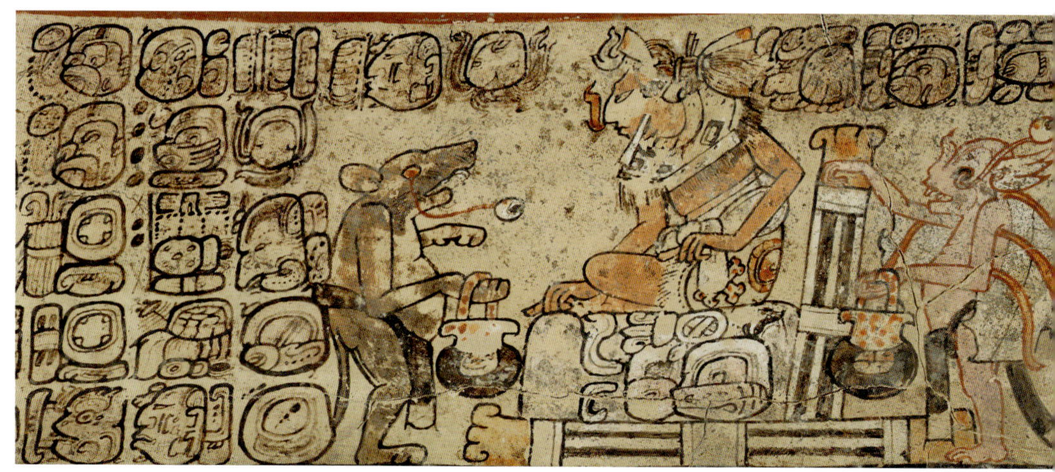

Dish

Maya, Late Classic Period, 700–750 CE
Central Petén lowlands, Department of El Petén,
Guatemala

Displaying one of the longest hieroglyphic texts on a Maya pottery vessel, this dish describes mythical events before the advent of humanity. It begins with a rite-of-passage event expressed as a birth on the Mayan calendar equivalent of January 2, 2440 BCE, perhaps referring to the primordial deity Hun Ixim (One Maize). The god's long name phrase comprises unique couplets that defy deciphering, and the phrase ends with his mother's name, which includes signs for a jade celt (a stone shaped like an axe), a maize sprout, wind, and a skeletal toad head. The text quickly becomes more opaque, beginning with a new date expressed only by the day and month position in the 260-day ritual calendar. The next Long Count date may be the equivalent of February 22, 2401 BCE. On this day was enthroned another deity (or deities), and the phrase ends with a lengthy series of couplets. Although their meanings remain a puzzle, they exemplify the lyrical poetics of Classic Maya ritual speech and religious doctrine.

The text concludes with the name phrase of the dish's painter, expressed in couplet form and including a title shared with the gods of creation, lending him a lofty association. It ends with the glyph for "paint/write" drawn as a hand holding a paint brush. The artist accentuated his "signature" by portraying himself seated above his name and wearing a head mask emblematic of the word for "lord" and the white head wrap of court scribes.

The dish's painted interior is uncommon for Maya vessels. On the inside of the rim, a row of crossed femurs and disembodied eyeballs floats in a black-painted band, below which is a wider red band. As symbols of primordial time and the preternatural realms, they reinforce the mythic nature of the events on the dish's exterior.

Earthenware with red, pink, black, and white
on cream slip paint ground
H. 9.4 cm (3¾ in.), diam. 25 cm (9⅞ in.)
Gift of Landon T. Clay   1988.1183

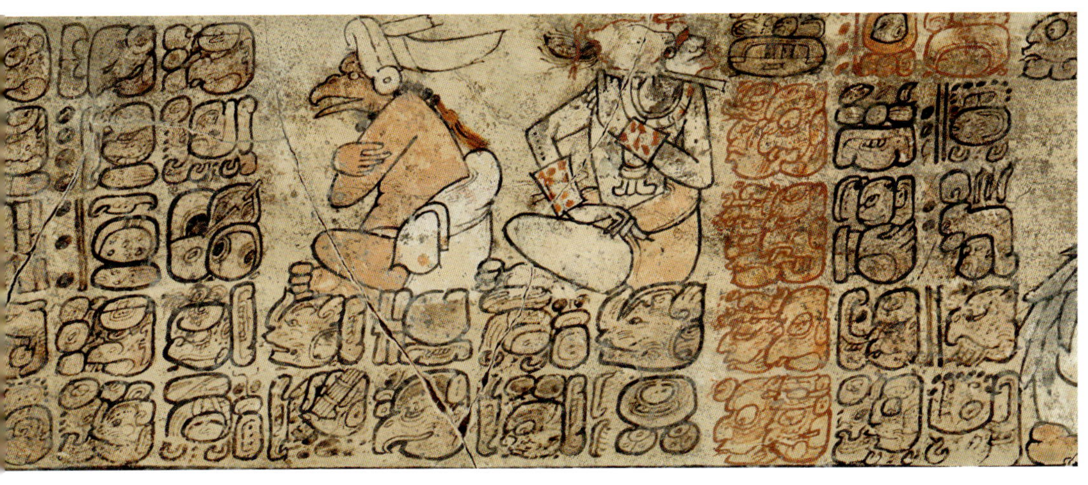

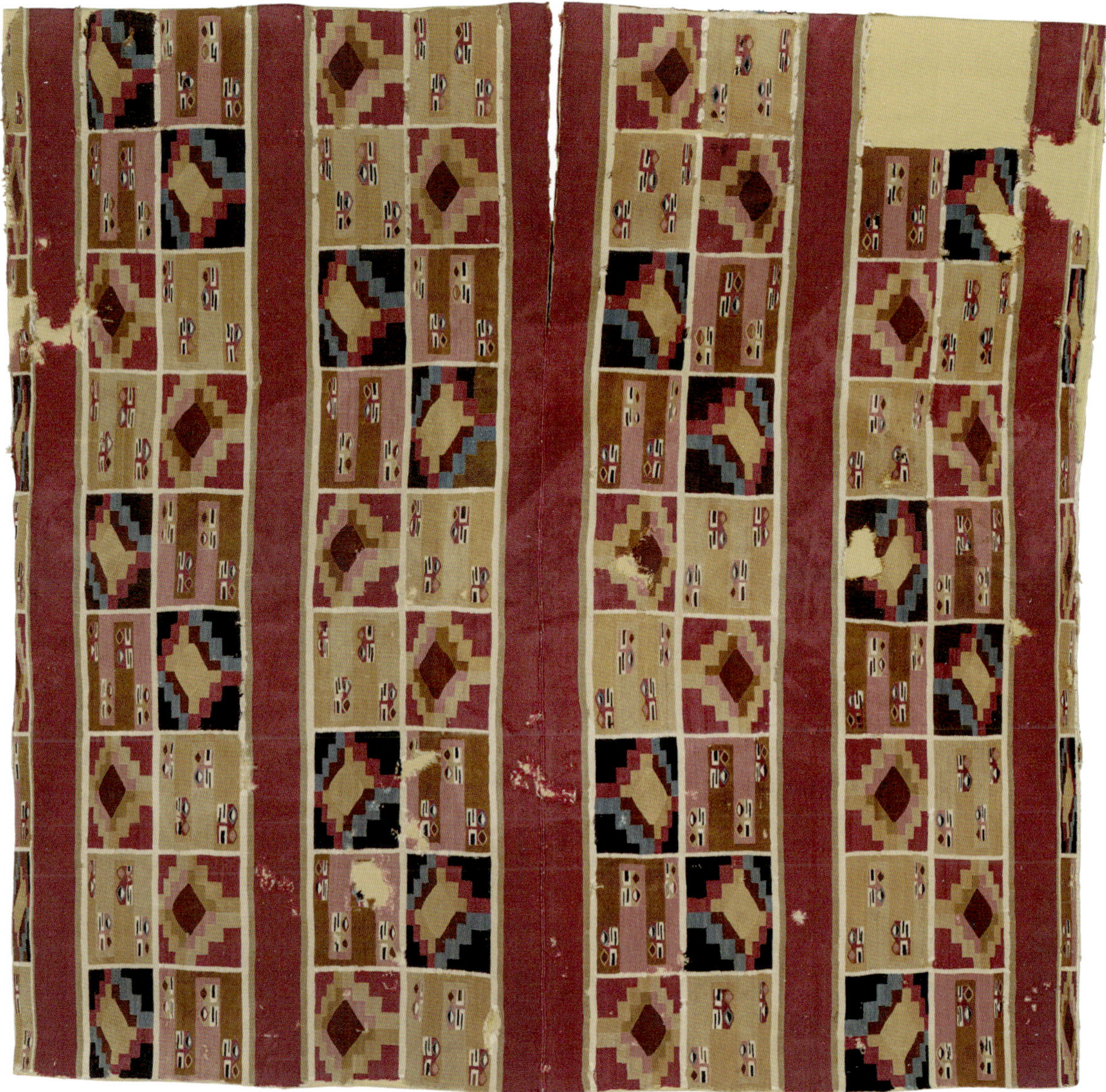

Tunic

Wari, Middle Horizon Period, Peru, 500–800 CE
South Coast, Peru

Fine textiles were among the most prized of all feasting gifts in Mesoamerica and Peru. Among the Inkas of the fifteenth century, the finest woven tunics featured exclusive designs signaling the wearer's rank, official role, or accomplishments on behalf of the state, which also controlled the production and distribution of these garments. The rigorously standardized Wari textiles, produced over seven hundred years earlier, also point to official patronage and state jurisdiction over the finest textiles.

Scholars suggest that Wari textile patterns express a fundamental numerical principle based on the common ratio of two and amplified by multiples thereof. This tunic features a version of the Wari conventional face-fret and interlocked U-shaped motif, arranged in twos and adhering to a strict color patterning of paired hues (red and gold, pink and tan, and so on). The brown-hued squares, alternating between pairs of light and dark brown fibers, are arranged in a vertical zigzag pattern. Wari fiber artists typically scattered indigo blue motifs throughout a fabric to break the otherwise repetitive layout. Here, the artist maintained the diagonal pairing of the blue- and black-hued squares and linked them to the darker brown quadrangles to construct a horizontal sub-pattern in contrast to the tunic's dominant verticality. The complex arrangement creates larger geometric patterns emphasizing opposed diagonals while maintaining the binary basis and four-part organization fundamental to Andean ideology.

Wool (camelid) and cotton interlocked tapestry
H. 100 cm (39⅜ in.), w. 103.5 cm (40¾ in.)
Charles Potter Kling Fund   1978.124

Tripod plate

Maya, Late Classic Period, 670–830 CE

Naranjo-Holmul area, Department of El Petén, Guatemala

This rare tripod plate resembles those used for serving tamales, although it has three small attached cups on its interior. Beyond being simply a food service vessel, it is a model of cosmic creation. Here the Maize god dances at Three-Stone-Place, the mythical hearth where the Maize deity erected the world tree to establish the three levels of the universe—the sky, the earth, and the underworld. The white cups represent the three hearth stones, and in the center the Maize god dances. The black bands at the base of the cups/stones are marked with sun glyphs, referring to the darkened sky before the sun's first dawning. A second reference to pre-creation times is the cormorants adorning the plate's walls, which symbolize the primordial waters from which the disk-like earth emerged.

The underside of the plate continues the creation allegory. Its three tall supports also represent the cosmic hearth stones, painted with the pan-Mesoamerican black and white stripes signifying stone. In the center, a large red-painted circle denotes the cosmic hearth's new fire, its embers burning with nascent life. The plate's distinctive painting style typifies ceramic production in eastern Guatemala, especially at the archaeological sites of Naranjo and Holmul. The texts on "Holmul-style" vessels often name local nobility, although the text on this spectacular example is not linguistically readable. Its only coherent section is a deity impersonation phrase having no known relationship to the pictorial imagery. The dichotomy between unreadable text and articulate composition is as remarkable as the artistic vision behind this matchless serving plate.

Earthenware with red, orange, and black on cream slip

H. 14 cm (5½ in.), diam. 33 cm (13 in.)

Museum purchase with funds donated by Lavinia and Landon T. Clay

2006.844

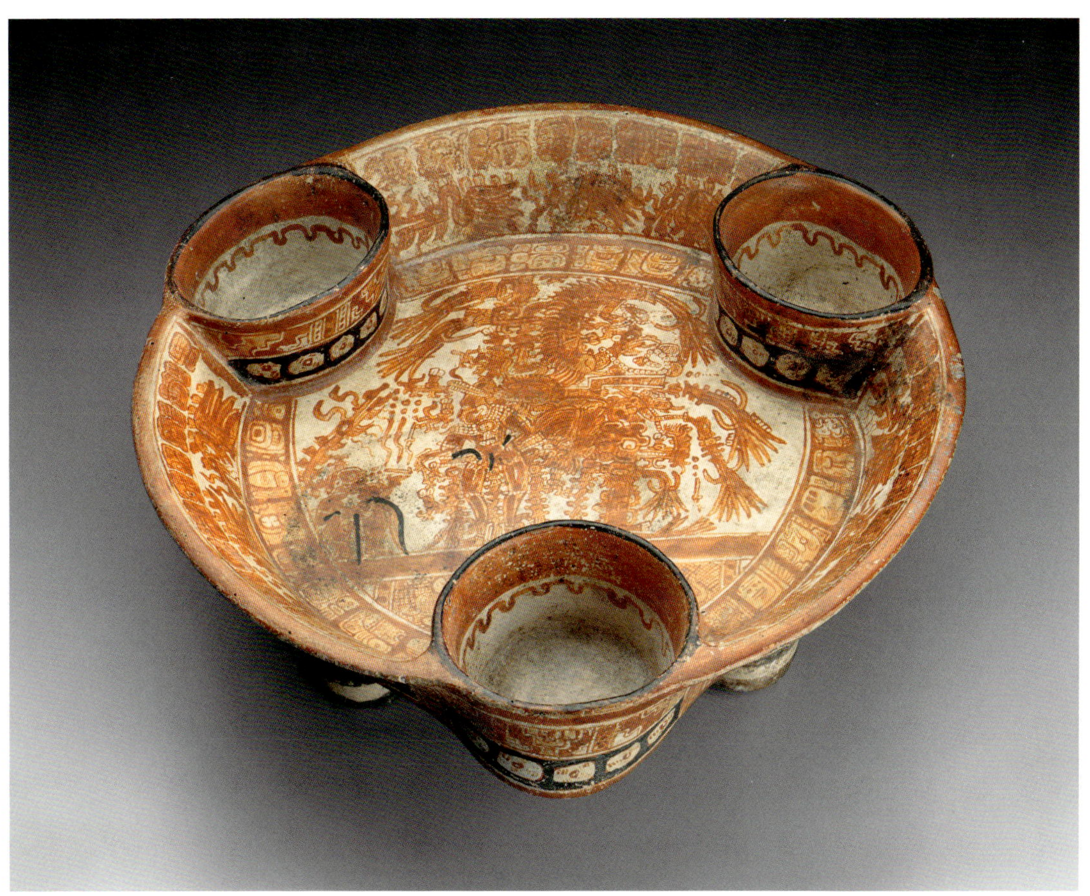

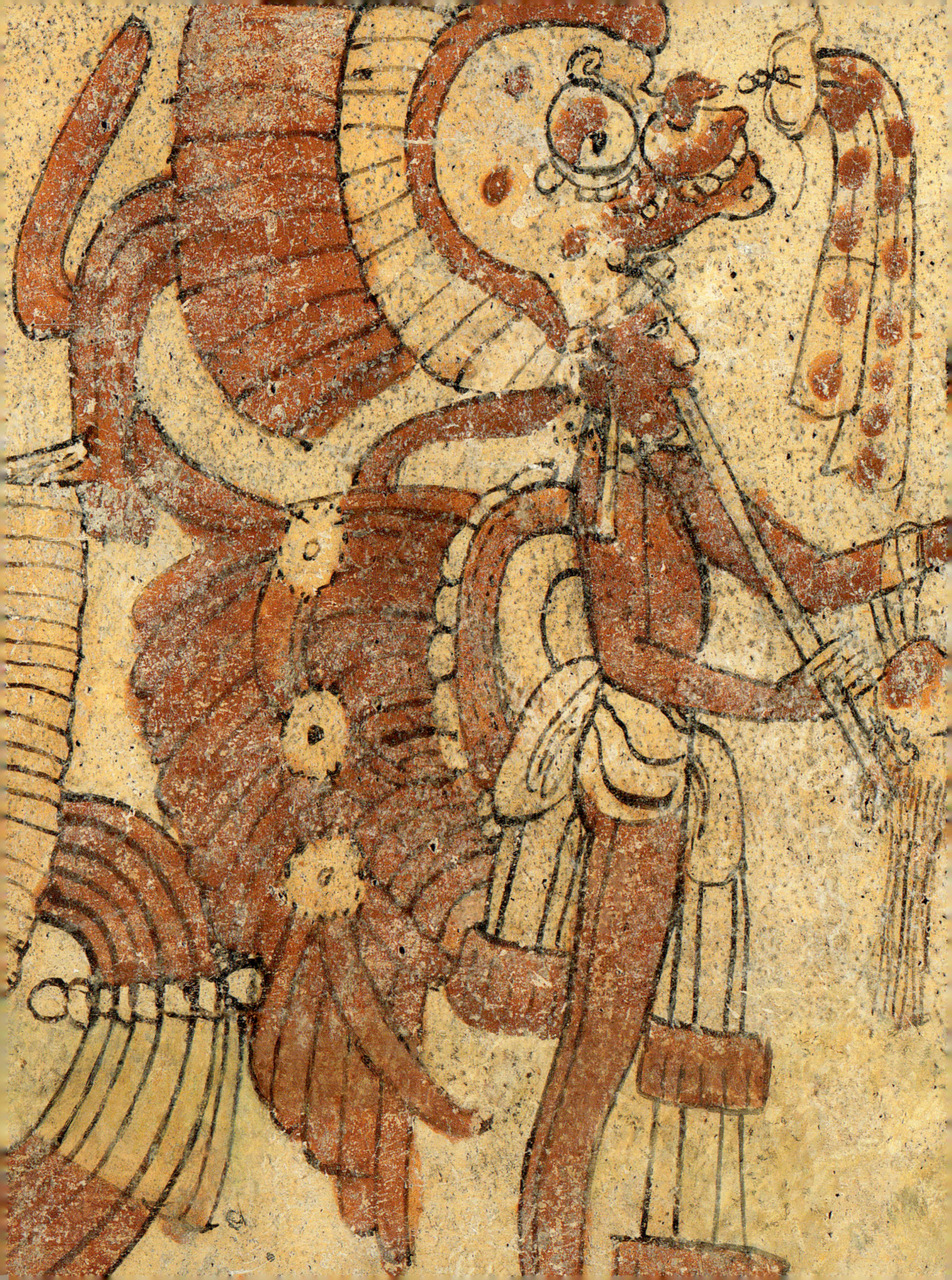

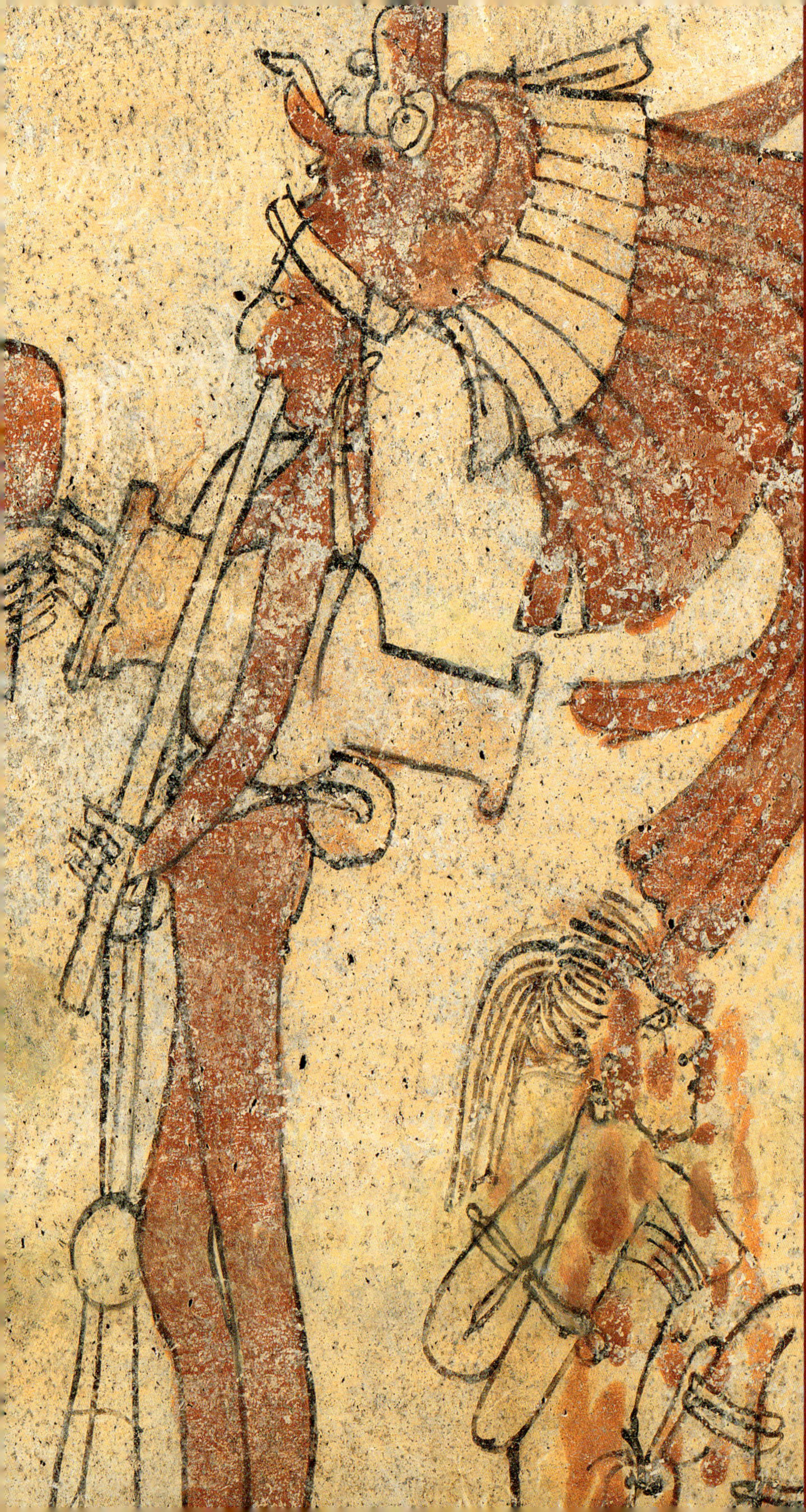

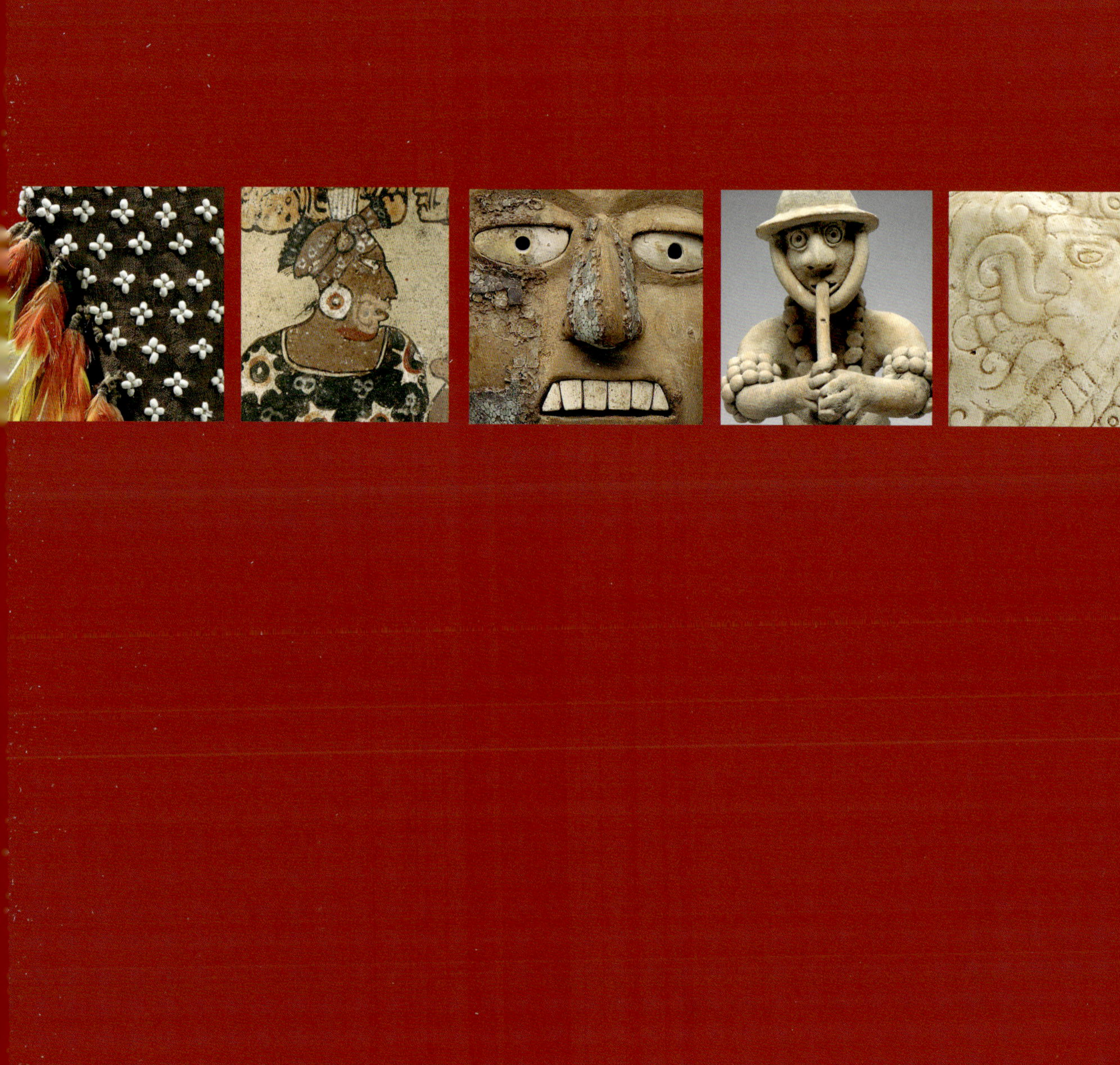

Performance

Music and dance were vital art forms among the cultures in the ancient Americas. Both were integral to all types of performances and public rituals that expressed religious, social, and political traditions. Performance is equally essential today among Latin America's indigenous communities, although the contemporary versions have been modified by more than five hundred years of contact with European, African, and Asian cultures. Fleeting elements of ancient practices can be found in these performances, such as the famous "Aztec" dancers of Mexico and the festival of the Virgin of Mamacha Candelaria in Peru, the latter being linked to ancient harvest festivals. To explore ancient performance in the Americas, we look to indigenous artworks and early Spanish accounts of this transitory art form.

Many ancient artworks portray performances with dancers and re-enactors, musicians, secondary participants, and onlookers. Among the most famous are the late eighth-century murals at the Classic period Maya city of Bonampak, Mexico, in which nobles dressed in elaborate regalia dance on the wide stairs of a civic building. Sixteenth-century accounts describe similar public pageants, although the reports are often imprecise and biased toward European expectations. For example, Diego de Landa, the first bishop of Yucatan, describes a performance in which eight hundred people holding little streamers danced to a beat with long "warlike steps" that were "heavy" and lasted all day. From even Bishop Landa's sketchy account, his description recalls the kind of elaborate event like that pictured in the Bonampak murals, which took place six hundred years earlier.

Public performances remain an important part of civic and religious events throughout Latin America. Many are rooted in ancient forms and most frequently are found in remote locales where the colonial Spanish presence was not overly strong. Further, many performances have survived because they coincided with ritual observances in the Catholic calendar. The early friars recognized the power of these observances and transformed them into public displays featuring the Christian and Spanish messages. The resulting hybrid pageants today draw crowds from around the world, especially those during the Christian celebrations of Carnival and Semana Santa (Holy Week), which were linked to ancient agricultural and fertility rites.

Ancient renderings of performances feature processions of musicians and dancers, who also are portrayed singing or reciting a narrative expressed by open mouths and "sound scrolls" issuing from the lips. This recalls the conquistador Francisco de Aguilar's description of pageants in highland Mexico during which people read aloud the epic fables and histories contained in the ancient Native books, chanted to the rhythmic accompaniment of a drum. Given the fragmentary glimpses from artworks, we can only wonder to what degree spoken word and song contributed to the aural landscape of the ancient Americas.

Performances were important vehicles for cultivating a sense of community and social well-being, and members of the elite participated in elaborate displays of status and authority. They re-enacted religious myths and ancient history, celebrated political triumphs, and amused with witty plays. The Bonampak murals narrate a battle and public victory celebration with dancing nobles, parading musicians, and the sacrifice of war captives. A Maya earthenware basin depicts warriors performing music at a sacrificial rite, one blowing a shell trumpet and others playing flutes, drums, and rattles (see pp. 166–67). Eight hundred years later, Spanish writers in central Mexico describe magnificent civic pageants commemorating military successes, with rulers and warriors dancing and displaying their captives to the gathered populace.

Music was essential to performances because its physical and psychological resonances enhanced the experience. The archaeological record has preserved some instruments, such as the bone flutes at Caral, Peru, dating to 2500 BCE, but most have been lost because they were made from wood, animal hide, and other perishable materials. The Spanish contributed to the loss by destroying what they deemed "pagan" instruments, illustrated by the report of one seventeenth-century Jesuit missionary smashing more than four thousand drums and flutes in a single Peruvian village. At the same time, early Spanish accounts illuminate the repertoire of musical forms and now-lost instruments. For example, Bishop Diego de Landa tells of a thin trumpet-like horn of hollow wood with a long twisted gourd at the end; his description closely resembles images of wooden trumpets in Classic Maya artworks. Yet Spanish writers typically did not make accurate records of the instruments or the music they heard, often dismissing it as meaningless noise. Most were not trained musicians and had little knowledge of or interest in such matters, and they regarded the performances as a pagan detriment to the apostolic mission of Catholic conversion. As a result, they largely banned native musical forms. Yet they understood the power of performance and transformed many into pageants explaining the Christian story.

In our modern world, cyclical pageants such as the Academy Awards and national political conventions are lavish events that bring together society in a shared experience. These performances always include music and personal displays of character and identity. In the ancient Americas, pageantry served the same goal of social unity via the staging of treasured rites. Public performances, with their theatrical and musical displays, provided the stage for affirming social norms, political hierarchy, and the sovereignty of the community. To catch a glimpse of these powerful events in the ancient Americas, we look to the few surviving musical instruments and infrequent representations of performance to recover something of this ephemeral art form.

This vase features a nobleman preparing to perform in the guise of an aged deity, perhaps Itzamnaaj, one of the gods of creation. A mask portraying this deity is offered by an elegant woman dressed in a black *huipil* (tunic dress) decorated with motifs associated with the moon goddess. A second lady stands in front of the lord ready to perform with him. She has a rattle in her right hand and the panache (or plume) of feathers worn on her back, a common performance costume accessory throughout Mesoamerica. Red body paint is being applied to the lord who glances into a mirror held by an attendant. The mirror closely resembles those used for divination rites, suggesting that the performance has a spiritual finale.

Music was essential to public ritual dance performances among the ancient Maya. Such performances also accompanied private events pertaining to the official and sacred duties of the nobility, which took place in palaces and ancestral shrines. Surviving instruments suggest the music was primarily rhythmic with some melodic content produced by flutes and ocarinas (vessel flutes). Public performances were spectacles of costume, sound, and choreography, with the dancers and musicians arrayed on the broad stairways of stately buildings to elevate the entourage above the crowds assembled in the plaza below. The pageants reenacted myths and epic tales that were the foundation of communal identity and royal power. Sixteenth-century accounts state that these types of performances typically were staged during political and religious gatherings.

Earthenware with orange, red, dark pink, brown, gray (originally green), and black on cream slip paint; traces of "Maya Blue" pigment
H. 17.2 cm (6¾ in.), diam. 11.8 cm (4⅝ in.)
Gift of Landon T. Clay   1988.1176

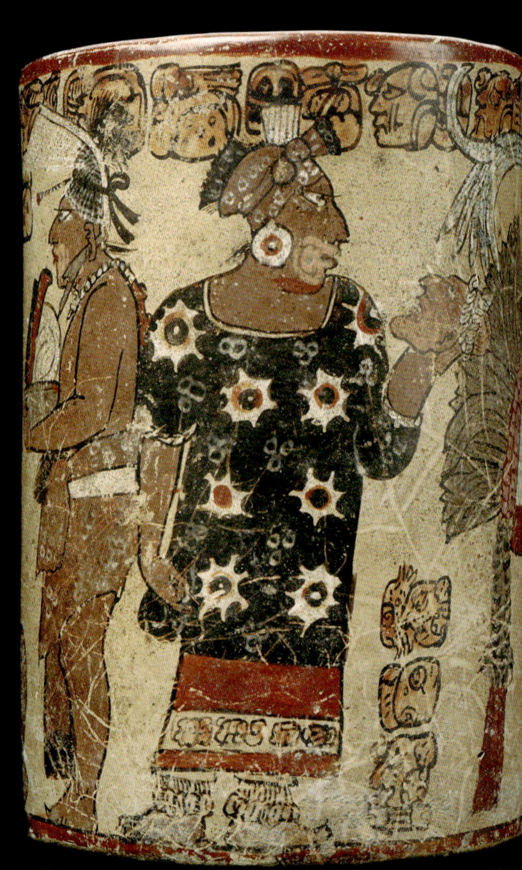

Mask

Aztec (Mexica) or Mixtec, Postclassic Period, 1300–1521
Central or Southern Highlands, Mexico

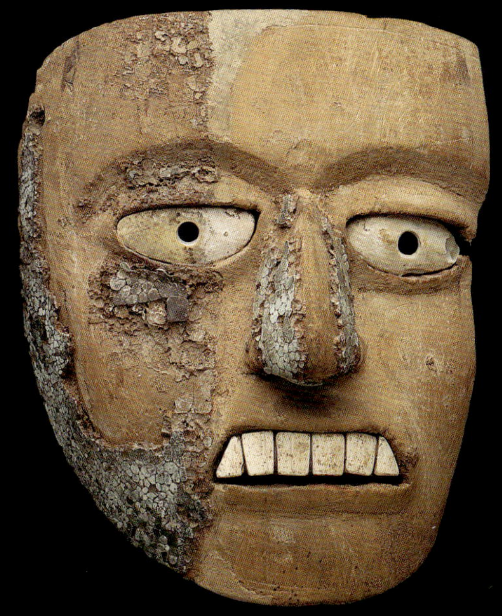

Wooden masks served two primary functions in ancient Mexico: they were used as performance masks and were also tied onto funerary bundles to represent the deceased's face. This mask could have served either purpose. Although only a small proportion remains, the entire front surface was adorned with an intricate turquoise and shell mosaic. The sixteenth-century Spanish commentators reported extensively on masks made by Mixtec artisans who excelled in creating mosaics using semiprecious stones, including turquoise imported from what today is New Mexico, and shell brought from the Gulf and Pacific Coasts. Most dance masks were made of wood, like this example, although others were fashioned of papier-mâché, animal hide, and cloth. Very few have survived due to their perishable materials and destruction by the Spanish, who deemed them relics of pagan rites. Some masks were carved from stone such as jadeite, alabaster, or obsidian, their heavy weight suggesting they were tied to a funerary bundle or onto wooden sculptures of deities.

Masks are far more than a simple costume element. They transform a person into a new persona by changing his or her face—the center of one's identity. By donning a mask, one's personality is eliminated and a new entity is created, often a spirit being or mythic character. Among many indigenous peoples in Mexico and Guatemala today, the ubiquitous dance or festival mask is a conduit for connecting with the historical past, the mythic ages of creation, and the spirit realm of sacred ancestors and gods—be they Catholic or indigenous. Thus it is not surprising that the mask survives today as a principal component of ritual performance during a variety of religious observances.

Wood with turquoise, black stone, shell, and mother-of-pearl
H. 16.8 cm (6⅝ in.), w. 14.1 cm (5½ in.), d. 4.5 cm (1¾ in.)
Gift of Landon T. Clay   1988.1207

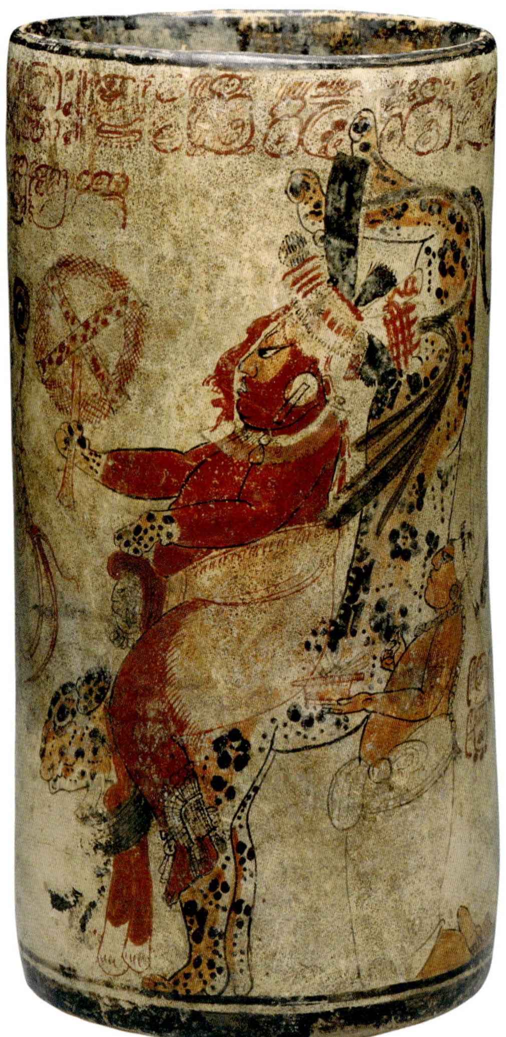

Cylinder vessel

Maya, Late Classic Period, 740–60 CE
Ik' Polity, Motul de San José area,
Department of El Petén, Guatemala

Yajawte' K'inich, the rotund ruler of the Ik' polity (present-day Motul de San José, Guatemala), participates in a blood sacrifice and vision quest performance on the Mayan calendar equivalent of November 20, 743 CE, as recorded in the hieroglyphic text around this vase's rim. Joining Yajawte' K'inich are two noblemen from the influential polities of Hix Witz and Tayasal located to the north and east of the Ik' polity. The leaders wear costumes portraying supernatural beings with attributes of the jaguar, eagle, and centipede, all powerful spirit beings in Maya religious ideology. The dramatic masks are rendered in "X-ray" fashion to reveal the lords' heads inside the helmet-like regalia.

The masked ruler seems to ride a jaguar spirit being, its rear legs arching over his head. Yet the beast's front legs mimic those of Yajawte' K'inich, signaling the merging of man and jaguar spirit. This transformation is described in the hieroglyphic text as the ruler dancing in jaguar form. A fourth masked figure, his body painted dark brown, grasps a feathered staff and extends his left hand in dance position. A kneeling figure, without a mask, holds a small dish containing blood sacrifice implements, and the prone body of a heart-sacrificed infant is superimposed on the chest of one of the performers. Yajawte' K'inich's name and royal titles end the rim text and establish his ownership of this vessel; short hieroglyphic texts scattered throughout the scene identify the participants.

Earthenware with orange, red, dark pink, and black on cream slip paint
H. 23.5 cm (9¼ in.), diam. 12.4 cm (4⅞ in.)
Gift of Landon T. Clay   1988.1177

Three musician-performers

Colima, Late Formative to Early Classic Periods,
Comala phase, 200 BCE–200 CE
Colima, Mexico

This ceramic tableau depicts three performers leaning forward with bent knees in the pan-Meso-american posture indicating dance. One plays a long flute and the other two shake rattles (maracas). The rattles' vertical ridges suggest they were made from gourds as is common throughout Mexico today. The performers' elaborate attire includes hats with chin straps, large necklaces and armbands of spherical beads, and decorated hip wraps covering long loin cloths. Pairs of wide disks adorn their lower legs. The flutist is the principal figure, distinguished by his larger size, adorned hip wrap, and distinctive fringed anklets. His duct flute resembles those found in the region, with four finger holes on the lower part of the pipe and played in the position seen here. All three figures are, in fact, vessel flutes (ocarinas), with the mouthpiece located at the top of their heads.

Ceramic figures like these are frequently found in the deep shaft tombs located throughout Colima, Nayarit, and Jalisco, situated in western Mexico. The domed tomb chambers housed multiple burials with a variety of grave offerings, especially ceramic sculptures portraying earthly life such as this group of musicians. The nearly perfect condition of these sculptures indicates they likely came from such a burial or tomb.

Earthenware
Tallest figure: h. 13.2 cm (5¼ in.), w. 6.5 cm (2½ in.),
d. 4 cm (1⅝ in.)
Gift of Timothy Phillips in honor of Matthew D. Teitelbaum
2015.2844.1-3

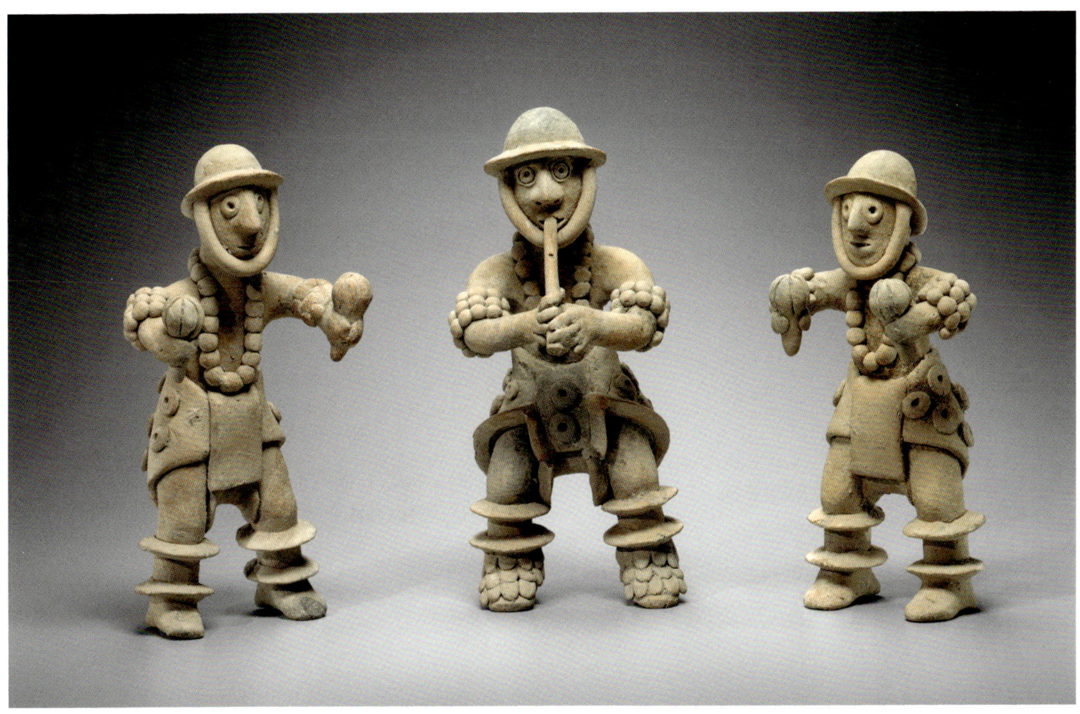

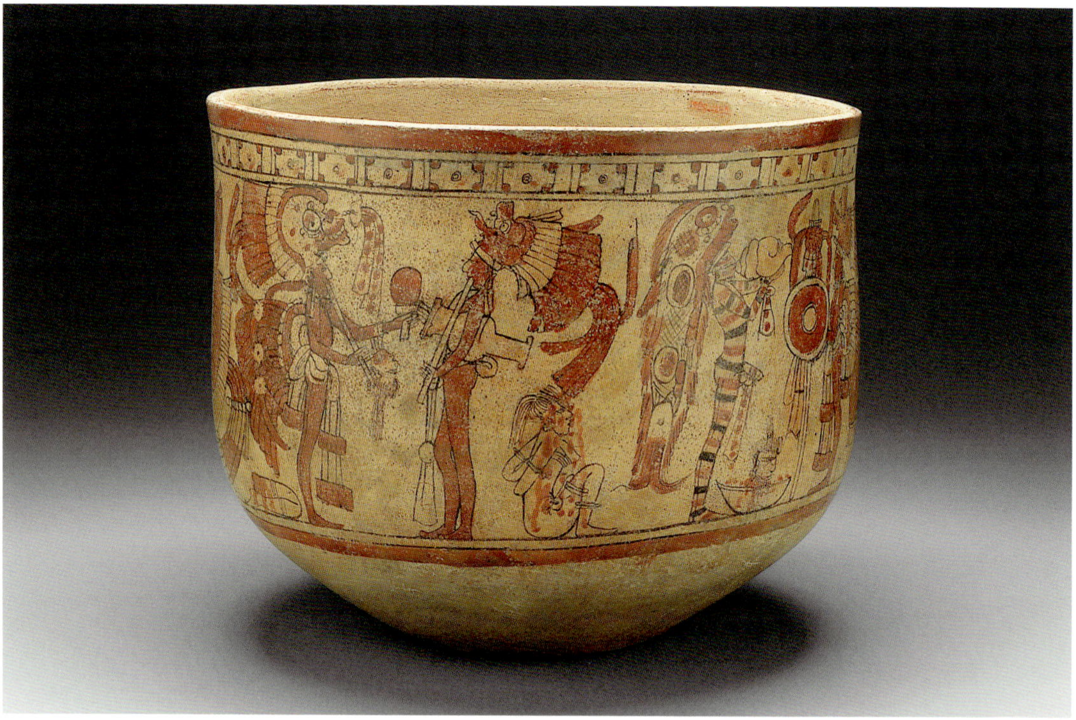

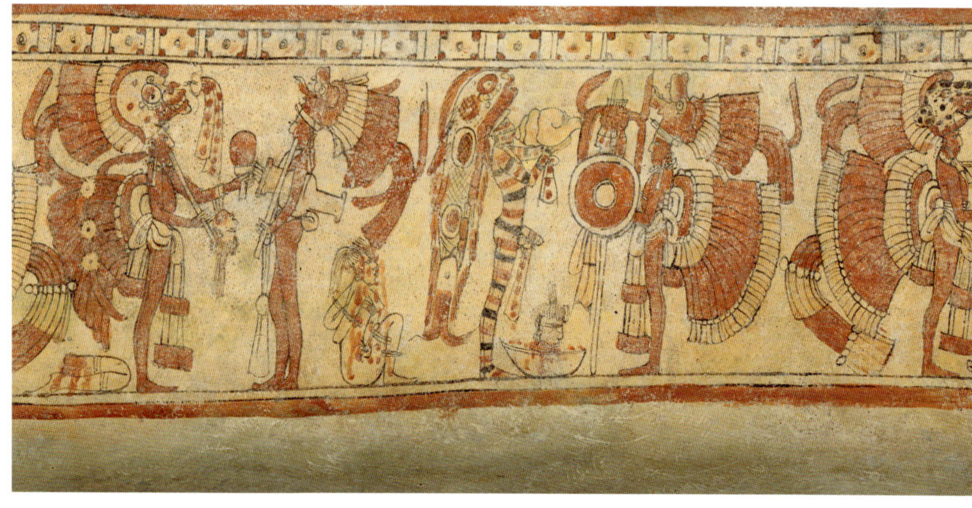

Basin

Maya, Late Classic Period, 550–750 CE
Belize

Music accompanies the sacrificial rite painted on this unusually large basin. Three musicians perform alongside two pairs of warriors, bound captives, and severed body parts. The warriors wear battle finery, including jaguar and puma headdresses, and brandish shields and long, bloodied spears. Nude captives sitting on the ground are covered with stab wounds, inflicted to spill their life-giving blood central to the rite's purpose. A fifth warrior faces a standing nude figure painted in red and black stripes and with a bloodied cloth binding his penis—penis-perforation was a sacrificial rite associated with Maya royalty. He blows a large shell trumpet like those used on the battlefield to drive the action, as described by Spanish chroniclers. Two other musicians play long flutes; the placement of their hands along the shaft suggests a small number of tone holes, which would produce a limited note range. One flutist shakes a spherical rattle, while a decapitated human head dangles upside down from his forearm.

The second flutist plays a small ceramic drum using his hand to strike the drum head. This flute-and-drum combination required practiced skill to produce music. The pairing is found among a surprisingly large number of ancient American cultures (e.g., those of Peru's North Coast) and elsewhere in the world. Notable among these are the flute-and-drum compositions preserved in the thirteenth-century Spanish *Cantigas de Santa María*, one of the largest collections of songs with accompanying illustrations from the Middle Ages. The tradition survives today in southern France and adjacent Cataluña (northeast Spain) as well as in Mexico and Peru.

Earthenware with red, orange, and black slip paint
H. 34.8 cm (13¾ in.), diam. 40.8 cm (16⅛ in.)
Gift of Landon T. Clay   1988.1240

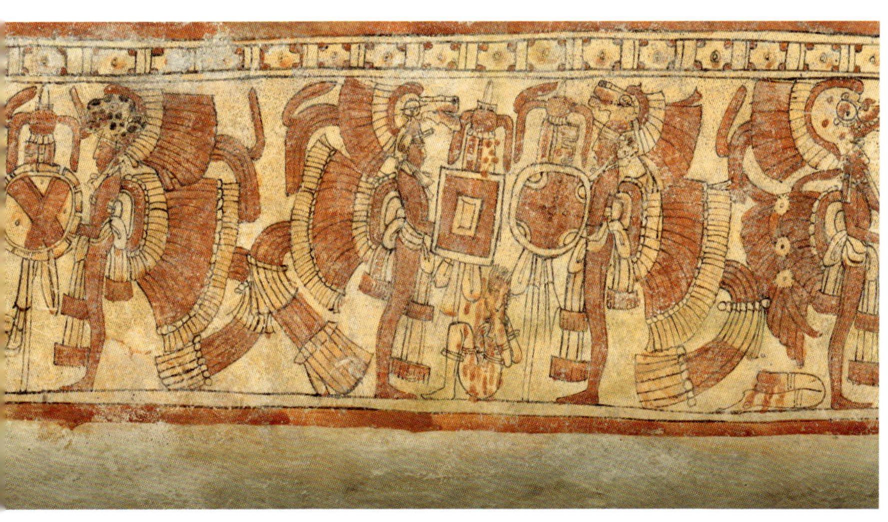

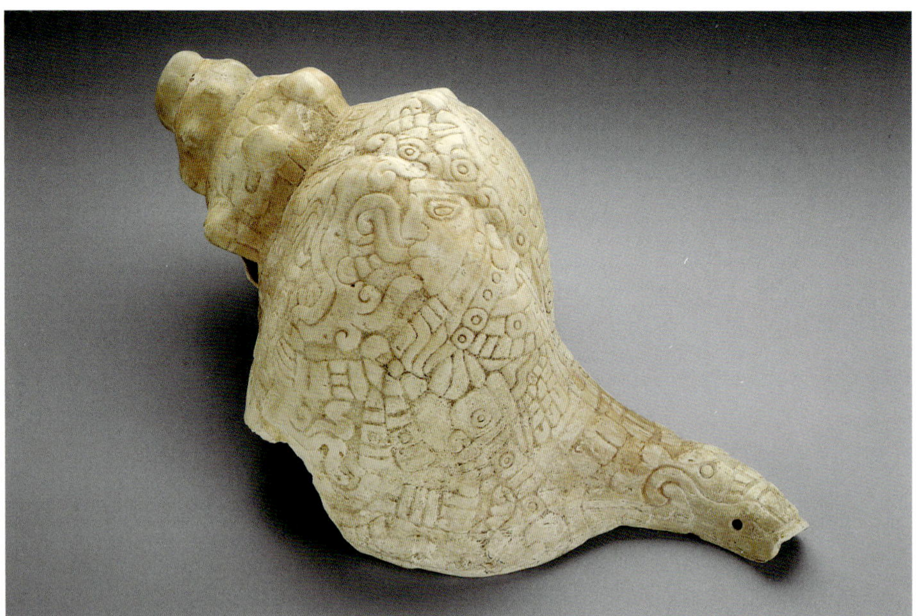

Shell trumpet

Aztec (Mexica) or Mixtec, Late Postclassic Period,
1425–1520
Central Highlands, Mexico

The blaring of shell trumpets punctuated the battle-field and public ceremonies among the Aztecs of central Mexico, as noted by the Spanish who were astounded by the shells' loud sounds, which traveled great distances. Trumpets varied in form and materials, and also differed in manner of playing, tonal qualities, and note ranges. Almost any material can be made into a trumpet—shell, ceramic, gourd, leather, or wood—and current archaeological and art historical data suggest all of these were used in the ancient Americas.

The player of a shell trumpet could produce a wide range and quality of notes by manipulating a hand inside the shell's cavity. Here the instrument maker chose a large conch from the *Pleuroploca* family of marine gastropods. Seashells, especially those with deep or iridescent coloration, were a luxury item throughout the ancient Americas, and were even used as currency. The artisan removed the end of the shell's spire near its apex to fashion the mouthpiece and pierced the elongated end for suspension on a cord or for attaching ornamental cloth, feathers, or beads.

The decorative carving features a dancing performer. The large scroll adorned with a flower bud emerging from his mouth signifies "flower and song" in the Aztec language Nahuatl, meaning poetry/singing.

The shell's fine workmanship suggests Mixtec artistry, although the imagery recalls that of the neighboring Aztecs. Mixtec artisans often worked in Aztec craft studios because they valued the superb Mixtec technical skills in pottery, shell, feathers, jadeite and stone mosaics, and gold.

Conch shell
H. 38.1 cm (15 in.), w. 20 cm (7⅞ in.)
Gift of Landon T. Clay   1988.1214

Trumpet

Tiwanaku, Middle Horizon Period, about 500–900 CE
Bolivia

This wooden trumpet may have survived because it was preserved by the arid environment of the Bolivian highlands. It is embellished with the image of a standing male figure whose broad face, almond-shaped eyes, and tall headdress typify the Tiwanaku (Bolivia) style of rendering deities and members of the ruling elite. His distinctive straight-sided headgear recalls the four-cornered hats typical of Middle Horizon (500–900 CE) male garb throughout northern Bolivia and southern Peru. Variously made of fancy brocade or interwoven with tropical bird feathers, these elaborate hats conveyed the elevated status of their wearers.

Tiwanaku was a thriving metropolis in northern Bolivia on the southeastern shore of Lake Titicaca, and its influence spread into neighboring Chile, Argentina, and Peru during the first millennium CE. Similarly shaped trumpets made of earthenware have been found in Tiwanaku temples and public ritual spaces, indicating a wide-ranging tradition of music played during ceremonies. Wood was a primary artistic medium for Tiwanaku artisans and their Wari counterparts in Peru, from which they fashioned containers, cooking implements, weaving tools, and hair combs, as well as sacred items such as snuff trays (for hallucinogenic powders) and divination mirror backs.

Wood
L. 33 cm (13 in.), diam. 3.2 cm (1¼ in.)
Mary L. Smith Fund   1986.603

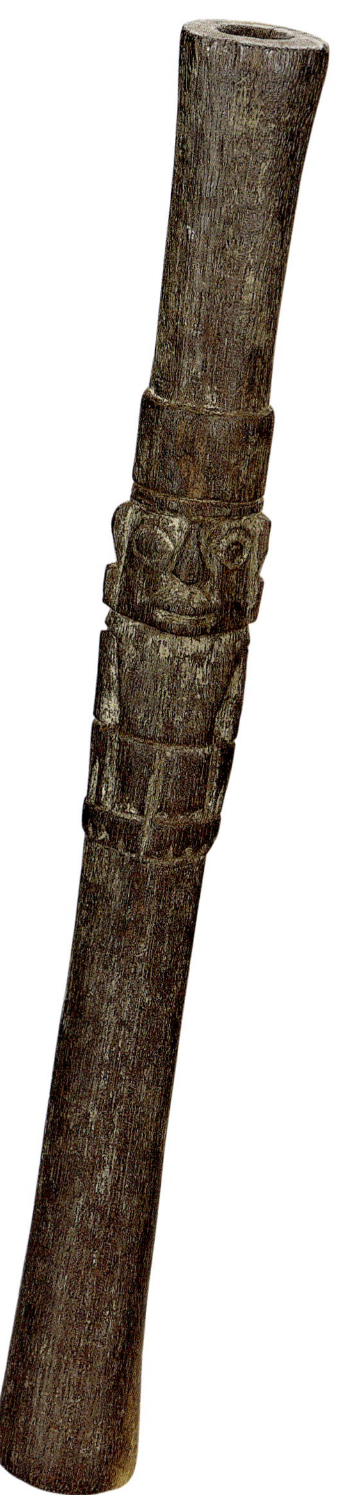

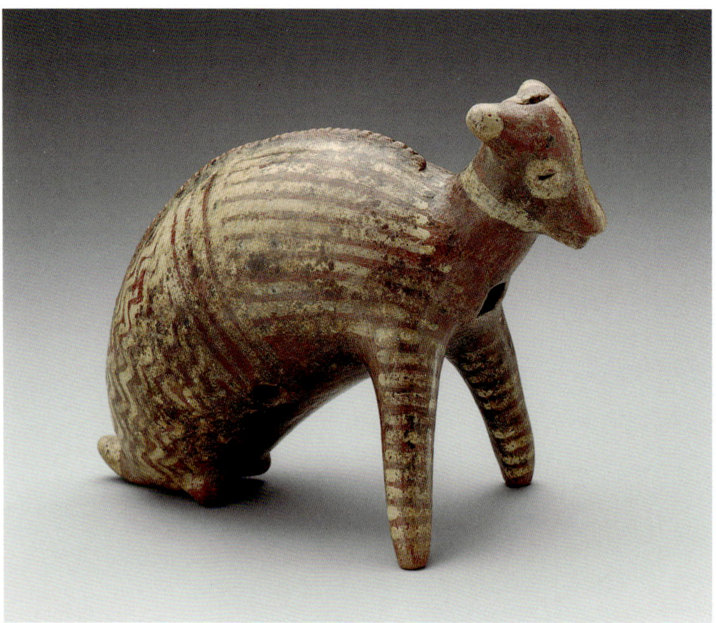

Vessel flute (ocarina)

Nayarit, Late Formative to Early Classic Periods,
200 BCE–300 CE
Nayarit, Mexico

According to Mesoamerican belief, a dog guided the soul of the deceased through the underworld. This canine effigy vessel flute exemplifies the zoomorphic ocarinas often found in tombs in West Mexico. These musical instrument tomb offerings suggest they were played during funerary processions, recalling the modeled clay representations of such processions, also found in the shaft tombs, depicting the mourners playing ocarinas and flutes. The mouthpiece of this version is located atop the canine's head. Three dog breeds are indigenous to Mexico: the *itzcuintli* (or *chichi*, the common dog), the *xoloitzcuintli* ("Mexican hairless"), and the smaller *tlalchichi* (later called *techichi*), which Hernán Cortés observed being sold as food and which Friar Sahagún described as "good to eat."

Today's popular chihuahua is a nineteenth-century cross between European dogs and the *techichi*.

West Mexico's portrayals of dogs range from highly realistic to evocative abstraction. Nayarit artists favored minimalism, seen here in the dog's head, which is reduced to a triangular form with only subtle indentations implying eyes and mouth. The dog's body is equally spare, with a simple notched ridge indicating its spine and lump-like conical forms representing hind legs and tail. In contrast to the restrained form, the dog's body is profusely decorated with painted designs, with four zones of abstract motifs alluding to the typically short to medium-long coats of Mexico's indigenous dogs.

Earthenware with cream on red slip paint
H. 15 cm (5⅞ in.), w. 24.4 cm (9⅝ in.), d. 8.5 cm (3⅜ in.)
Helen and Alice Colburn Fund   1984.359

Duct flute
Zenú (Sinú), 900–1500
Colombia

Constructed in two conical sections joined at the middle, this type of vessel flute is characteristic of those of the Tairona and Zenú (Sinú) cultures of Colombia's northern Caribbean lowlands. The Zenú were skilled goldsmiths, renowned for intricately cast-gold body ornaments and ceremonial figurines. Many of the same decorative patterns found on the gold works were also used for earthenware objects, including braid-like forms and bands of delicate punctates or short incisions as seen here. Modeled animals are prevalent in Tairona and Zenú artworks; the most common ones on vessel flutes are crocodiles and jaguars or pumas. These fearsome predators symbolically represent strength and sovereignty over their respective realms—the wetlands and the forest—although each can invade the other's territory. Caimans and large felines also served as family totems and sometimes represented the spirit companions of shamans. The playing of flutes during all types of rituals invoked the qualities inherent to the animals embellishing the instrument.

The mouthpiece of this flute is the short, pronged end, which has a duct located on the underside. The flute's body is pierced by four finger holes, three of which pass through the jaguar effigies. A small hole just below the mouthpiece allows the user to suspend the instrument on a carrying cord.

Earthenware
L. 26.7 cm (10½ in.), w. 6 cm (2⅜ in.), h. 8.3 cm (3¼ in.)
Gift from the Collection of Shirley and Hy Zaret
2008.186

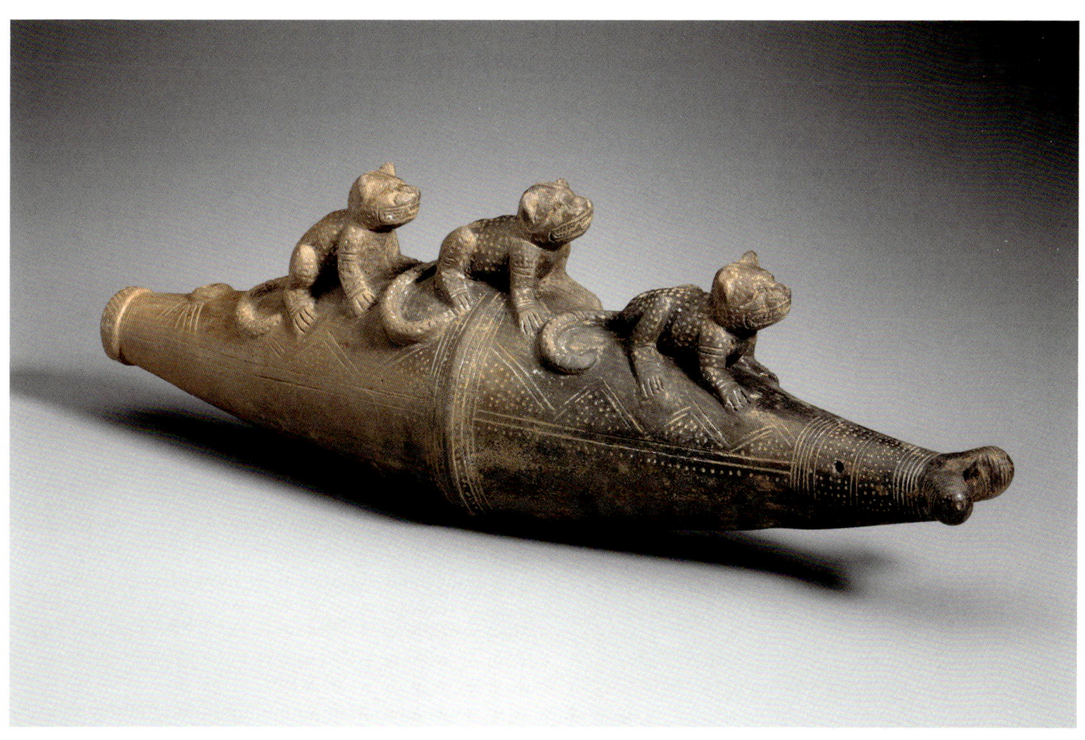

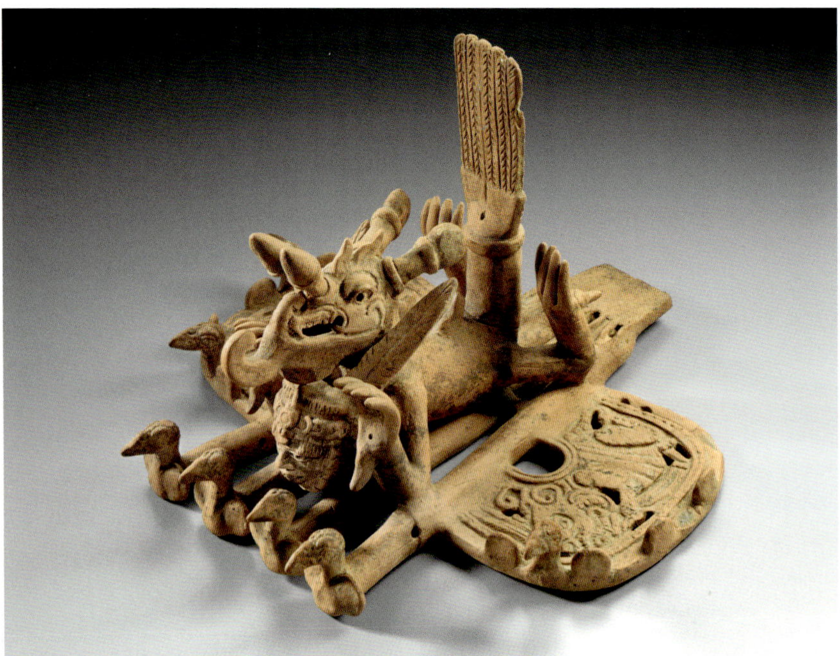

Quadruple duct flute

Veracruz, Late Classic Period, 550–950 CE
Veracruz, Mexico

Ancient Veracruz is renowned for its wide array of wind instruments, especially flutes with multiple tubes. This flute's four tubes merge into a single mouthpiece for simultaneous playing. The resulting tones, often discordant to the Western ear, are high and shrill; loose clay cylinders inside each tube also create a slight warbling sound. Both qualities are known to generate psychological and physiological effects in the brain. The flute portrays an iguana-based mythical being with five long tail feathers and a human figure emerging between its clawed feet and below its head. Two large, wing-like flanges serve as handles adorned with the image of a skeletal feline. The wing-flanges and the four pipes terminate in vulture heads; together these create a flying bier or litter for the mythical iguana being and its companion.

Multiple-pipe flutes are played today in Veracruz by its famous Voladores ("flyers"), who spin down a tree-like pole suspended by their ankles from ever-lengthening ropes tied to its top. The upside-down performers, dressed in ornate clothing and plumed headdresses, play their flutes to imitate birds as they spin to the ground. This unique ritual originated as a springtime rite of rain-bringing at the beginning of the planting season; the similarity in sound between the modern flutes and this ancient instrument suggests it may have been played during such ceremonies.

Earthenware with traces of white stucco and blue pigment
H. 18.5 cm (7¼ in.), w. 27 cm (10⅝ in.), d. 29 cm (11⅜ in.)
Promised gift of Timothy Phillips in honor of Matthew D. Teitelbaum

Panpipes (*antara* or *zampoña*)

Nasca, Early Intermediate Period, 200–600 CE
South Coast, Peru

Panpipes are a kind of multiple-tube, end-blown flute. The closed pipes have no finger holes and are played by blowing air across their open end. Panpipes have a long history in Peru dating back before the Early Horizon period (800 BCE–1 CE), and continue today as the predominant indigenous instrument throughout the Andes. Most ancient examples are made from clay, although cane, silver, stone, and animal bones, including those of llamas and other camelids, were used. The surviving stone versions date to Inka times (post-1300) and, although relatively rare in the archaeological record, more have been found in Chile and Argentina than in Peru.

Ancient panpipes made of ceramic are superbly constructed to ensure accurate tuning of each pipe. Such precision suggests they were made using standardized molds. Panpipes emphasize intervals of notes including octaves and fifths or minor and major thirds; microtones ("between-pitch" notes) are prevalent in the shorter pipes, which produce higher-pitched notes. Panpipes have been found in pairs or groupings, each one with a different note range but of similar intervals. Such tonal exactitude strongly suggests they were made and played as an ensemble and for a specific musical form or composition. The groupings also imply they were used during particular rites or events.

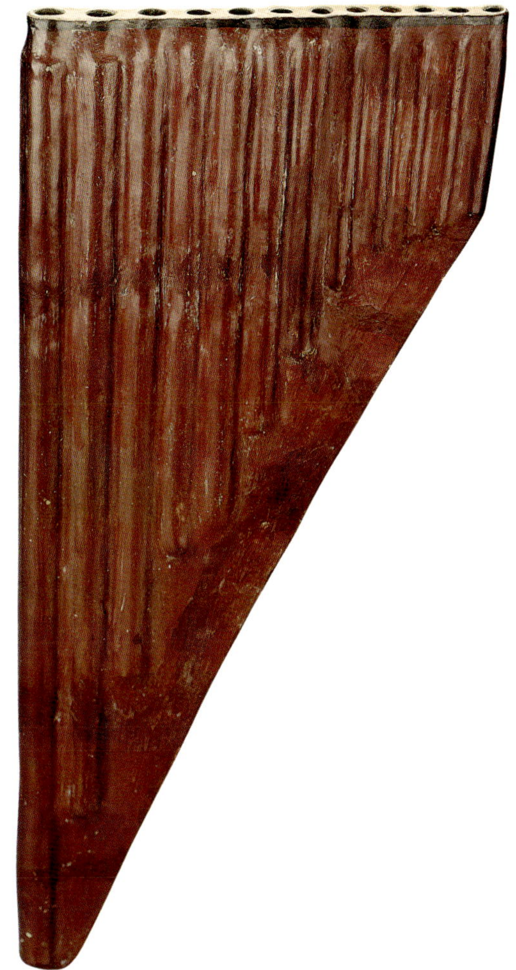

Earthenware with red slip paint
H. 46 cm (18⅛ in.), w. 18 cm (7⅛ in.), d. 2.5 cm (1 in.)
Helen and Alice Colburn Fund   1984.332

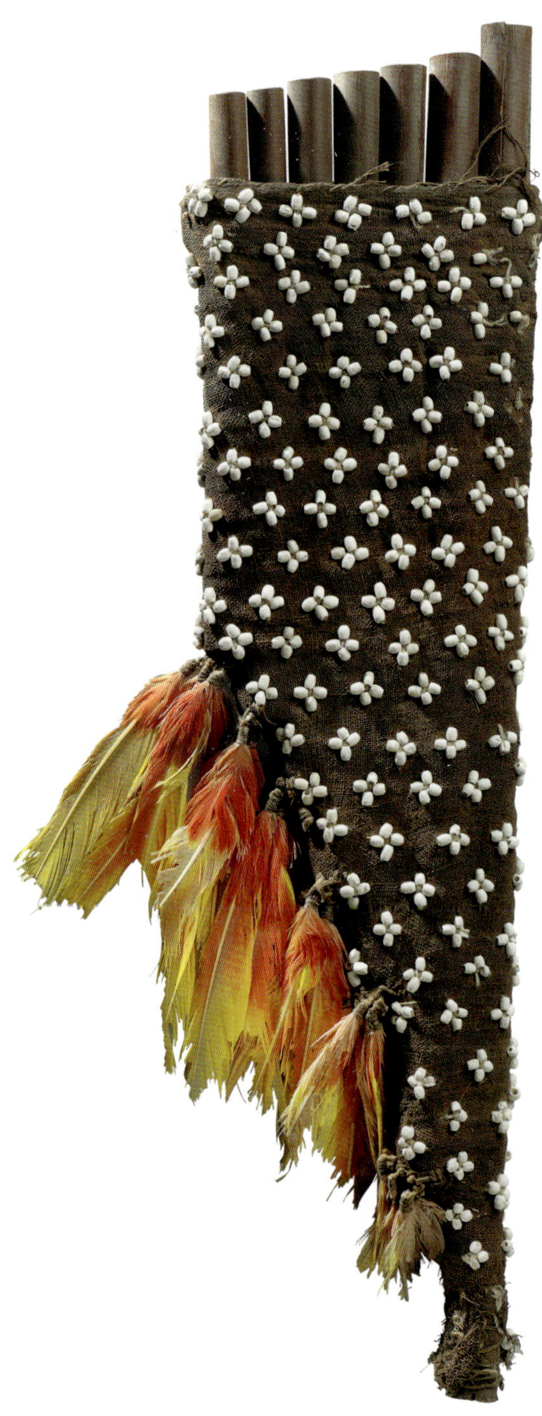

Panpipes (*antara* or *zampoña*)

Nasca, Early Intermediate Period, 200–600 CE
South Coast, Peru

The carefully selected reed tubes of this panpipe were cut to specified lengths, and their blowing edges were skillfully shaped to facilitate precise sound production. The instrument maker relied on the naturally occurring nodes between sections of the plant to block the lower end of each tube. They were lashed together with fine yarn, and then a brown cotton fabric was wrapped around the instrument. Tiny shells were stitched to the fabric to create the cross-shaped pattern, present on the front and back sides in keeping with Andean aesthetic traditions. The bottom end is embellished with bundles of tropical bird feathers, likely imported from the Amazon Basin on the eastern side of the Andes.

The fine craftsmanship of this panpipe, including its uncommonly ornate decoration, points to its being a valued instrument created for a special client or function. Caches of panpipes are known from ceremonial contexts at the large center of Cahuachi, located on Peru's South Coast. Described as the most important Nasca ritual center, the floors of many rooms in its Great Temple were covered with hundreds of intentionally broken panpipes. This pattern is found elsewhere in Peru and Bolivia, implying a widespread use of panpipes during rituals such as those venerating sacred ancestors, dedicating temples, and inaugurating rulers.

Cane, cloth, feathers, shell
L. 44.8 cm (17⅝ in.), w. 12.7 cm (5 in.)
Gift of Douglas Deihl   2010.616

Jaguar bell pendant

Coclé, 750–1500

Panama

This bell pendant portrays a feline, perhaps a jaguar, although the smooth surface lacks indications of the jaguar's spotted pelt. The feline clasps a human skeletal forearm in its mouth, while the tip of its tail sprouts an animal head. These elements evoke shamanic spirit beings and the life/death allegory of shamanic transformation. The sound, material, and representational forms of bell pendants conveyed status and carried symbolic messages while also contributing to the aural landscape by producing sound when the wearer moved. Cast in a single piece, this bell pendant contains a small metal pellet that jingles inside the bulbous chamber of the feline's torso. The metalsmith likely produced the free-moving ball by enclosing a cast-metal pellet inside the pendant's core material (probably clay), which was later removed to free the tinkler.

Gold body adornments were commonly worn in ancient Costa Rica and Panama, where social status was conveyed by the relative quantity of an individual's gold ornaments. Chiefs and other members of the ruling elite donned prodigious amounts of golden adornments, embellished with widely recognized symbols of power and authority. An early sixteenth-century Spanish account of a chief's burial in Parita, Panama, describes his body wrapped in cloth and completely covered in gold adornments like this jaguar pendant.

Gold alloy

H. 3.2 cm (1¼ in.), w. 7.6 cm (3 in.), d. 5.1 cm (2 in.)

Maria Wharton Wales Fund   22.306

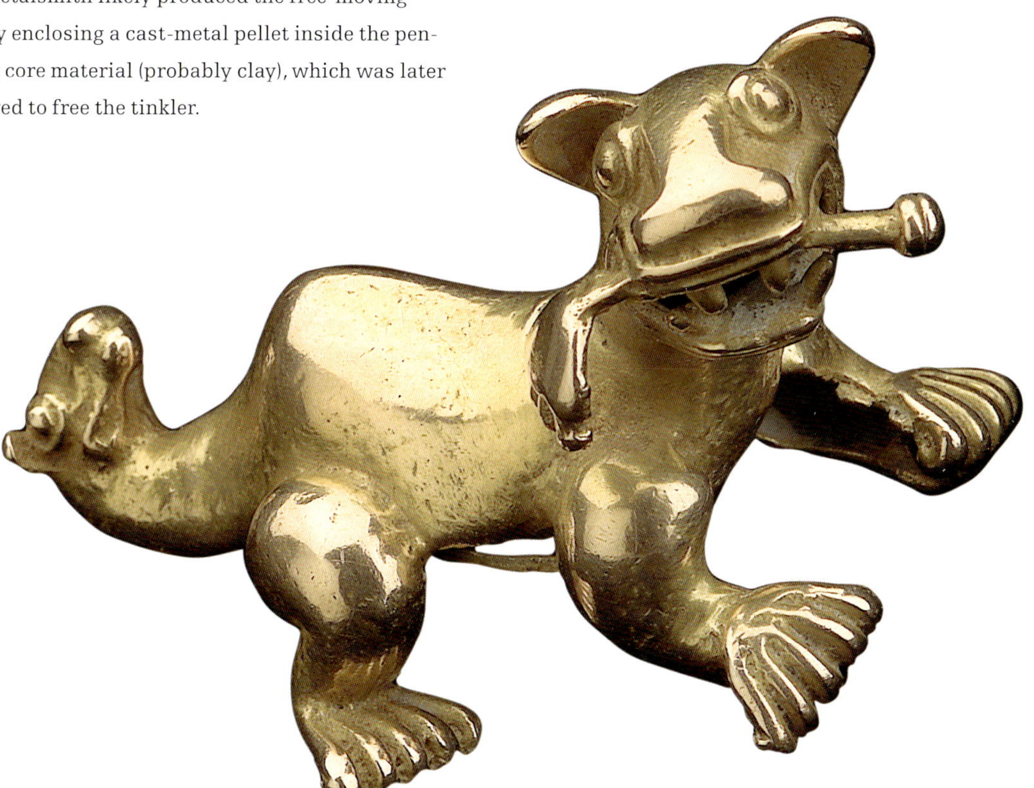

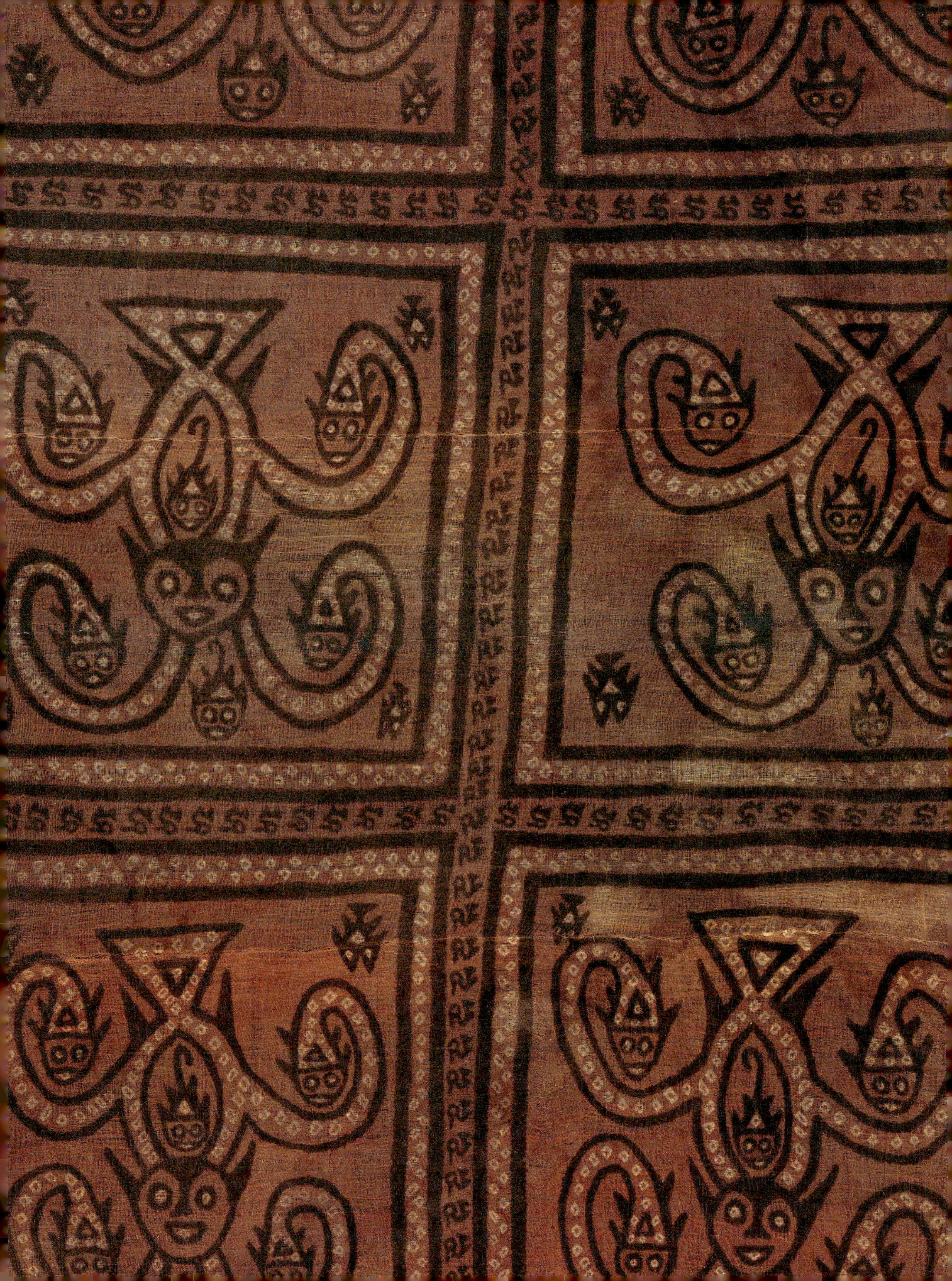

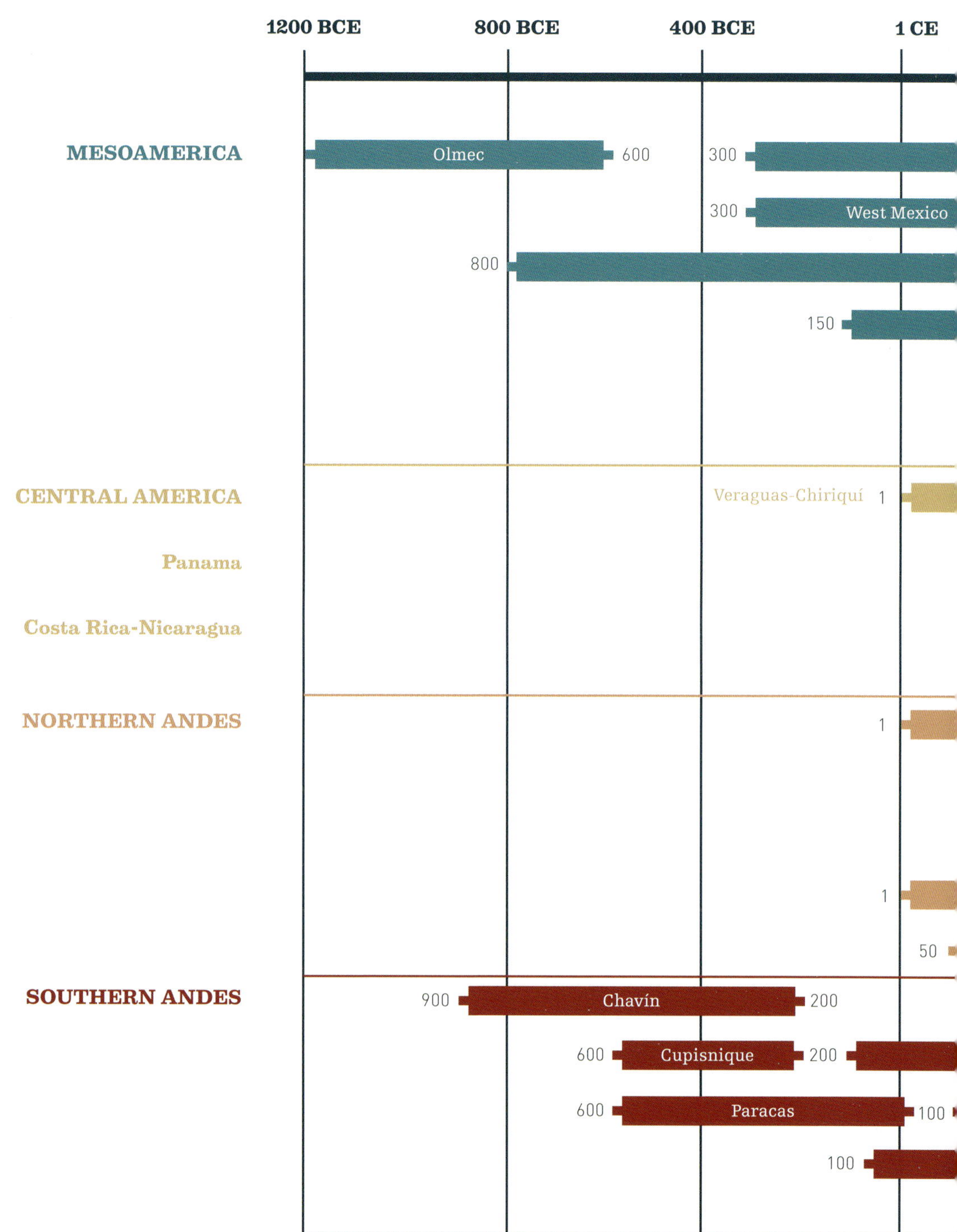

1200 BCE
800 BCE
400 BCE
1 CE
MESOAMERICA
Olmec
600
300
300
West Mexico
800
150
CENTRAL AMERICA
Veraguas-Chiriquí
1
Panama
Costa Rica-Nicaragua
NORTHERN ANDES
1
1
50
SOUTHERN ANDES
900
Chavín
200
600
Cupisnique
200
600
Paracas
100
100

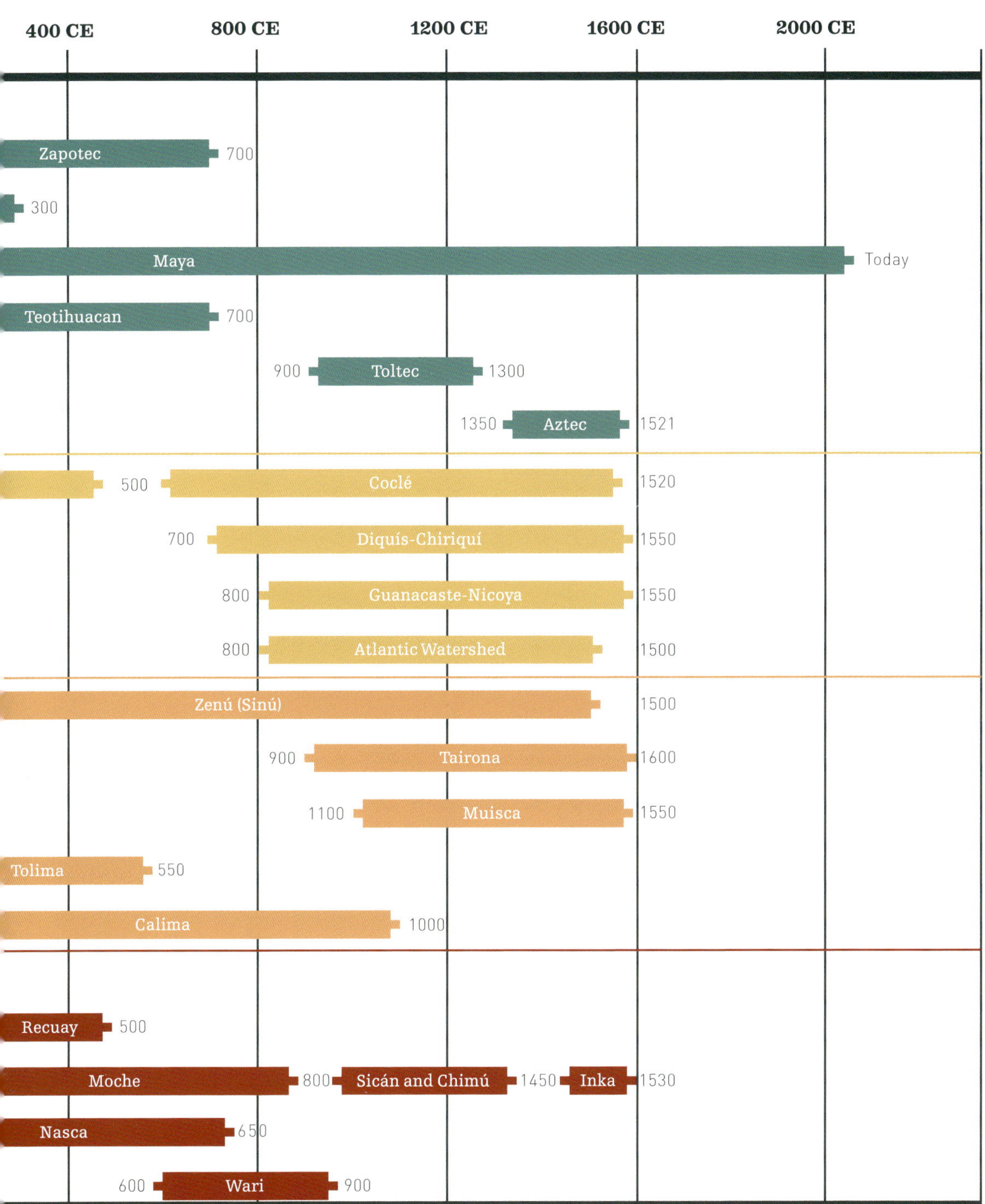

400 CE
800 CE
1200 CE
1600 CE
2000 CE
Zapotec
700
300
Maya
Today
Teotihuacan
700
900
Toltec
1300
1350
Aztec
1521
500
Coclé
1520
700
Diquís-Chiriquí
1550
800
Guanacaste-Nicoya
1550
800
Atlantic Watershed
1500
Zenú (Sinú)
1500
900
Tairona
1600
1100
Muisca
1550
Tolima
550
Calima
1000
Recuay
500
Moche
800
Sicán and Chimú
1450
Inka
1530
Nasca
650
600
Wari
900

The Cultures of Mesoamerica

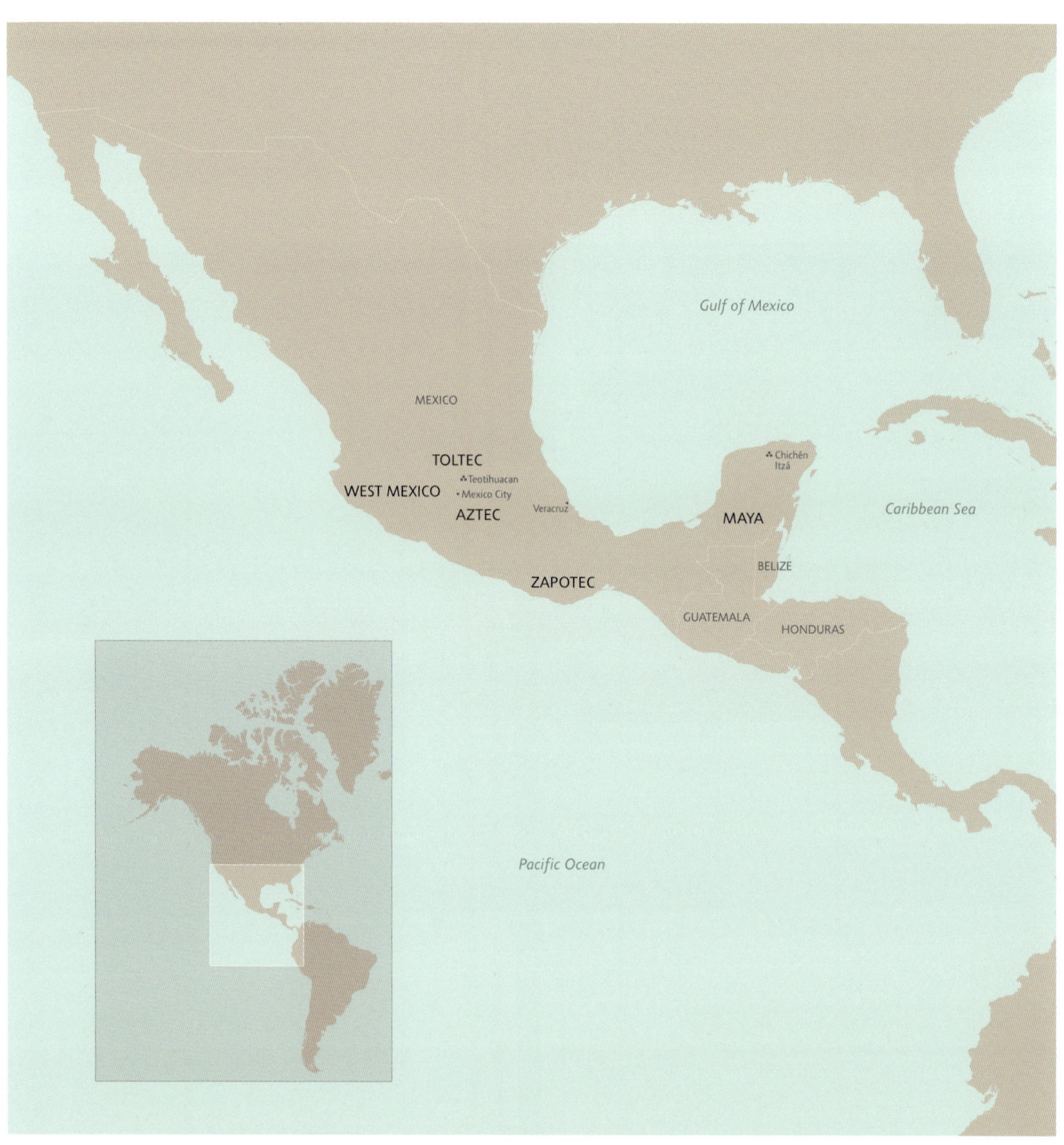

The Cultures of Central America and the Andes

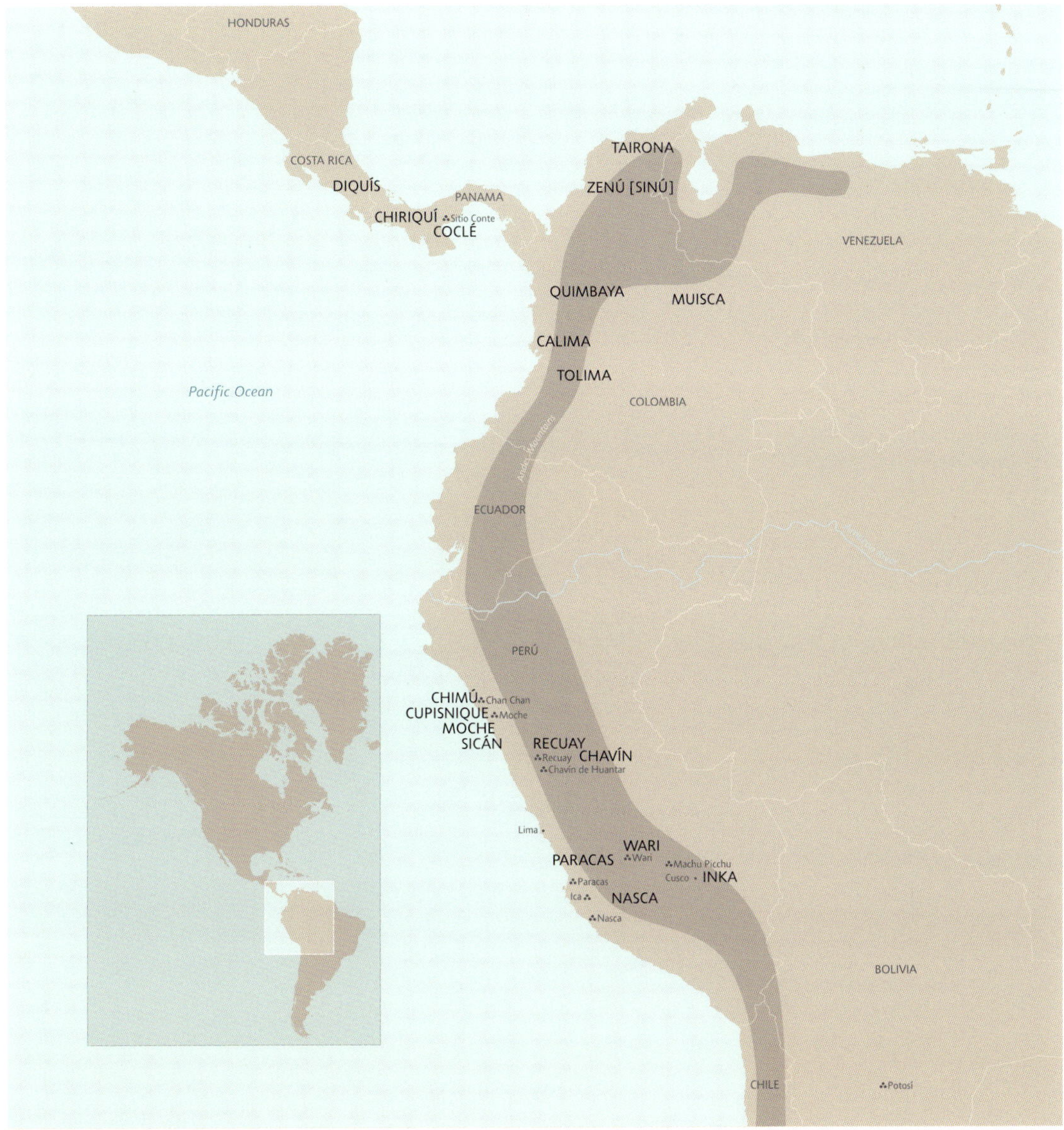

Further Reading

The Earliest American Arts

Abel-Vidor, Suzanne, et al. *Between Continents/Between Seas: Pre-Columbian Art of Costa Rica*. New York: Abrams, 1981.

Coe, Michael, and Rex Koontz. *Mexico: From the Olmecs to the Aztecs*. 7th edition. New York: Thames and Hudson, 2013.

De la Vega, Garcilaso. *Royal Commentaries of the Incas; El Inca*. Austin: University of Texas Press, 1966.

Sahagún, Bernabé de. *Florentine Codex: General History of the Things of New Spain*. Translated and edited by Arthur Anderson and Charles Dibble. Santa Fe: School of American Research; Salt Lake City: University of Utah Press, 1950–82.

Sharer, Robert, and Loa Traxler. *The Ancient Maya*. 6th edition. London and New York: Thames and Hudson, 2006.

Stone, Rebecca. *Art of the Andes: From Chavin to Inka*. 3rd edition. London and New York: Thames and Hudson, 2012.

Tozzer, Alfred M. *Bishop Diego de Landa's Relación de las Cosas de Yucatán*. Papers of the Peabody Museum of American Archaeology and Ethnology, no. 18. Cambridge, MA: Harvard University, 1941.

Spirit and Cosmos

Botero, Clara Isabel, Roverto Lleras Pérez, Santiago Londoño Vélez, and Efraín Sánchez Cabra. *The Art of Gold: The Legacy of Pre-Hispanic Colombia*. Bogotá: Museo del Oro, 2007.

Headrick, Annabeth. *The Teotihuacan Trinity: The Sociopolitical Structure of an Ancient Mesoamerican City*. Austin: University of Texas Press, 2007.

Labbé, Armand. *Colombia before Columbus: The People, Culture, and Ceramic Art of Prehispanic Colombia*. New York: Rizzoli, 1986.

Paul, Anne, and Solveig A. Turpin. "The Ecstatic Shaman Theme of Paracas Textiles." *Archaeology* 39, no. 5 (1986): 20–27.

Stone, Rebecca. *The Jaguar Within: Shamanic Trance in Ancient Central and South American Art*. Austin: University of Texas Press, 2011.

Urton, Gary. *At the Crossroads of the Earth and the Sky: An Andean Cosmology*. Austin: University of Texas Press, 1998.

Portraiture

Coe, Michael, and Mark Van Stone. *Reading the Maya Glyphs*. London and New York: Thames and Hudson, 2001.

Labbé, Armand. *Guardians of the Life Stream: Shamans, Art and Power in Prehispanic Central Panamá*. Seattle: University of Washington Press, 1995.

Martin, Simon, and Nikolai Grube. *Chronicle of the Maya Kings and Queens: Deciphering the Dynasties of the Ancient Maya*. London and New York: Thames and Hudson, 2000.

Reents-Budet, Dorie. "Elite Maya Pottery and Artisans as Social Indicators." Pp. 71–89 in *Craft and Social Identity*, edited by Cathy Costin and Rita Wright. Washington, DC: American Anthropological Association, 1998.

Steiner, Wendy. "Portraits: The Limitations of Likeness." *Art Journal* 46, no. 3 (Fall 1987): 173–77.

Stone, Andrea, and Marc Zender. *Reading Maya Art: A Hieroglyphic Guide to Ancient Maya Painting and Sculpture*. London and New York: Thames and Hudson, 2011.

Regalia

Labbé, Armand. *Shamans, Gods, and Mythic Beasts: Colombian Gold and Ceramics in Antiquity*. New York: American Federation of Arts; Seattle: University of Washington Press, 1998.

McEwan, Colin, ed. *Precolumbian Gold: Technology, Style and Iconography*. Chicago: Fitzroy Dearborn Publishers, 2000.

Quilter, Jeff, and John Hoopes, eds. *Gold and Power in Ancient Costa Rica, Panama and Colombia*. Washington, DC: Dumbarton Oaks Research Library and Collections, 2003.

Schele, Linda, and Mary Ellen Miller. *Blood of Kings*. Fort Worth, TX: Kimbell Art Museum, 1986.

Fabrics of Power

Anawalt, Patricia. *Indian Clothing before Cortés: Mesoamerican Costumes from the Codices*. Norman: University of Oklahoma Press, 1981.

Bergh, Susan E. *Wari: Lords of the Ancient Andes*. New York and London: Thames and Hudson, 2012.

D'Harcourt, Raoul. *Textiles of Ancient Peru and Their Techniques*. Seattle: University of Washington Press, 1962.

Stone-Miller, Rebecca. *To Weave for the Sun: Andean Textiles in the Museum of Fine Arts, Boston*. Boston: Museum of Fine Arts, 1992.

Feasting

Bruman, Henry J. *Alcohol in Ancient Mexico*. Salt Lake City: University of Utah Press, 2000.

Coe, Sophie D. *America's First Cuisines*. Austin: University of Texas Press, 1994.

McNeil, Cameron, ed. *Chocolate in Mesoamerica: A Cultural History of Cacao*. Gainesville: University of Florida Press, 2007.

Poma de Ayala, Felipe. *El primer nueva crónica de buen gobierno* (1615). Edited by John Murra and Rolena Adorno. Mexico: Siglo Veintiuno Editores, 1980.

Reents-Budet, Dorie, Joseph Ball, Ronald Bishop, Virginia Fields, and Barbara MacLeod. *Painting the Maya Universe: Royal Ceramics of the Classic Period*. Durham, NC: Duke University Press, 1994.

Staller, John, and Michael Carrasco, eds. *Pre-Columbian Foodways: Interdisciplinary Approaches to Food, Culture, and Markets in Ancient Mesoamerica*. New York: Springer, 2010.

Performance

Adje Both, Arnd. "Aztec Music Culture." *Journal of the Department of Ethnomusicology, Otto-Friedrich University* 49, no. 2 (2007): 91–104.

Aguilar, Francisco de. *The Chronicle of Fray Francisco de Aguilar [Relación breve de la conquista de la Nueva España]*. Edited by F. Gómez de Orozco, preface by Howard D. Cline. New York: Orion Press, 1963.

Izikowitz, Karl Gustav. *Musical and Other Sound Instruments of the South American Indians: A Comparative Ethnographical Study*. Göteborg: Elanders Boktryckeri Aktiebolag, 1935.

López de Cogolludo, Diego. *Historia de Yucatán*. Barcelona: Lingua Publishers, 2014.

Olsen, Dale. *Music of El Dorado: The Ethnomusicology of Ancient South American Cultures*. Gainesville: University of Florida Press, 2002.

Figure Illustrations

1

Inti Watana residential group, Pisac,
Peru, 1982
Photograph courtesy of Dorie Reents-
Budet

2

Double-spouted vessel
Designed by Christopher Dresser (Scottish, 1834–1904)
Made at Linthorpe Art Pottery, Middlesbrough, England, about 1879–82
Glazed earthenware with incised
decoration
H. 17.5 cm (6⅞ in.), w. 16 cm (6¼ in.),
d. 15 cm (5⅞ in.)
Gift of Nicholas Johnson
1996.222

3

Drinking vessel
Maya, 675–750 CE
Guatemala
Earthenware with slip paint
H. 12.8 cm (5 in.), diam. 12.3 cm (4⅞ in.)
Gift of Landon T. Clay
1900.1205

4

Bird effigy pendant
Veraguas–Gran Chiriquí,
1st–4th century CE
Veraguas or Chiriquí Province, Panama
Gold alloy
H. 10.8 cm (4¼ in.), w. 8.5 cm (3⅜ in.)
Maria Wharton Wales Fund
22.284

5

Effigy bottle
Lambayeque (Sicán) or early Chimú, Late
Intermediate Period, 900–1470
North Coast, Peru
Earthenware
H. 24.8 cm (9¾ in.), w. 15.1 cm (16 in.),
d. 22.9 cm (9 in.)
Everett Fund 79.1

6

Man on litter effigy
Muisca, 1100–1550
Departments of Cundinamarca and
Boyacá, Colombia
Gold and copper alloy
H. 7.3 cm (2⅞ in.), l. 22.9 cm (9 in.)
Gift of Landon T. Clay
1975.139

7

Drinking vessel (detail)
Maya, Late Classic period, 675–750 CE
Lake Petén-Itzá region, Guatemala
Earthenware with slip paint
H. 21.5 cm (8½ in.), diam. 13.2 cm (5½ in.)
Anonymous loan

Details

pp. 2–3: p. 114; p. 5: p. 112; p. 10: p. 57;
p. 19: p. 43; pp. 20–21: p. 50; p. 25: p. 35;
pp. 52–53: p. 65; pp. 76–77: p. 86;
pp. 106–7: p. 132–33; pp. 134–35: p. 141;
p. 139: p. 152; pp. 156–57: p. 166;
pp. 176–77: pp. 130–31.

Index

Page numbers in *italics* refer to illustrations.